LIVING DEEP

A 365 DAY JOURNEY
THROUGH GOD'S WORD

The day I got my first bike was the first day I felt free. I had acquired the opportunity to explore and connect with others who lived on the small Outer Banks island where I grew up.

My mom often testified that, after that day, it was impossible for me to stay home. I always needed to be with friends. I guess that is how God created me. I knew it then but I am convinced now that relationships are what bring true wealth to a person.

Fast forward decades later. This devotional project is a revelation of this truth. We truly are better together. This 365-day devotional is comprised of many different voices from various walks of life. Each is extremely important because each testifies to the goodness of God and the power of His Word to bring radical transformation. I pray that in the pages of this devotional you will encounter our friend Jesus in order that you may "live deeply."

Stephen Willis
President, Lead Deep

To request permissions, contact the publisher at info@leaddeep.org.

Paperback: ISBN 978-1-7359143-3-6
Ebook: ISBN 978-1-7359143-4-3

First paperback edition September 2023.

Edited by Emily Heady and Rachael Kamm
Cover art, layout, and design by Caleb Atkins
All photographs are used with permission from www.unsplash.com.

All Scripture quotations are taken from the Holy Bible, *New International Version, NIV* ®, unless otherwise noted. Other versions include: *The Voice*, The Voice Bible Copyright © 2012 Thomas Nelson, Inc. The Voice™ translation © 2012 Ecclesia Bible Society All rights reserved.

Printed by Lead Deep in the United States of America.

Lead Deep
110 Wyndview Drive
Lynchburg, VA 24502

Leaddeep.org

THE LEAD DEEP COLLECTIVE

The following authors contributed to the production of this book.

Caleb	Atkins	Lynchburg	VA	United States
Angelica	Atkins	Bowmanville	Ontario	Canada
Janette	Berge	Lewisburg	PA	United States
Brad	Billet	West Point	VA	United States
Clay	Bryan	Forest	VA	United States
Jennifer	Burgett	Lynchburg	VA	United States
Cavan	Carlton	Lynchburg	VA	United States
Alan	Carlton	Tulsa	OK	United States
Jim	Chapman	Lake Saint Louis	MO	United States
Russanna	Cook	Forest	VA	United States
Doug	Fry	Lynchburg	VA	United States
Bruce	Gardner	Appomattox	VA	United States
Ashley	Gomez	Poquoson	VA	United States
Lynne	Goodwin	Lynchburg	VA	United States
Steven	Guizar	Front Royal	VA	United States
Chene	Heady	Appomattox	VA	United States
Emily	Heady	Appomattox	VA	United States
Andrew	Horseman	Gladys	VA	United States
Deborah	Huff	Forest	VA	United States
Dani	Huizar	Durham	NC	United States
Nan	Jacobs	Lynchburg	VA	United States
Tabitha	Jernigan	Crewe	VA	United States
Deirdra	Jones	Forest	VA	United States
Divanna	Junkert	Lynchburg	VA	United States
Bobbie Jo	King	Virginia Beach	VA	United States
Marlon	King	Virginia Beach	VA	United States
Wynne	Lankford	Chesterfield	VA	United States
John	Lawson	Bridgewater	VA	United States
Matthew	Lesniak	Forest	VA	United States
Mike	Lyle	Forest	VA	United States

Brian	Marker	Forest	VA	United States
January	Marshall	Palmyra	VA	United States
Darcy	Mcalinn	Lynchburg	VA	United States
Jenn	McCamant	Lititz	PA	United States
Chad	Moler	Palmyra	VA	United States
Gary	O'Shell	Lynchburg	VA	United States
Reenie	Peppers	Fredericksburg	VA	United States
Steven	Peppers	Fredericksburg	VA	United States
Carla	Pollard	N. Chesterfield	VA	United States
Brad	Robertson	Lynchburg	VA	United States
Andy	Scoles	Lynchburg	VA	United States
Chris	Shalter	Denver	PA	United States
Linda	Shepherd	Lynchburg	VA	United States
Camelot	Shuff	Suffolk	VA	United States
Torrie	Slaughter	Lynchburg	VA	United States
Gary	Smith	Goode	VA	United States
John	Swales	Bedford	VA	United States
Todd	Thomas	Timberville	VA	United States
Priscilla	Tomlin	Lynchburg	VA	United States
Matthew	Waggoner	Montoursville	PA	United States
Kerry	Willis	Cape May	NJ	United States
Stephen	Willis	Lynchburg	VA	United States
Lisa	Willis	Lynchburg	VA	United States
Billy	Willis	Kingsport	TN	United States
Nick	Willis	Jacksonville	FL	United States
JJ	Wyzinski	Ephrata	PA	United States

The Prodigal Father | John C. Bowling

"But while he was still a long way off, his father saw him and was filled with compassion for him; he ran to his son, threw his arms around him and kissed him."
–Luke 15:20

Charles Dickens famously called this the greatest short story ever written. And it is a great story, both in terms of its literary craft and its enduring meaning and impact. The storyline is simple enough for a child to follow, yet it is the subject of several classical book-length studies.

Scholars have spent centuries pouring over this text line by line. Of all Jesus' parables, this is the most richly detailed, dramatic, and personal. It brims with emotions ranging from sadness to triumph to shock, and finally, to an unsettling wish for more. It is, perhaps, the greatest five minutes of storytelling ever.

As the story unfolds, the focus shifts from one character to another, building in intensity as it progresses. The younger son is the focus at the beginning; the father takes center-stage at the magnificent moment of reconciliation; and finally, the focus shifts to the elder brother's response, which unsettles the story's end and leaves the reader hanging.

With each movement, the plot takes a turn. The image of a boy who becomes so desperately hungry that he scavenges husks from pig slop would have been particularly offensive to Jesus' Jewish audience since pigs were unclean according to Levitical law. This part of the story reminds us that our choices have consequences—a lesson that too many people learn the hard way.

However, what makes this tale unforgettable is the poignancy of the father's response to his son: "But while he was still a long way off, his father saw him and was filled with compassion for him; he ran to his son, threw his arms around him and kissed him." What a picture of love and grace—what a portrait of God, who is the prodigal (extravagantly generous) father! Who wouldn't be moved by that kind of love and forgiveness?

God's love for each of us is unfailing. It does not change, regardless of our actions. He waits patiently for us to turn back to Him. You need not wonder how the Lord will respond. This story makes it clear that God, like the Father in the story, is "filled with compassion."

Lion of Judah | Jennifer Burgett

"Abraham was the father of Isaac, Isaac the father of Jacob, Jacob the father of Judah and his brothers." –Matthew 1:2

I grew up hearing the story of Joseph. His is an easy story to like. He fled from sin and endured hard times but never wavered in his faith. He was clearly blessed by God and he helped to save God's people.

I always loved Judah, though. He made countless mistakes, embraced sin, and hurt those around him. It was his idea to sell Joseph into slavery, his sons were so wicked God killed them, and he had to be deceived to do the right thing by Tamar.

I think that encounter humbled him; it made him realize he had spent his life treating his family poorly. Why do I think this? Well, after that he returns to his father and brothers.

Truthfully, Judah has one truly great moment in his life, and we usually overlook it. Here is what Judah says to Joseph, who wants to hold his brother Benjamin hostage: "Now then, please let your servant remain here as my lord's slave in place of the boy, and let the boy return with his brothers" (Genesis 44:33).

Judah didn't know Benjamin hadn't stolen anything. He didn't know Joseph was actually his brother. He could have explained to Jacob what happened, and he wouldn't have been wrong. His brothers would have backed him up. But he didn't.

Instead, Judah asked to take the punishment for the sins of another. He was willing to lay down his life so that a sinner could go home to his father.

It's easy to write Judah off. It's easy to overlook this moment and focus on Joseph's joy over getting his brothers back. But we serve a God who sees all—who wanted Judah to be in the lineage of His Son and blessed him because of this moment.

And it's important to understand this, because you might feel like you screw up more than you ever get it right. Or that you are always in the shadow of greater men. Or that your decisions don't matter. But they do. God sees all, and He wanted Judah's story to be told too. He doesn't just want to bless the Josephs of the world; He wants to bless and use the Judahs too.

LORD, MAKE ME AN INSTRUMENT OF YOUR PEACE

"If it is possible, as far as it depends on you, live at peace with everyone." –Romans 12:18

Lord make me an instrument of your peace;
where there is hatred, let me sow love;
where there is injury, pardon;
where there is discord, union;
where there is doubt, faith;
where there is despair, hope;
where there is darkness, light;
where there is sadness, joy;
O Divine Master, grant that I may not so much seek to be consoled as to console,
to be understood as to understand, to be loved as to love.
For it is in giving that we receive.
It is in pardoning that we are pardoned,
and it is in dying that we are born to eternal life.
Amen.

St. Francis of Assisi

Faithfulness | Alan Carlton

"Look at the proud! They trust in themselves, and their lives are crooked. But the righteous will live by their faithfulness to God." –Habakkuk 2:4

This is one of the most important verses in the Old Testament. It is important because it is quoted in three key verses of the New Testament: Romans 1:16-17, Galatians 3:11, and Hebrews 10:38.

In Habakkuk, God spells out for us the two options for how to live our lives. We can either be full of ourselves, living as we want, or faithful to God, living as He instructs. Those are the only two choices . . . and the only path to eternal life is living by faithfulness. "Emunah" is the important word here. It can be translated as "faith" or "faithfulness," but because it is in the continuing tense, faithfulness is the best choice. We must LIVE by our EMUNAH. It can't be something we once recognized but have failed to put into daily practice.

In Romans, Paul demonstrates that the good news of Christ teaches us how we are to live. It is "The Manufacturers Handbook to People." We are to live by what Christ taught and how He lived. As such, we can live confidently because we trust God and inherit Christ's righteousness when He truly lives within us.

In Galatians, Paul uses it to prove that God does not justify by our works or by the law, but by our continuing faith in Jesus Christ—our faithfulness.

The author of Hebrews uses the third quote much as Habakkuk himself did. He shows us that there are two ways we can choose to live. We can live faithful to God and achieve the reward of eternal life, or we can listen to our own counsel, live contrary to God's wishes, and be destroyed.

In 2 Corinthians 5:7, Paul states, "We walk by faith, not by sight." By LIVING DAILY in our continuous faith in God and HIS plan in faithfulness whatever circumstances may befall us, we are counted among the righteous.

We must daily choose a side: my way or His? Ask yourself if you are living in your faith, filled with the Holy Spirit. If you are not, today is the day to begin.

What's on Your Schedule? | Brian Charette

"Then He said to them all: 'Whoever wants to be my disciple must deny themselves and take up their cross daily and follow me.'" –Luke 9:23

Got plans for today? If you're average, you'll spend most of your time working and sleeping, at least according to Our World in Data. Of your 1440 minutes today, 80-90% of that time will be spent on paid work, housework, leisure, eating, and sleeping. Of course, it varies across the world. For instance, South Koreans sleep the least, and people in India sleep the most. (Americans average about six and a half hours of sleep per night and two and a half hours per day on social media.)[1]

But biblically, something else should occur every day. If you are a believer, the Lord, well acquainted with a cross-call, has established the rules for true discipleship—deny yourself and take up your cross daily.

Daily. There is a cross for you today. Have you considered what it means to take up a cross daily? In the Luke text, this daily cross carrying is a condition of being a disciple. So, if one wants to be Jesus' disciple (do you?), this cross carrying is part of the deal. And, since we know Jesus isn't talking about a literal cross—175 pounds of splintering wood—we know that this cross carrying happens in our hearts. It means the act of crucifixion is part of a disciple's life every day. We crucify temptation, faithless thoughts, our desire for control, our lack of compassion for others, our fear, etc. Every day, something else gets nailed to the cross we carry. And there, Jesus accepts it and cleanses us. But there is no discipleship without your daily, personal cross.

So, got plans for today?

------

1 Ortiz-Ospina, Esteban, Charlie Giattino, and Max Roser, "Time Use." 2020. Our World in Data. https://our-worldindata.org/time-use. Accessed May 30, 2023.

I Can Never Be the Christian You Are | Joyce Grambo

"When someone becomes a Christian, he becomes a brand-new person inside. He is not the same anymore. A new life has begun!" –II Corinthians 5:17

I have heard the comment, "I can never be the Christian you are" many times over the course of my life. The funny thing is I have never asked anyone to be the Christian I am. And yet these very people use this comment as an excuse to not even try to be the Christian God designed them to be.

I believe this happens for a variety of reasons: First, the people who made this comment don't want to give up control of their lives and become obedient to Christ. It's too hard, too demanding. Second, the world has a hold on them that is so deep they don't even recognize it. Third, they don't believe in heaven and hell, or that they will spend an eternity in one place or the other. And fourth, they just want to enjoy life and will eventually get around to becoming a Christian.

Jeremiah 29:11 says, "'For I know the plans I have for you,' declares the Lord." God's plan for your life is not the same as His plan for my life. You have to embrace your identity in Him.

When I became a Christian, I became a new person in Christ, and I have tried my best to walk the path to which God has called me. It has not always been easy, but I know that Christ has been with me every step of the way. Some days my walk looks messy, while other days it seems grace-filled and beautiful. All of the ups and downs, good days and bad, baby steps and giant leaps account for my personal relationship with Christ.

I pray that you will become a new person in Christ and walk the path that He has chosen for you. Don't try to measure up to someone else's relationship with Christ. Focus on your personal relationship with Him and take it one day at a time. If you fall, get up! If it gets messy, brush yourself off and keep going. Then you can say that you may never be the Christian I am, but are the Christian God designed you to be! And it gets better every day.

SABBATH

A RHYTHM
OF REST

[1] It is good to praise the Lord

and make music to your name, O Most High,

[2] proclaiming your love in the morning

and your faithfulness at night,

[3] to the music of the ten-stringed lyre

and the melody of the harp.

Psalm 92:1-3

Ingredients for Epiphany: Awareness | Mike Lyle

"After Jesus was born in Bethlehem in Judea, during the time of King Herod, Magi from the east came to Jerusalem and asked, 'Where is the one who has been born king of the Jews? We saw his star when it rose and have come to worship him.'" –Matthew 2:1-2

The Church calendar is marked by various movements based on the life of Jesus. Through these, Christians are invited into different rhythms of waiting and active seeking. Advent, which is the season just before Christmas, is characterized by waiting. It is a time of longing and acknowledging our need for a Savior. Epiphany, the season following Christmas, marks a shift in our posture. With the story of the Magi as its touchstone, Epiphany invites us into a time of active seeking. During the season, we are challenged to establish new rhythms that open us to deeper revelation of who Jesus is. This week, let us use the story of the Magi to guide us on our journey into Epiphany. Like a good 90s preacher, I'll walk us through this story with a bit of alliteration. We'll explore the role of Awareness, Arrangement, Adoration, Acknowledgment, and Alignment as the main ingredients of Epiphany.

The first thing we see in this story is an Awareness. The Magi have to notice a difference in the sky. Noticing is hard. We would like to have more epiphanies of who Jesus is, but we have soccer practice, music lessons, school dances, a report that is due tomorrow, and dinner that needs to be prepared. Life demands that we keep our head down and plunge forward. But, with our heads down, it is hard to see the new star in the sky.

Any epiphany we might have is contingent upon Jesus' revelation of who He is. Why do you think the Magi saw the star appearing in the sky? It wasn't because they were educated. It was because they were looking for it. Perhaps the first movement of Epiphany is an awareness of something new. The star in the sky was a giant invitation for the Magi to come looking for a king. What are the stars in your sky? Have you noticed something new in your life that might be acting like an invitation from the Lord to come looking for Him? If not, lift up your head.

Ingredients for Epiphany: Arrangement | Mike Lyle

"After Jesus was born in Bethlehem in Judea, during the time of King Herod, Magi from the east came to Jerusalem and asked, 'Where is the one who has been born king of the Jews? We saw his star when it rose and have come to worship him.'" –Matthew 2:1-2

We are exploring the ingredients of Epiphany this week. We want to know Jesus. Epiphany is the time of year when we move from a rhythm of waiting and start actively seeking Jesus by opening our hearts to newer and deeper revelations of who He is. The first ingredient to this is Awareness: We practice paying attention to God's invitations to pursue Him. Today, we will talk about the arrangement required in Epiphany.

My family are notorious over-packers. We bring the same amount of bags if we are going to be gone for two days or for two months. No matter how long we will be gone, I am left playing Tetris in the trunk of our minivan trying to fit everything in. So, I know a thing or two about making arrangements for a trip. The Magi in our story are no different. They were leaving on a trip. They didn't know where they were going or how long they would be gone. I promise, this trip took some arrangement.

Often, when we see the star or an invitation to a journey with God, we fail to make arrangements for that journey. For example, we might notice the invitation to read the Scriptures. However, if we don't plan a time to read them, this invitation will go unanswered. We might sense a desire to spend more time in prayer and communion with the Lord. But, if we don't set aside a specific time in our day to do so, it will never happen. Journeys take arrangement. Our spiritual journey is no different. Are you arranging your life for epiphany?

Ingredients for Epiphany: Adoration | Mike Lyle

"After Jesus was born in Bethlehem in Judea, during the time of King Herod, Magi from the east came to Jerusalem and asked, 'Where is the one who has been born king of the Jews? We saw his star when it rose and have come to worship him.'...Then Herod called the Magi secretly and found out from them the exact time the star had appeared. He sent them to Bethlehem and said, 'Go and search carefully for the child. As soon as you find him, report to me, so that I too may go and worship him.' After they had heard the king, they went on their way, and the star they had seen when it rose went ahead of them until it stopped over the place where the child was. When they saw the star, they were overjoyed. On coming to the house, they saw the child with his mother Mary, and they bowed down and worshiped him." –Matthew 2:1-2, 7-11

Epiphany is a time of actively seeking Jesus. We have come into an awareness of His invitation to know Him better, and we have made arrangements to answer that invitation. Today, we will discuss the reason behind our movement—Adoration.

In his account of the story of the Magi, Matthew tells us they left their country to go and worship a king. I wonder if any motivation less than worship is strong enough to sustain our movement toward Epiphany. I think it is possible to desire new patterns in our lives out of misguided motives. There are plenty of self-help books on the shelves that promise a newer, better version of ourselves. It would be easy to think that I need to see Jesus more clearly so that I can be a better disciple or have more intimacy in my marriage or be a better parent. However, the motivation behind the journey of the Magi was nothing less than worship. They left their hometown to worship a king, not to become better Magi.

What would change in your journey toward Epiphany if your motivation were worship? By worship I don't mean singing songs you hear on the radio (although that can be a form of worship). I mean ascribing the value and worth to Jesus that He deserves. When this journey gets hard, you'll need to proclaim, "He's worth it." That's worship.

Ingredients for Epiphany: Acknowledgment | Mike Lyle

"After they had heard the king, they went on their way, and the star they had seen when it rose went ahead of them until it stopped over the place where the child was. When they saw the star, they were overjoyed. On coming to the house, they saw the child with his mother Mary, and they bowed down and worshiped him. Then they opened their treasures and presented him with gifts of gold, frankincense and myrrh."
–Matthew 2:9-11

Today, we turn toward another ingredient of Epiphany—Acknowledgment of a King. I feel like every epiphany should lead us to this great one: Jesus is Lord. The wise men were not unfamiliar with kings. Their position, wealth, and knowledge would have given them access to many kings of different nations. In fact, they spoke with King Harod on their way to Jesus. I think it is significant that these learned men went in search of a king. I wonder if we are all in search of a king. We know the mess we make when we are in charge of our own lives and we know the disaster that comes from putting other fallen humans in the position of absolute authority. Perhaps the gifts of the Magi were not only given to acknowledge the birth of a king, but also to point to the kind of King that Jesus would become—a better king than Herod.

First, they gave gold. Gold is a good, kingly gift. It denotes royalty and position. By giving gold, the Magi were acknowledging that Jesus was royal and had the authority to rule. Second, they gave frankincense, an incense used in temples that were dedicated to the divine. Incense was a priestly gift that denoted prayer and praise. Third, they gave the gift of myrrh, an oil used in burial. It points to death and suffering.

I don't know how much the Magi knew or didn't know. But I think it is fitting that their gifts point to a king who has the authority to rule but uses that authority in a priestly way and is willing to lay his life down for the people in his kingdom. That's my king—King Jesus. Will you acknowledge Him as your king today?

Ingredients for Epiphany: Alignment | Mike Lyle

"And having been warned in a dream not to go back to Herod, they returned to their country by another route." –Matthew 2:12

Did you catch that? The Magi didn't return home the same way they came to Bethlehem. I believe there is more to this little verse than meets the eye. There is a transformation that happened in this story. Let's remember the story from the beginning.

The story begins when the Magi noticed a star. They didn't hear a voice or even discern the prompting of the Holy Spirit. They merely noticed a new star in the sky and recollected some prophecy about what that might mean. In the beginning of this story, we might say that God's invitation to them was outside of them. They pursued Jesus not from personal connection but out of a knowledge of prophecy and a belief in the word of other people concerning the birth of a new king.

Then, something changed. After seeing Jesus and worshiping Him for themselves, they received instruction from within them in the form of a dream. They went from curiosity about a nameless king to receiving specific instruction from the Holy Spirit. No longer can we say that these Magi were merely following a star. They were following God. I think this is the normal end of Epiphany.

The end of Epiphany is not its finish line but its purpose or goal. Every year, the Church calendar invites us to enter the season of Epiphany. How is this rhythm something we do every year without getting tired of it? Because Jesus has so much to reveal. We could spend the rest of our lives having millions of little epiphanies and we would never exhaust the depths of who Jesus is. The goal isn't to simply go on a journey to learn more about Jesus. The goal is to be transformed by this King and to return to our lives as different people. This is how we come into greater alignment with Jesus as Lord.

What the Wise Men Saw | Emily Heady

"On entering the house, they saw the child with Mary his mother; and they knelt down and paid him homage." -Matthew 2:11

In the Church Calendar, the Feast of the Epiphany, celebrated January 6, commemorates the visit of the Three Wise Men to the infant Jesus. More broadly, it reminds us of what that visit meant—that Christ had come not just for Jews but for all of us. The Epiphany changed the rules by which salvation history was playing out.

In the study of literature, an "epiphany" refers to a moment when a character has a sudden insight about something that has happened to him. Typically, the epiphany shifts a character's perspective so radically that it results in a life change—he does things differently after it. A good example of an epiphany comes from T.S. Eliot's poem "The Journey of the Magi," which is narrated from the perspective of one of the three wise men. The poem is full of biblical imagery that mixes the Old and New Testaments—three trees, vine-leaves, a lintel, pieces of silver, empty wine-skins, and so on. All of these familiar images point to stories we know well. But encountering them here for the first time, the wise men find them hard to absorb: "We had evidence and no doubt. I had seen birth and death,/But had thought they were different; this Birth was/Hard and bitter agony for us, like Death, our death./We returned to our places, these Kingdoms/But no longer at ease here, in the old dispensation"[1] (ll. 40-43).

Epiphany brings a birth—the birth of the Christ child in the lives of those who had been outsiders to God's grace. And that birth changes everything. It changes how we see the world, and it asks us to let go of—to kill—some things that belong to our old lives.

Jesus, thank you for bringing new birth. As we welcome you in, may we also put to death the things that don't belong in our kingdoms any longer. May your kingdom come and your will be done.

---

1. Eliot, T.S. "The Journey of the Magi." 1927. *Collected Poems.* New York: Faber, 1974.

SABBATH

A RHYTHM
OF REST

When Jesus spoke again to the people, he said, "I am

the light of the world. Whoever follows me will never

walk in darkness, but will have the light of life."

John 8:12

Just Believe | Deirdra Jones

"Jesus said to Thomas, 'You believe because you've seen me. Blessed are those who haven't seen me but believe.'" –John 20:29

To believe in someone or something you have never seen or understand takes faith.

In John 20:24-29, all of the disciples except Thomas saw Jesus after the resurrection. They told Thomas, "We've seen the Lord" (v. 25), but Thomas refused to believe it until he had seen Jesus with his own eyes and stuck his fingers in His wounds. Eight days later, Thomas gets his wish as Jesus joins the disciples in their hidden upper room. He tells Thomas to touch His wounds with his fingers and to stop doubting—just believe. As a result, Thomas declares that he does believe. Jesus tells Thomas that he believes because he has seen Him, but blessed are those who believe without seeing Him.

Blessed. Blessed are we who believe Him without physically seeing Him. We are blessed. It will go well for us because we have believed without seeing.

I have never seen Jesus with my physical eyes, but I have seen His effects in my life and in the lives of others. I have never physically touched Jesus with my fingers, but I have felt His Presence around me closer than the air I breathe. I have felt the atmosphere in the room change at the mention of His name. His Presence has been palpable—though I cannot see Him, I know He is there. I have not physically been with Jesus like the disciples were, but I know that I know that I know He has been and is with me...always. Always leading, loving, guiding, redirecting, reminding, whispering, speaking, teaching, enlightening, correcting, disciplining, and changing me.

He's alive. I just believe. I believe He's alive in me. How do I know? I know I am not who I used to be—praise God! I am a changed life. My life, who I am and how I live out daily and not-so-daily doings, comings, and goings—He is the only explanation. I've tried doing things my way. It did not turn out well...ever. I always came up short.

I just believe. I have not seen Him with my eyes, but I just believe. I have beheld Him in my heart so I just believe, and Jesus calls me blessed.

Stop doubting. Just believe.

Jesus' Family | Camelot Shuff

"Whoever does God's will is my brother and sister and mother." –Mark 3:35

In Mark 3, Jesus heals and casts out a demon. Meanwhile, with the crowds pressing in on this miracle worker, His mother, Mary, and his two brothers were trying to get to Jesus. This scene unfolds as people relay that Jesus' family had arrived to see Him. I can imagine that this would make the crowds give way—of course, these important people should be given access! However, Jesus' answer surprised all who heard: "Who are my mother and brothers? Whoever does God's will is my brother and sister and mother." What a teaching moment for those in the crowd, but also for Mary and the brothers!

Mary knew from all of her experiences that Jesus was the Son of God, but at this point in time, the brothers did not believe. It was almost as if Mary the believer was taking her other boys out of their hometown, out of the place that gave Jesus no honor, in order to show them just who and what their brother, Jesus, really was.

Most people have had some experience of either being dragged into Jesus' presence or dragging someone else to Him. If we could only pray over them enough, or have them sit with other believers, or hear pastor so-and-so preach, then they would see—that's what we tell ourselves. While this human effort seems so hopeful at the time, Jesus was quite clear: There is no relationship, no special gimmick, no kind or convincing word that will bring people close to Him.

Do you have people in your life who need to meet Jesus? Pray and trust. Pray that their eyes and ears would be opened, pray that God would send laborers in His way and in His timing. Trust God. Trust God with them.

No More Missed Opportunities | Kerry Willis

"Then if my people who are called by my name will humble themselves and pray and seek my face and turn from their wicked ways, I will hear from heaven and will forgive their sins and restore their land." –II Chronicles 7:14

Summertime, to me, seems to be a season of spiritual opportunity in so many ways.

I have a present and future fervent prayer as summertime approaches. From the depths of my being, I fervently plead: No more missed opportunities, Lord, I pray.

I am heavily leaning on these New Testament words: "The earnest prayer of a righteous man has great power and wonderful results" (James 5:16, NLT).

I don't want these Old Testament words becoming reality in my lifetime: "The harvest is finished; the summer is over, and we are not saved" (Jeremiah 8:20, NLT).

God forbid! Yes, I fervently plead and repeat over and over: No more missed opportunities, Lord, I pray.

I rest in God's promise: "Then if my people who are called by my name will humble themselves and pray and seek my face and turn from their wicked ways, I will hear from heaven and will forgive their sins and restore their land" (II Chronicles 7:14, NLT).

As our inheritance, give us the lost, Lord. Help us to spiritually seize the summer season and to experience a harvest of souls for Your glory alone.

Amen.

Miracle Message | Stephen Willis

"As you go, proclaim this message: 'The kingdom of heaven has come near.' Heal the sick, raise the dead, cleanse those who have leprosy, drive out demons." -Matthew 10:7-8

I awoke one morning with a significant burden. There was a specific prayer request that I prayed about, and it seemed that morning that the situation just wasn't going to resolve. Hope was nearly dead—but still, I found myself in my familiar morning prayer spot longing for God to provide solace for my heavy heart. As I got into the Word that morning, I read the words of Jesus in Matthew 10:7-8. As I read it, I felt like the Spirit prompted me to read it again. Then I felt I should read it again. As I continued to read it over and over, the Spirit brought to me two specific questions: "Are you proclaiming it?" and "Do you believe it?"

It truly is a miracle message. Do we believe Jesus heals the sick? Do we believe He resurrects dead things? Do we believe He can cleanse the unclean and drive out demons? In my brokenness, I found myself saying, "Yes, I do believe! Forgive any residue of unbelief." I am convinced that on that one particular morning the Spirit simply wanted me to proclaim the miracle message to myself. Read it again! Read it again! Yes, He heals the sick! Yes, He resurrects dead things! Yes, He can cleanse the unclean and drive out demons! At the end of my morning prayer time, I felt the burden lift. At that very moment, I had this assurance in my soul that something had changed in that situation that had seemed dead just moments before. Yes, I testify to you that despite my not fully understanding how it happened, God broke in and not only lifted the burden, but also answered the prayer. I found myself exalting Him that day for proving to me once again that He and His message are miraculous.

Our Prayer: Lord Jesus, help me to not only proclaim your miracle message but also to believe it and experience it. I live in a world full of brokenness, pain, and death. In the midst of it all, I know that you are good and that your miracle message of healing remains. I trust you! Amen!

Contagious Discipleship | Chad Moler

"...teach these truths to other trustworthy people who will be able to pass them on to others." -2 Timothy 2:2

I remember when I was growing up, we would often visit my grandparents at their home in Pennsylvania. My grandfather was a pastor and lived in a parsonage attached to the church building. My sisters and I would have a blast throughout the week, exploring all of the rooms in the church and having a huge church parking lot where we could ride our bikes.

But one of the best memories I have is helping my grandfather around the house and church. When he washed the car, I was knocking over the bucket of water. If he cleaned the windows, I was right there making streaks on them again. If he swept the floors, he would have a "helper" making another mess right behind him. OK, so maybe I was not exactly helping, but I was right there with him every step of the way. And for every misstep I made, never once did he ever scold me.

Francis Chan said, "We reduce discipleship to a canned program, and so many in the church end up sidelined in a spectator mentality that delegates disciple making to pastors..."[1]

One of the things we are called to do as Christians is to disciple others. To model through both word and deed what it means to follow Jesus. It does not mean that we are perfect, nor is the expectation that others be perfect. As people on a journey of discipleship, we walk with others through the high and low points of life. We do exactly what Paul instructed Timothy: We take what we have learned from Scripture and other godly people and we teach others, who teach others.

I wholeheartedly believe that there is room in every Christian's life to take on the mantle of discipleship, both learning from following Jesus and teaching others to do the same. This faith that we have is not a spectator sport, but requires full participation, even when mistakes are made.

Heavenly Father, I pray that you would help us to embrace this life of discipleship. That we would take what we have learned and entrust it to others.

Amen.

———————

1 Chan, Francis. *Crazy Love: Overwhelmed by a Relentless God.* Colorado Springs: David C. Cook, 2008.

"Come and Listen..." | Deirdra Jones

"Come and listen... let me tell you what He has done for me." -Psalm 66:16 (NLT)

As a believer, the greatest thing you possess is your relationship with Jesus Christ as the Lord and Savior of your life. One of the next greatest things you possess is your testimony.

One of my favorite scenes in the series The Chosen was a conversation between Mary Magdalene, who had been possessed and tortured by demons to the point of trying to take her own life, and Nicodemus, a prominent Jewish leader and Pharisee. The last time Nicodemus had seen her was when he had been asked by the Romans to perform an exorcism on her. However, Nicodemus was unsuccessful. Mary said to Nicodemus, "It wasn't anything that you did; it was Someone else. He called me Mary, and He said I am His and I am redeemed. I don't even understand it myself, but I was one way and now I am completely different. And the thing in between...was Him."

Mary didn't have all the church lingo down or all of the theology figured out. She simply testified to what Jesus had done in her life.

As for me, I don't have to understand or know exactly how God works or moves to testify that He does move and has moved in my life.

From Genesis to Revelation, we read about one miracle after another, and those miracles continue to happen, even today. Every time someone comes into the saving knowledge of Christ and accepts Christ as their Lord and Savior, a miracle has occurred. Every breath you take and every beat of your heart is a testament to the miraculous beauty, awe, and wonder of our Creator.

Miraculous things are still happening in the world today. Miracles are still happening. They are happening right here, right now. We are simply called to tell others what He has done in and for us.

Like Mary Magdalene, I don't even fully understand it myself, "but I was one way and now I am completely different. And the thing in between...was Him."

Call to Action: Pray for the opportunity to tell someone what He has done in and for you, and then act on it.

SABBATH

A RHYTHM
OF REST

Then Jesus declared, "I am the bread of life.

Whoever comes to me will never go hungry, and

whoever believes in me will never be thirsty."

John 6:35

When the Answer Hasn't Come Yet, I Will Still Believe | Linda Shepherd

"And He spake a parable unto them to this end, that men ought always to pray, and not to faint." -Luke 18:1

Have you ever given up the thought of prayer before you even started because you felt something was impossible for God to answer? Have you ever thought someone had gone too far to be saved and you lacked the faith to believe in their redemption? Did you know ever think about the fact that sometimes God saves people after we have gone to be with the Lord? He'll still be working, even when we aren't here to participate! Do you also know that sometimes God surprises us and saves people long before we ever dreamed He would? God's ways are not ours, so He reminds us that we always need to pray and not give up. God is often working something in the spiritual realm, and we must believe that and wait patiently for Him.

When we pray, we must strive to see things happening with the spiritual eye. How do we do this? First, we must not get discouraged and let our feelings rule us. We must let our faith keep us strong. We must keep our eyes on Jesus as we pray and thank Him for the answer even before it comes. We must also remember to have a heart of thanksgiving and praise.

What seems impossible for you right now? Remember with God all things are possible. Keep praying unto the end. We must not waver and focus on the situation. Instead, we must keep looking to God. And when God does answer, make note of it! Perhaps we could journal our prayer requests and the times God does answer, so we will not take God for granted or be tempted to give up when the answer doesn't arrive as soon as we would like. We must persevere in our prayer life, and then we will grow in our faith.

Father, help me to pray always and not to faint. I choose to keep up the faith and persevere in prayer. I praise you that the answer is coming. I praise you for working on my behalf even when I don't see the answer yet.

"Thou Hast Made Me" | Emily Heady

"Know that the LORD is God. It is he who made us, and we are his; we are his people, the sheep of his pasture." –Psalm 100:3

The poet John Donne wrote a cycle of 19 sonnets, most of them prayers, that offer an in-depth and brutally honest look at the spiritual life. Donne moved from career to career until he finally realized his vocation and took orders as a clergyman in the Church of England (he eventually became Dean of St. Paul's Cathedral in London, in fact).

Some background: Sonnets are 14-line poems with regular rhyme schemes. Typically the first eight lines (or octave) describe the situation or problem, and the next six (the sestet) describe the answer or resolution.

The first of these sonnets (included below), offers Donne's prayer on his deathbed. In the first line, he asks a hard question: Why, if God made him, his body should decay? He describes the pains of sickness and begs for God to come near; he feels the pull of despair and fear. In line 8, though, things begin to look different, as he speaks in faith, saying that yet he knows that when God enables him to look upwards, to see the Lord, his heart will be strengthened. He has no illusions about his own strength—he knows that only God keeps him strong of heart and faithful—but he reiterates his faith in God even in the midst of his difficult circumstances.

Here is Donne's poem:

Thou hast made me, And shall thy work decay?
Repair me now, for now mine end doth haste,
I run to death, and death meets me as fast,
And all my pleasures are like yesterday;
I dare not move my dim eyes any way,
Despair behind, and death before doth cast
Such terror, and my feeble flesh doth waste
By sin in it, which it t'wards hell doth weigh;
Only thou art above, and when towards thee
By thy leave I can look, I rise again;
But our old subtle foe so tempteth me,
That not one hour my self I can sustain;
Thy Grace may wing me to prevent his art,
And thou like Adamant draw mine iron heart.

God, please turn our eyes to you; please sustain us, for we cannot trust ourselves.

Mountains and Timber | Steve Peppers

"'Go up into the mountains and bring down timber and build my house, so that I may take pleasure in it and be honored,' says the Lord." –Haggai 1:8

In the mountains, Abraham met with God, who gave him a ram to sacrifice. In the mountains, Moses talked with God and received instructions. In the mountains, Jesus went for prayer with His Father and called His twelve apostles. The mountains often symbolize God's presence.

While the original book of Haggai was directed to the Jewish leaders in 520 BC, I believe God can use such Scripture to quicken a new and personal meaning for those who seek Him. Forty years ago, God used Haggai 1:8 to speak to me and my engaged wife. God encouraged us to keep meeting with Him so He could give us the timber for our marriage.

Just as timber provides form and strength to a physical house, God's timber provides form and strength to our house of marriage. The end goal is to please and honor God. Such an awesome promise from an awesome God! I don't know anything more fulfilling than pleasing and honoring God. Of course, that doesn't mean we have escaped all problems. We've had some hard trials, but God brought us through as we continued to meet with Him, learn from Him, and trust His counsel. And we still believe it pleases and honors Him as we "go up into the mountains."

So, is this life verse only for me and my wife? Are we the only ones for whom God can quicken this verse? I doubt that. Maybe you also need to recognize God speaking to you about your house. Maybe marriage doesn't apply to you. Maybe yours is a different sort of house—a house of your career, your health, your children, your extended family... Is God asking you to "go up into the mountains" to meet with Him and to bring down His timber to strengthen and give form to your house?

Prayer: Lord, help us hear whatever you may be saying. Help us commit to go up and meet with you and to listen to you through Scripture and prayer. And show me how to apply the timber you give so you will take pleasure in it and be honored. Amen.

Mountains | Andrew Horseman

"Jonathan said to his young armor bearer, 'Come, let's go over to the outpost of those uncircumcised men. Perhaps the LORD will act in our behalf. Nothing can hinder the LORD from saving, whether by many or by few.'" –I Samuel 14:6

In front of Jonathan stood two mountains he would need to cross to reach the Philistine outpost on the other side. Trusting in the Lord and taking a step in faith, Jonathan set out against the detachment of Philistines. He knew God was with him, so he and his armor bearer scaled the cliffs looking for the Lord's leading as they reached the outpost. The Lord delivered the Philistines into Jonathan's hands, making him and his armor bearer victorious.

Even as Christians, as we go through life, we will face mountains—mountains that sometimes seem too big for us to climb, or mountains that are full of danger. When we are up against those mountains, whether they be addictions, finances, health struggles, or something else, we know God is with us. For me personally, He has brought restoration to all three of those areas in my life.

What a celebration it ought to be when we reach the top of that mountain that seemed so impossible!

But all too soon, the moment can fade. What happens when we reach the summit, when we overcome? Do we remember who it was that got us there? Often, we easily revert back to living for ourselves once God has gotten us over the mountain we were struggling to climb. A mentor of mine once wrote in a devotion, "We are quick to accept Christ as our savior but reluctant to accept Him as Lord."

Once he reached the Philistines, Jonathan stopped and looked for the Lord's leading. As the Lord gets us past the mountains in our lives, let's make it our mission to remain surrendered and look to Jesus as Lord.

"I Arise Today" | St. Patrick

"God...is not far from any one of us. 'For in Him we live and move and have our being.'"
–Acts 17:27-28

Jesus Christ, may we be ever aware of your presence.

I arise today
Through the strength of heaven;
Light of the sun,
Splendor of fire,
Speed of lightning,
Swiftness of the wind,
Depth of the sea,
Stability of the earth,
Firmness of the rock.

I arise today
Through God's strength to pilot me;
God's might to uphold me,
God's wisdom to guide me,
God's eye to look before me,
God's ear to hear me,
God's word to speak for me,
God's hand to guard me,
God's way to lie before me,
God's shield to protect me,
God's hosts to save me
Afar and anear,
Alone or in a multitude.

Christ shield me today
Against wounding
Christ with me, Christ before me, Christ behind me,
Christ in me, Christ beneath me, Christ above me,
Christ on my right, Christ on my left,
Christ when I lie down, Christ when I sit down,
Christ in the heart of everyone who thinks of me,
Christ in the mouth of everyone who speaks of me,
Christ in the eye that sees me,
Christ in the ear that hears me.

I arise today
Through the mighty strength
Of the Lord of creation.

Stewarding God's Answers to Prayer | Bruce Gardner

"I tell you, you can pray for anything, and if you believe that you've received it, it will be yours." –Mark 11:24

How often do we pray for something, but when God answers that prayer, we don't hold up our end of the bargain? When we go through good times we may feel we have all the answers and forget how God has provided the means for us to be there. Then we find ourselves in the bad times and we reach out to God for His blessing and answers to our problems because we have reached the end of ourselves.

Why do we go to God at the end of ourselves rather than at the beginning of each day? Chris Tiegreen offers us some perspective:

> *James O. Fraser, missionary to the Lisu of China in the early 20th century, developed much of his prayer life from a fascinating contemporary illustration. At the time, the Canadian government offered incentives for British citizens to emigrate to Canada and claim territory in the west. There was plenty of territory waiting to be cultivated; all that was needed were people who would boldly come, claim as much land as they could reasonably cultivate, commit to care for the land, accept the conditions of the government, enter into it, and then be faithful to work it. It was an open invitation to spread out and steward resources for the benefit of the realm.*
>
> *That's a lot like prayer. We have an open invitation from God to ask and receive—to claim territory for his kingdom. But there are conditions. We ask specifically. We commit to steward the gift faithfully. We get up and go into the promise, and then we cultivate what we've been given. It's how God has chosen to expand his kingdom and entrust it into the hands of those who represent him well.*
>
> *Pray with that kind of definition and commitment (Mark 11:24). Understand the terms of God's promises—that his gifts are free, but once given must be handled with care. Develop a vision for the territory of your calling, and then ask God for it. Then take definite steps, by faith, to enter in.*[1]

How are you praying today?

---

1 Tiegreen, Chris. "A Model for Asking," iDisciple.org. https://www.idisciple.org/post/a-model-for-asking

SABBATH

A RHYTHM
OF REST

Exalt the Lord our God

and worship at his holy mountain,

for the Lord our God is holy.

Psalm 99:9

Prayers of the Righteous | Doug Fry

"The prayer of a righteous person is powerful and effective." –James 5:16

It was a Saturday afternoon in August 1965 when I received a letter from the U.S. Army informing me that I had been selected to serve my country. I was instructed to report to our local Army Induction Station for active duty on September 29, 1965. It was that day that my life would change forever.

About 30 of us young men were flown to Fort Jackson, South Carolina, that night. It took about two days for me to realize that this was very serious, and that life was precious. The Vietnam War was at its peak.

In preparation for the battlefield, we had to get physically fit, learn hand-to-hand combat, throw a hand grenade, and qualify with an M14 rifle. Our instructors reminded us every day that if we were not well trained and physically fit there was good chance that we could be injured or killed in the line of duty.

One night after a couple of weeks, I was lying in my bunk bed unable to sleep, thinking that I could lose my life on the battlefield. I wasn't living for the Lord and thinking that I could die and go to hell. I had grown up with godly parents and had been in church most of my life. I received Jesus as my Lord and Savior but had wandered away from my faith.

That night in my bunk, I prayed and promised the Lord if He would protect me and keep me close to home that one day, I would serve him. I heard Him say to me as if He were there in person, "I will always take care of you and keep you close to home." My mother would send me letters telling me of all the people in our church who were calling her to say that God had placed me on their hearts and they were praying for me on a specific day at a specific time.

I completed my training and was assigned to Aberdeen Proving Grounds, Maryland. After completing my classes there, I was assigned to permanent staff and then sent to instructors' school to be trained to teach in the classroom. I am convinced that my church family's prayers made the difference: "The prayer of a righteous man or woman is powerful and effective" (James 5:16).

Listening for the Conn | Nick Willis

"Listen to me, you descendants of Jacob, all the remnant of the people of Israel, you whom I have upheld since your birth, and have carried since you were born. Even to your old age and gray hairs I am he, I am he who will sustain you. I have made you and I will carry you. I will sustain you and I will rescue you." –Isaiah 46:3-4

The United States Navy's powerful warships have a mission to protect the world with their presence—and a single voice guides these ships. Every pilothouse in the Navy contains upwards of eight people at all times, but the most important interaction is between the Conning Officer and the Helm. The Conning Officer relays clear and concise orders to the Helm to manipulate rudder angles and propeller speeds. The Helmsman, who works in the chaotic and stressful pilot house, makes all the changes as ordered. In almost all cases the Helmsman cannot see where he or she is steering. How easy for the Helmsman to get distracted and listen to the wrong voice!

Life is like the open ocean: busy, equal parts glorious and dangerous. And we, like a Helmsman, are steering on faith based on the commands that we hear. Be it culture, peer pressure, or even our own judgment, we listen to every voice in the bridge of our hearts, and many of these could lead us into danger. However, there is great hope! In Isaiah 46:3-4, God cuts through all the voices to tell a faithless Israel to listen specifically to Him. He reminds them of their identity and His own character. He is a trustworthy guide.

Elsewhere in John 10, we see Jesus identify as the Good Shepherd, explaining that the sheep know His voice, that He calls them by name, and that they will not listen to the voice of another. Praise God for His Word and His Spirit, both of which He implants deeply in our hearts, directing us when and where to "turn our rudder" and when and where to "slow down." He is our faithful Conn, and though we cannot often see clearly, He will bring us safely to shore.

Prayer: Lord, grant me wisdom to know your voice and faith to follow as you command, trusting that you will lead me for my good and your glory!

Locked Doors...Open Doors | Melba Willis

"Jesus often withdrew into the wilderness to pray." –Luke 5:16

By the grace of God, my sons speak of how I often locked them out of the house on Saturday mornings or on summer days, a time in which I sought the Lord in prayer. And while they found the door to our home locked many times, it was in the prayer closet where I discovered Jesus opens all the doors of life.

Early on in my walk with Jesus, I read of how He often withdrew to lonely places to seek His Father. I read what Jesus said about entering your prayer closet, of how He answers the prayers that are prayed behind locked doors. As a young wife and mother, I soon discovered that He was the only One I could go to with my problems and pains, sicknesses, and sorrows. I also found out that you don't have to have the right words, that He alone understands the deep cries of your heart and life.

Speaking of the cries of my heart, I expressed my heart's desire that God would save the souls of my sons and make something out of their lives. As a young mother, I saw how other young men were living their lives without God. This led me to call desperately out to God for my sons, prayers which were often wordless, prayers expressed with profound groans from the depths of my heart.

In the gospels we read of how Jesus and His disciples departed for solitary places. So often I have found myself in lonely, desperate places, only to realize that Jesus was always with me. I have also learned that Jesus uses these places to draw His children closer to Him and to help us empathize with the pain and sorrow of others, in particular the loneliness and pain experienced by the lost, by those who don't know Him.

Remembering back to when my children were very young, I recall the hot summer days. I think back to how they often knocked on the back door, asking for a drink of water, as I prayed and sought intimacy with Jesus, the Water of Life.

Prayer of the 23rd Psalm | Deirdra Jones

"The Lord is my shepherd; I have all that I need." -Psalm 23:1

The Psalms are beautiful, raw, honest, and sometimes hard prayers. Over the years, I have heard pastors encourage people to pray the Psalms. This practice has helped the Psalms come alive for me, to have a reality beyond the pages of my Bible. One of my favorites is the 23rd Psalm, and I turned to it and wrote out my prayer in response to a particularly difficult situation I was facing.

"The Lord is my Shepherd whom I am dependent on to provide, guide, and protect me. He already knows about everything I need and has prepared for it, so I trust Him to meet my needs as they arise. He has a plan for my life that I cannot fully see at any given moment, but because I trust Him completely, I will follow Him wherever He leads me—even into the hard places. Every leading is intended for me to fully embrace His will. The hard places will be used to refine me, and the quiet, smooth places He will use to refresh and restore me. He guides me in the paths of righteousness for His glory and my good and best. I don't need to fear the desert or dark places. I don't need to fear the attacks or presence of the enemy at my door because the Father is with me at all times— even when I don't think I can hear Him, see Him, or feel Him. His Word says His presence is with me always—I believe it and I trust it. God has set a table for two, meant just for me and Him—it is good and pleasant. The enemy is lurking, but he is not invited, and he does NOT have permission to sit down. Father, you have anointed my head with oil; you promise to protect me. My life has overflowed with and is evidence of your goodness and your blessings. I am so very grateful. I know and believe that your goodness and love will follow me all of the days of my life. With my whole self, I long and wait for the day that I will get to dwell in your house and in your presence, forever. Amen."

Turn a psalm into a prayer today.

The Surprising Simplicity of Prayer | J. Philip Fuller

"'Lord, teach us to pray!' the disciples pled with Jesus." –Luke 11:1

I have been a Christian for more than 50 years. Let me confess, I have struggled to find the best way to pray. I have never found it practical to be in the same place at the same time every morning for prayer. Yet when I have been at my best for Jesus, I have found both great simplicity and profound meaning in prayer.

My mother had just died. My father, already in the earliest stages of dementia, welcomed his neighbor who stopped by to deliver a casserole—a kind gesture filled with love. Dad, in a moment of incredible lucidity and in typical southern fashion, thanked her profusely for how good it was (though he hadn't tasted it yet!). Then, with a tear in his eye, he asked his neighbor to pray for him, "because this is the hardest thing we've ever known." She politely acknowledged that she would indeed pray for him and turned to head home. Dad reached out to her and kindly, but firmly, asked, "I meant right now, would you pray for us right now?"

Obviously, she was quite uncomfortable with the idea of praying publicly. She stuttered something like, "I...I...don't...don't pray...out loud..."

"Sure you can," Dad told her with such love.

His words were at once disarming and empowering. Perhaps it was his grief or possibly his Christlike demeanor, I'm not sure. Maybe it was both. Nonetheless, the simplicity of it all overcame her. She turned toward my father and grabbed both of his hands in hers as my father said to her, "If you'll just start, He will help you!"

She did start. He did help her. It wasn't fancy. It was genuine. It wasn't flowery. It was heartfelt. It wasn't complicated. It was profoundly simple.

Jesus' disciples learned the simplicity of prayer from Him—prayer about daily bread, about our Father in heaven, about His will, about trespass forgiving, and prayer that what is in heaven can be on earth. (See Luke 11.)

Lord, teach me to pray—simply, powerfully, consistently, corporately, and increasingly.

Why Prayer? | Ashley Gomez

"Rejoice always, pray continually, give thanks in all circumstances; for this is God's will for you in Christ Jesus." –I Thessalonians 5:16-18

Sometimes it seems like we are in a season of little prayer. Or perhaps it is our lack of faith in how powerful prayer really is. My family and I have been praying for my sister and her family for several years. In response, God miraculously healed one of my sister's daughters from a vegetative state, and, when my sister's difficult pregnancy threatened both her own life and the life of her son, both mother and child were protected and given treatment at one of the top facilities in the area. The hand of God is heavily evident upon my sister's life and that of her family. And yet, we yearn for their salvation, for these miracles have not yet resulted in her or her children receiving the love of Christ. The grief felt, especially for the children, feels almost too heavy to bear at times.

The challenge is to keep praying, rejoicing, and giving thanks, no matter how hopeless the situation may seem. God's power can break through even the darkest mind, chained down in its mires of self and the confusion and difficulties of failing health and life. This is why we must pray, resisting the urge to think despondently, "All I can do is pray." Yes, exactly. That is all you can do; but it is not all He can do.

SABBATH

A RHYTHM
OF REST

The Lord is my shepherd, I lack nothing.

He makes me lie down in green pastures,

he leads me beside quiet waters,

he refreshes my soul.

Psalm 23:1-3

Joy | John Swales

"I tell you that in the same way there will be more rejoicing in heaven over one sinner who repents than over ninety-nine righteous persons who do not need to repent." –Luke 15:7

It was the summer of 2014 when my oldest son, JT, joined a tee-ball team through a local rec league. His first two at-bats, he could only hit the stand. Eventually, he touched the ball, and it dribbled a few feet in front of him. His third at-bat was very different. He hit the ball dead-on, and it rolled all the way to the pitcher's mound. That's when mayhem broke out on the field. JT and the entire opposing team were running to get the ball. We yelled for him to go to first base, and the other coaches were trying to get the kids to stay in their positions. It was a futile attempt because those five-year-olds were on a mission. JT was the first to get to the ball and was so happy! He picked it up and start jumping for joy. Then, the rest of the opposing team got there, and they started jumping up and down with JT! It was the purest form of joy I have ever witnessed. Even though they were on opposing teams, these kids were genuinely joyful for JT.

This is the type of joy Jesus is speaking of in the Parable of the Lost Sheep. It's an unadulterated, pure joy that gives you goosebumps. Try to recall how you felt when you gave your life to Christ. Remember the sense of relief and joy you felt knowing your sins were forgiven? You have a clean slate. Remember how you felt the instant you came out of the water during your baptism? Jesus tells us about the rejoicing in heaven when one lost soul is found.

After some time, though, we become complacent. We clap our hands when we hear about someone turning their life over to Christ or witness someone's baptism, but it's not the same anymore. It's time for us to start sharing heaven's joy with the world. Do you rejoice like heaven when you see/hear of someone being saved or baptized? Are you filled with the same joy you had the day you turned your life over to Christ?

If not, then what can you do today to rekindle that joy?

Divine Discontent | Stephen Willis

"How precious is your steadfast love, O God! The children of mankind take refuge in the shadow of your wings. They feast on the abundance of your house, and you give them drink from the river of your delights. For with you is the fountain of life." –Psalm 36:8-9

When John D. Rockefeller was asked, "How much money is enough?," he responded, "Just a little bit more." This man owned one percent of the U.S. economy and 90 percent of the gas and oil industry. Yet it wasn't enough. His response reveals that no matter how much of something you have, it seldom satisfies. The lack of satisfaction can drive us to enormous success, but it also can become a trap that steals our soul. We must be on guard when we have feelings of selfish discontent. This selfish discontent was the genesis of Satan's sin that had him cast out of heaven (Isaiah 14:12-15). It wasn't good enough for Satan to be near to God and to bask in His goodness. His selfish discontent led to a desire to be worshiped himself.

As I grow in my relationship with God, I am discovering that the discipleship process helps replace selfish discontent with divine discontent. Our selfish desires can wreck our souls, but a greater longing for the things of God leads us into increased Christlikeness. It is for this reason that the psalmist proclaims the steadfast love of God, our protection within His care, and the abundant life that is a result of God's presence. These truths bring tremendous joy.

The apostle Paul discovered the abundance that the psalmist proclaimed in Psalm 36. Paul testified, "Indeed, I count everything as loss because of the surpassing worth of knowing Christ Jesus my Lord. For his sake I have suffered the loss of all things and count them as rubbish, in order that I may gain Christ" (Phil. 3:8). When studying the life of Paul, we find that he lost everything that the world considered valuable. Yet Paul considered it rubbish in comparison to truly knowing Jesus.

As we examine our own desires let us not forget that Rockefeller and Paul lived with a longing for "just a little bit more." One never found satisfaction while the other found the only one who truly satisfies—Jesus.

Prayer: Lord Jesus, I simply long for more of you.

Longing for the Courts of the Lord | Torrie Slaughter

"For the Lord God is a sun and shield; the Lord bestows favor and honor; no good thing does he withhold from those whose walk is blameless." -Psalm 84:11

Psalm 84 is a beautiful song of longing for God's presence and a desire to worship Him. It is a psalm that expresses the writer's deep longing for the courts of the Lord and the joy of being in His presence. The psalmist writes, "My soul longs, yes, faints for the courts of the Lord; my heart and flesh sing for joy to the living God" (Psalm 84:2).

The writer describes the beauty of the temple and how blessed are those who dwell in it, for they continually praise God. He writes, "Blessed are those who dwell in your house, ever singing your praise!" (Psalm 84:4). The psalmist's desire for worship is not just a desire for an experience but a desire to be in God's presence, to dwell in the house of the Lord and to be close to Him. The psalmist also recognizes the blessings of being in God's presence. He writes, "For a day in your courts is better than a thousand elsewhere. I would rather be a doorkeeper in the house of my God than dwell in the tents of wickedness" (Psalm 84:10). Being in God's presence brings joy and peace that cannot be found anywhere else.

As believers, we should also deeply desire to worship God and be in His presence. Our longing should be not only for the experience of worship, but also for a deeper connection with God. We should strive to be in His presence continually, seeking after Him in prayer, reading His Word, and worshiping Him with all our hearts.

As we read and meditate on Psalm 84, let us be inspired to deepen our desire for worship and our longing for God's presence. May we seek after Him with all our hearts and find joy and peace in His presence.

The Sound of Silence | Caleb Atkins

"Be still and know that I am God. I will be exalted among the nations; I will be exalted in the earth." –Psalm 46:10

Think about hearing a beautiful piece of music, or your favorite worship song. What comes to mind? Maybe it's the lyrics that capture your heart. Maybe it's the intricate melody that floats through the air. Maybe it's even the harmonies that compliment that melody.

But how often do you think about the role of silence in music? Famous jazz musician Dizzy Gillespie said, "It's taken me all my life to learn what not to play." This is someone who spent countless hours practicing what to play in order to create good music—yet he had the wisdom to know the role of silence.

Silence is the great canvas that invites beauty into the world. Silence provides space for the next note to land. Silence provides tension and calls for resolution. Silence invites other musicians into the conversation. Silence is necessary.

How about the role of silence in our relationship with our Father? How often do we take the time to listen? How often do we take the time to be silent before our God?

We are so accustomed to noise in our culture. It seems like the very world we live in is screaming for our attention. And we often scream back.

But when we quiet our souls, when we sit in silence before our God, that's when we might catch His still small voice that reveals His name and whispers meaning into our soul. When we are silent is when we can have ears to hear.

The Soul and a Jar of River Water | Mike Lyle

"I have calmed and quieted myself, I am like a weaned child with its mother; like a weaned child I am content." –Psalm 131:2

What is this psalmist calming and quieting? The Hebrew word is "naphesh." In English, we could translate it to "soul." When he uses the word "soul," the psalmist is not talking about some abstract, amorphous thing with no definition, but the part of him that is the most real—the very essence of who he is.[1] This is what he is calming and quieting—his very self. Isn't this the part of us that is most often in need of being calmed and quieted?

We are bombarded daily by images of success, beauty, and counterfeit sources of identity. We receive blows to our souls as we reveal the truest part of ourselves only to be rejected or found wanting. We experience trauma in life that sends our souls into hiding. All of this produces a kind of tumult within us that makes us feel like our souls are screaming and unsettled. As a result, we reach for anything that will offer us a measure of peace and comfort: the opinion of others, a job well done, a candy bar, a drink, a high, or a movie. But all this does is medicate our souls when what they need is to be calmed and quieted.

Now, imagine a jar of river water. When you first scoop it out of the river, it is wild brown with dirt and soil stirring within it. However, if you were to set it down and allow it to be still for a while, all of that debris would settle and reveal clear water. I think this is what it looks like to calm and quiet our souls. The disciplines of solitude and silence invite us to sit still long enough to settle our souls. Then, our souls can find rest in God like a weaned child rests in its mother's arms.

Is your soul screaming within you? Try practicing solitude and silence today. Spend 15 minutes with God and God alone without the pressure to say anything.

---

1 Barton, Ruth Haley. "When Leaders Lose Their Souls." Transforming Center. 2008. Accessed August 1, 2023, https://transformingcenter.org/2008/06/when-leaders-lose-their-souls/

Ears to Hear His Voice | Bruce Gardner

"The sheep recognize his voice and come to him. He calls his own sheep by name and leads them out." –John 10:3

"'Go out and stand before me on the mountain,' the Lord told him. And as Elijah stood there, the Lord passed by, and a mighty windstorm hit the mountain. It was such a terrible blast that the rocks were torn loose, but the Lord was not in the wind. After the wind there was an earthquake, but the Lord was not in the earthquake. And after the earthquake there was a fire, but the Lord was not in the fire. And after the fire there was the sound of a gentle whisper." –I Kings 19:11-12

Have you ever prayed to hear God's voice? Most people would love to hear God's voice clearly and consistently, with step-by-step instructions on how to live their best life and get the most out of it—but few think it's even possible.

This is not what the Scriptures tell us though. The Bible is full of examples of how God spoke to kings who worshiped pagan gods. Pharaoh and Nebuchadnezzar come to mind, as do people from idol-worshiping families, such as Abram (whom God renamed Abraham) and Gideon, a long list of unwilling prophets from which there are so many to choose, and, of course, even the chief persecutor of the early followers of Jesus, Saul, who became Paul.

He has spoken and continues to speak to addicts clinging to one last hope, and to rebels headed in the wrong direction in their stubbornness. He speaks to Muslims fighting against believers in Jesus, to materialists who finally ask the question, "Is this life all there is?," and even to normal, everyday people who just pray to Him for direction.

You should never assume you are unable to hear God's voice. All you have to do is ask. It may take some practice and fine-tuning to hear Him well, but you can. You probably already do but haven't yet learned to distinguish what He is saying. He speaks through scripture, conversations, prayer, desires, patterns of circumstances, and even the parables written into your everyday experiences. Ask for ears to ear, and then open them. The world will come alive with the sights and sounds of his voice.

Do you have ears to hear?

SABBATH

A RHYTHM
OF REST

You prepare a table before me

in the presence of my enemies.

You anoint my head with oil;

my cup overflows.

Surely your goodness and love will follow me

all the days of my life,

and I will dwell in the house of the Lord

Forever.

Psalm 23:5-6

Delight | Bobbie Gardner

"Take delight in the Lord, and he will give you the desires of your heart." –Psalm 37:4

Many years ago, I learned an acronym for the word DELIGHT;
Daily - **E**verything - **L**aid - **I**nto - **G**od's - **H**ands - **T**riumphantly

This acronym came from Dr. Earl Lee, who once pastored the Pasadena First Church of the Nazarene. He shared this with us during a revival while I was a student there, and I wrote it in a Bible I used during my college years.
It sounds simple, doesn't it? I used to think something like this: "The Lord is great, and I'm a good person, so He will surely bring me whatever I ask Him for!" In my youth, I asked for a great-looking spouse, a successful job, a house full of beautiful and perfectly well-behaved children, and of course a skinny body. (If you know me, surely you're laughing aloud right now!)

Over time, though, I learned great—but tough—lessons about taking delight in the Lord. My will was often NOT aligned with God's will, and I know that because it was NOT aligned with God's Word. I had to learn that our delight in and from the Lord comes with our surrender. When we study the Word of God and align our will to God's Word, then our delight is found in Him.

Doing this takes discipline and time. What are we willing to surrender? Is it TV, sports, social media, or job responsibilities? Could it be family or financial worries? These things may steal our joy if they distract us from being in God's Word and spending time in His presence daily.
Daily – Take up praying and reading God's Word.

Everything – Envision all of it; not just picking and choosing things, but the good, the bad, and the ugly laid before the Lord.

Laid – Picture all those things surrendered, let go of, released, gone, fully handed over.

Into God's Hands – Imagine your little hand in God's big hand and hold on to Him, hold your hands out, palms up. Say, "I surrender to you, Lord."

Triumphantly – Give God the glory and praise for He is worthy; He has given you the strength you need to take delight in Him. Our greatest desire is to love, serve, and be open to His will.

Famine and Feast | Emily Heady

"Then the disciples of John came to Him, asking, 'Why do we and the Pharisees fast, but Your disciples do not fast?' And Jesus said to them, 'The attendants of the bridegroom cannot mourn as long as the bridegroom is with them, can they? But the days will come when the bridegroom is taken away from them, and then they will fast.'" –Matthew 9:14-15

Mardi Gras, or Fat Tuesday, doesn't look all that much like a holy feast from the outside—at least if you take the New Orleans version of it as your standard. Early in its history, however, Mardi Gras was celebrated as a sort of last hurrah before the penitential season of Lent began, with its traditional fasting and somberness. And it represented more broadly the biblical pattern of feasting and fasting that characterizes so much of Christian history.

If you spend much time in Leviticus (and don't we all?), you will notice a series of seven ritual feasts that God prescribes for His people. Feasts serve many functions: marking a place for gratitude (the Feast of First Fruits, Leviticus 23:10; the Feast of Weeks or Pentecost, Leviticus 23:16); taking time to remember when God delivered His people (Passover, Leviticus 23:4-8; the Feast of Unleavened Bread, Leviticus 23:6; and the Feast of Tabernacles or Booths, Leviticus 23:34); resting and reflecting at the beginning of a new year (Leviticus 23:24); and making a space to thank God for His forgiveness (The Day of Atonement, Leviticus 16, 23:26-32). The Day of Atonement, in fact, was both a feast and a fast—a ritualized celebration of God's forgiveness that also involved abstaining from food.

Feasts and fasts set the rhythm of life for Old Testament Israel, reminding them of the goodness of God and prodding them toward greater holiness. In our own lives, times of joy and celebration alternate with seasons of grief and mourning, and the Church calendar helps us to remember that this is a divine rhythm. Mardi Gras, poised as it is right before the penitential season of Lent, gives us a space to celebrate the many blessings God bestows on us, while also preparing us to reflect on all the ways we need His forgiveness.

Dear God, as we move throughout the seasons of our lives, help us to remember that you are the God of the mountains and the valleys, and both are holy.

Are You Paying Attention? | Brian Charette

"I confess my iniquity; I am troubled by my sin." –Psalm 38:18

Yes, your attention span is shrinking. In fact, the average person doesn't have the attention span needed to read this devotion. (But try.) In the book Attention Span: A Groundbreaking Way to Restore Balance, Happiness and Productivity, Dr. Gloria Mark writes, "In 2004, we measured the average attention on a screen to be 2 1/2 minutes. Some years later, we found attention spans to be about 75 seconds. Now we find people can only pay attention to one screen for an average of 47 seconds."[1] Another study found that diagnosed Attention Deficit Disorder almost doubled between 1997 and 2016.[2]
So, what are you paying attention to?

So many things now demand our attention that there is less of it to go around. We live in a time when the concept of being "starved for attention" is real. Maybe that's why the season of Lent is important: It calls our attention back to the cross—back to the work of Christ on our behalf—and paves the way for the celebration of His resurrection. We honor this season every year to do battle against the forces which pull at us to the point of distraction. Our minds drift away from the one who is worthy of our focus.

Ash Wednesday is a day to begin to look our sin squarely in the face—attending to it—and taking the first step of repentance. Specifically, the biblical practice of sprinkling oneself with ashes symbolizes deep sorrow for sin. See Mordecai (Esther 4:1), Job (Job 42:6), the inhabitants of Nineveh (Jonah 3:5-6), or Daniel (Daniel 9:3-4). Forgiveness for sin, purchased by Jesus on the cross, is available in this moment. The opportunity to repent lays before us, if we are paying attention.

---

1 Mark, Gloria. *Attention Span: A Groundbreaking Way to Restore Balance, Happiness and Productivity*. Toronto: Hanover Square P, 2023.
2 Xu, Guifeng, Lane Strathearn, and Buyun Liu. "Twenty-Year Trends in Diagnosed Attention-Deficit/Hyper-activity Disorder among US Children and Adolescents, 1997-2016. JAMA Network Open. 2018. doi:10.1001/jamanetworkopen.2018.1471.

"LET ME KNOW MYSELF AND KNOW YOU"

"I want to know Christ and the power of His resurrection." –Philippians 3:10

Lord Jesus, let me know myself and know you,
And desire nothing, save only you.
Let me hate myself and love you.
Let me do everything for the sake of you.
Let me humble myself and exalt you.
Let me think of nothing except you.
Let me accept whatever happens as from you.
Let me banish self and follow you,
And ever desire to follow you.
Let me fly from myself and take refuge in you,
That I may deserve to be defended by you.
Let me fear for myself, let me fear you,
And let me be among those who are chosen by you.
Let me be willing to obey for the sake of you.
Let me cling to nothing, save only to you,
And let me be poor because of you.
Look upon me, that I may love you.
Call me, that I may see you,
And forever enjoy you.
Amen.

Lord Jesus, please help us to know ourselves insofar as seeing ourselves accurately helps us to know you more. Draw us near, for we are inclined to wander. Amen.

St. Augustine

I Give Up | Todd Thomas

"If anyone would come after me, he must deny himself and take up his cross and follow me." –Matthew 16:24

Winston Churchill rose to world-wide fame for his courage in the face of the advancing armies of the Third Reich. On October 29, 1941 he visited Harrow School, his alma mater. He made a few remarks which included these words: "Never give in, never give in, never, never, never, never—in nothing, great or small, large or petty—never give in except to convictions of honor and good sense. Never yield to force; never yield to the apparently overwhelming might of the enemy." Even to this day, we admire these words of courage and echo them in our own expressions: Don't quit, don't give up, keep going, finish what you started, stick to it, hang in there.

Then we encounter these words of Jesus—words that are like a sign over the entry of the narrow way, words that set the expectations we must consider before we begin the journey with Jesus.

Give up your self will.
Give up your life.
Give up your plans.

There is so much more to following Jesus than making room in our schedules to spend a few minutes a day with Him, a few hours a week. There is so much more to following Jesus than a few focus-days of disciplined restraint throughout the year. There is so much more to following Jesus than a temporary denial of meaningful or enjoyable portions of our routine.
Following Jesus calls for total, abject surrender.

This is saying, "Not my will but yours." This is saying, "I am crucified with Christ, yet I live." This is saying, "Only your purpose expressed in and through me, Lord."

This is the life of living sacrifice.

Convicting. Challenging. Contrary.

If we are going to follow this crucified and risen Savior we must bow humbly and whisper through our trembling—"I give up."

Clutter | Gary O'Shell

"He told them: 'Take nothing for the journey—no staff, no bag, no bread, no money, no extra shirt.'" –Luke 9:3

"Deserts unclutter the soul." –Alicia Britt Chole

Though all my walk with Him has been a journey, I think the first true spiritual adventure I undertook with Him was leaving my "homeland" for Bible College. Everything I owned was in that car. I was unencumbered, ready to go anywhere with and for Him. I felt so free. Thirty-nine years later, upon retirement, I entered upon a new journey and was considerably more "encumbered" with goods than the first time. We accumulate a lot of "stuff" over time, a lot of "clutter." That clutter pertains to far more than our possessions. A great deal of clutter can gather in our hearts and souls.

Jesus knows this. We see it in His sending of the disciples out to minister in the surrounding area. He commanded them to take nothing—NOTHING—to fall back upon. His Father would be their Source. It was His intention that in their going out with nothing, they would gain everything. Seeing everything, He saw into the clutter of their divided hearts. He saw what was lacking and He knew that the way to gain all things was to be divested of everything else that blinded them to what they had in Him. As Jesus had walked out into the wilderness, led of the Spirit, so too were the disciples entering their own kind of desert with the obeying of His command. He meant to unclutter their hearts through what they experienced in this radical new adventure.

If Jesus were to look into our hearts this season of Lent, what would He say needed to decrease so that He could increase? What attitudes, desires, jealousies, habits, and false idols do we need to let go of in order that we may complete the calling He's placed upon us? What spiritual clutter needs to be thrown out? What clogs our spiritual arteries and keeps us from His fullness? Are we really willing to shed anything in order that we might have His everything?

No one likes a cluttered house, but we get used to it, just as we do a cluttered heart. We know where we need the housecleaning. Are we willing to acknowledge where we need the heart cleaning?

SABBATH

A RHYTHM
OF REST

He says, "Be still, and know that I am

God; I will be exalted among the nations,

I will be exalted in the earth."

Psalm 46:10

The Kitchen Table Altar | Reenie Peppers

"For where your treasure is, there your heart [your wishes, your desires; that on which your life centers] will be also." –Matthew 6:21

We all have that surface in our home where things accumulate—the unopened mail, the overdue library book, and the pair of scissors that never gets returned to the desk drawer. That surface in my house is the kitchen table. Right now on my table is a plastic tub labeled 'lab reports for DE-Chemistry', a calculator and stapler, a sleeve of 20-sided gaming dice, the book Alice I Have Been by Melanie Benjamin, and a pair of superhero socks.

From my kitchen table, you might realize that my husband is a high school chemistry teacher, that my son is an avid gamer, that I love to read and am in a book club, and that we are a family of Marvel enthusiasts.

My kitchen table, in a manner of speaking, is an altar to what my family values. My husband values his role as a teacher and the positive influence he can have on his students. My son's gaming is significant to him as it keeps his mind sharp and is his main social community. Books keep my mind sharp, my person relaxed, and my soul nourished.

However, am I giving these things too much importance, especially at the cost of something else? For example, reading is a beneficial, worthwhile activity. However, is it pursued at the cost of having coffee with a friend who is having a rough time with their teenager? Is it at the cost of fixing my family a home-cooked, nutritious dinner? Ouch!

This question of what I value and give my time to brings to mind the verse, "For where your treasure is, there your heart [your wishes, your desires; that on which your life centers] will be also" (Matthew 6:21). That which I treasure, that which I value, that which is altar worthy, is that on which my life centers. The things represented by my 'kitchen table altar' are neither wrong nor unimportant. However, there is a cost in giving an activity or pursuit undue precedence over another activity or pursuit. We only have a limited amount of time, energy, and resources to invest in those things that we value most.

What is on your 'kitchen table altar'?

Provision in the Desert | Emily Heady

"The Lord said, 'During the forty years that I led you through the wilderness, your clothes did not wear out, nor did the sandals on your feet. You ate no bread and drank no wine or other fermented drink. I did this so that you might know that I am the LORD your God.'" –Deuteronomy 29:5-6

Lent is a hard season, a long one. The forty days preceding Easter call to mind forty days of rain that cleansed the earth from sin in Noah's time, the Israelites' forty-year wandering in the wilderness, and Jesus' forty days of temptation in the desert. Each of these was a season of famine rather than feast; each narrowed down the scope of experience of those living through them until there was nothing much left except God. Lent is a season to remind us that God is all we need—and sometimes, all we have.

But, as the Deuteronomy passage records, we can rest in knowing that God is all we have because He is in charge of everything—He is able to provide, and He will. Yet it is easier to say this sometimes than to believe it. I imagine myself in the literal shoes of the Israelites in the desert. They had no spare food—only enough for the day. They had no second tunic and no extra sandals to put on in case of bad weather or blisters. Me, I find it hard to pack for a weekend without at least three pairs of shoes and a few layers to add to my outfits. And at any given time, I have a stash of snacks with me. I think of it as being prepared, but in truth, it's also me wanting to control my circumstances—to make sure that whatever happens, I won't be caught off guard. I don't trust God well.

This year during Lent, I'm setting aside some of the things that typically help me to feel secure. I'm not doing this because I think there's anything magical in making a sacrifice but because I want to be reminded that God is enough, that He will provide, and that I can trust Him.

Jesus, as we go through desert times in our lives, help us to be grateful for how they teach us to rely on you.

Holy Brokenness | Dani Swords Huizar

"Truly, truly, I say to you, unless a grain of wheat falls into the earth and dies, it remains alone; but if it dies, it bears much fruit." –John 12:24

In the little apartment I had moved into during my divorce, my life crumbled before me. The custody battle was brutal, filled with dirt and despair. My tears formed actual puddles on the floor as I cried out to God from the depths of my heart. My adulthood had been marked by a shallow Christianity where I pretended to have it all together, particularly as a mother. But God, in His loving wisdom, allowed everything to collapse around me.

I lost everyone. God brought me to a place of solitude where He granted me the gift of brokenness, along with the precious commodity of time. I spent that time in repentance, but the blows kept coming. I sought the Lord earnestly, died to myself, studied, prayed, worshiped through the pain—but the hits continued. Yet in that season, I learned to trust God. I grew to say, "Lord, even if You choose not to fix this, I will live for You."

It took a while for things to turn around. I faced some truly terrible moments. But by then, the brokenness had worked a powerful cleansing in my life. I stood tall, knowing that no weapon formed against me would prevail (Isaiah 54:17). The old me had been replaced by someone who had walked through the fire and emerged refined.

God's love for me was so great that He allowed me to be broken. He let the consequences of my sin bring me to my knees and draw me back to His loving heart. Since that breaking, I have witnessed miracles unfold in my life— restoration, forgiveness, and a new calling. It all begins with crucifying our flesh and surrendering it on the altar each and every day. Obedience is God's love language, and as you choose daily to obey, you'll discover that He always had an amazing purpose wrapped up in your pain, and that above all, it was to make you holy.

Lord, it's so hard to see in the darkness. The big picture is lost on me, and I don't see the way out. But I do know that you are the way, the truth, and the light! I trust you. Amen.

When All You Have Are Bad Choices | Brad Billet

"David left Gath and escaped to the cave of Adullam. When his brothers and his father's household heard about it, they went down to him there. All those who were in distress or in debt or discontented gathered around him, and he became their commander. About four hundred men were with him." –1 Samuel 22:1-2

David had done everything right. He obeyed God. He was anointed to be king. He killed Goliath from Gath. He lead Israel's army to triumphs. This path took him from shepherd to the king's son-in-law with a chart-topping song—which is why the hurt was real when the triumphant army began hunting David because Saul was jealous.

Alone, fearing for his life, David had zero good options. Fleeing Israel, the next best place to hide was Goliath's hometown, Gath. He pretended to be insane to escape there and hid in a cave deep in the wilderness, far from the promised crown and comfort of family.

Have you been left with only bad choices? Have you echoed David's cries: Has God abandoned me? Whom can I trust? What future do I have?

In the place of desperation, God can turn bad choices into His best. The text shows God working for David: "You feel abandoned; here is your family. You feel alone; here are 400 who feel the same as you." The faith, friendships, and leadership required to be king were forged when David only had bad choices.

My friend spent New Year's Eve drunk and in jail. The damage done partying meant no one was coming to get him. With only bad choices left, he aimlessly walked. Sixteen miles later, he found himself climbing the railings of a high bridge. Abandoned, alone, he was done. Instead, a gust blew him onto the road. He rose, realizing the church of his youth was near. A New Year's miracle happened: He actually found people there. They fed him and showed him Jesus. God with him in desperation turned the worst into the best. This transformed my friend, enabling him to achieve sobriety, enjoy a loving family, and regularly welcome co-workers to his garage when they feel hopeless like he has.

Don't lose heart. The God who is with you can turn even bad choices into the best.

Prayer: Father, help me know that even in desperation you can give me hope.

VERSES UPON THE BURNING OF OUR HOUSE, JULY 10TH, 1666

"The Lord gave, and the Lord hath taken away; blessed by the name of the Lord" –Job 1:21

In silent night when rest I took,
For sorrow near I did not look,
I wakened was with thund'ring noise
And piteous shrieks of dreadful voice.
That fearful sound of "fire" and "fire,"
Let no man know is my Desire.
I, starting up, the light did spy,
And to my God my heart did cry
To straighten me in my Distress
And not to leave me succourless.
Then, coming out, behold a space
The flame consume my dwelling place.
And when I could no longer look,
I blest His name that gave and took,
That laid my goods now in the dust.
Yea, so it was, and so 'twas just.
It was his own, it was not mine,
Far be it that I should repine;
He might of all justly bereft
But yet sufficient for us left.
When by the ruins oft I past
My sorrowing eyes aside did cast
And here and there the places spy
Where oft I sate and long did lie.
Here stood that trunk, and there
that chest,
There lay that store I counted best.
My pleasant things in ashes lie

And them behold no more shall I.
Under thy roof no guest shall sit,
Nor at thy Table eat a bit.
No pleasant talk shall 'ere be told
Nor things recounted done of old.
No Candle e'er shall shine in Thee,
Nor bridegroom's voice e'er heard
shall be.
In silence ever shalt thou lie,
Adieu, Adieu, all's vanity.
Then straight I 'gin my heart to chide,
And did thy wealth on earth abide?
Didst fix thy hope on mould'ring dust?
The arm of flesh didst make thy trust?
Raise up thy thoughts above the sky
That dunghill mists away may fly.
Thou hast a house on high erect
Frameed by that mighty Architect,
With glory richly furnished,
Stands permanent though this be fled.
It's purchased and paid for too
By Him who hath enough to do.
A price so vast as is unknown,
Yet by His gift is made thine own;
There's wealth enough, I need no more,
Farewell, my pelf, farewell, my store.
The world no longer let me love,
My hope and treasure lies above.

Lord, may we hold lightly what we have been given.

Anne Bradstreet

Obedience | Janette Berge

"If you love Me, keep My commandments." –John 14:15

"Therefore, since we have these promises, dear friends, let us purify ourselves from everything that contaminates body and spirit, perfecting holiness out of reverence for God." –II Corinthians 7:1

As a parent, I can relate to the desire for my children to simply do what I ask without them questioning every instruction. Of course, I value their opinions, but sometimes I just know what's best for them, even if they can't see it yet. Similarly, there are times when God asks us to do things that we don't fully understand or agree with. But just like with our kids, God doesn't need us to like it; He just wants us to trust and obey Him. In fact, the Greek word for obedience in the Old Testament also means "to trust." So, when we obey God, we're demonstrating our trust in Him and His plan for our lives.

Jesus lived His entire life in complete obedience to God, even to the point of death on the cross, making Him the perfect example of obedience. In John 14:15, He calls us to follow His example and obey His commandments. Obedience goes beyond merely following rules, as it is an act of worship and a demonstration of our love for God. While it's true that obedience can be challenging and uncomfortable at times, we can trust that as we allow the Holy Spirit to transform us from the inside out, we'll grow in obedience and holiness. The more we trust and obey God, the more we become like Him.

Psalm 119 reminds us that those who obey God's laws and seek Him with all their hearts will find joy. And in 2 Corinthians 7:1, we're encouraged to strive for complete holiness because of our reverence for God. So, let's choose obedience today. Let's trust that God's plan for our lives is good and let our obedience be an act of worship and gratitude for His love and salvation.

It's important to remember that obedience is not a skill we learn overnight, but rather a daily choice to trust and obey God. Let's seek to grow in our obedience and trust in Him, knowing that He always has our best interests in mind.

SABBATH

A RHYTHM
OF REST

Even though I walk

through the darkest valley,[a]

I will fear no evil,

for you are with me;

your rod and your staff,

they comfort me.

Psalm 23:4

I Resign Myself to Thee | Emily Heady

"Do you not know that your bodies are temples of the Holy Spirit, who is in you, whom you have received from God? You are not your own; you were bought at a price. Therefore honor God with your bodies." –I Corinthians 6:19-20

John Donne's second Holy Sonnet describes his recovery from serious illness, probably typhus, in this poem. Donne's large point here is one that we would all do well to remember: that he belongs to God, and that although Satan continues to tempt and bother him, he knows that the love of God keeps him secure.

In the poem, the first eight lines focus on the fact that he belongs to God. Donne knows that legally, God has made him and holds the rights to him (lines 1-3). He knows that when he was in a state of decay and sin, Christ's blood bought him back, in order to display the glory of God in him (lines 3-5). He knows that he is God's servant, a sheep following the shepherd, and the very reflection of the image of God—except during those times when he has willfully disobeyed (lines 6-8).

Given that the poet clearly belongs to God, why, Donne asks, does the devil try to "usurp" or claim him? Yet Donne rests in the knowledge that God will rise and fight for His beloved creation, for God is love, and Satan, though he wants to claim Donne, does not love him at all. God's love will save His children.

Take a look at Donne's words:

As due by many titles I resign
My self to thee, O God, first I was made
By thee, and for thee, and when I was decay'd
Thy blood bought that, the which before was thine;
I am thy son, made with thy self to shine,
Thy servant, whose pains thou hast still repaid,
Thy sheep, thine Image, and, till I betray'd
My self, a temple of thy Spirit divine;
Why doth the devil then usurp on me?
Why doth he steal, nay ravish that's thy right?
Except thou rise and for thine own work fight,
Oh I shall soon despair, when I do see
That thou lov'st mankind well, yet wilt'not chose me,
And Satan hates me, yet is loath to lose me.

Kissing Your Cross | Brian Charette

"Then Jesus said to his disciples, 'Whoever wants to be my disciple must deny themselves and take up their cross and follow me.'" –Matthew 16:24

Someone once said that, as Christians, we should always be pulling splinters out of our lips. They should be there, metaphorically at least, because we spend so much of our time kissing the old rugged cross. We should know its taste, its smell, its power, its pain. This doesn't mean we should mimic the tradition of our Catholic friends who actually kiss the crucifix on Good Friday. But it means we should be well acquainted with the cross, our cross, not fleeing from it but taking it up.

We understand the call to take up our cross, don't we? We know Bible verses such as 1 Peter 4:13, which says, "But rejoice inasmuch as you participate in the sufferings of Christ, so that you may be overjoyed when his glory is revealed." We may not pursue the suffering symbolized by our cross, but, intellectually at least, we know that it is part of the life of the disciple of courage. As leaders, one of the most important things we do is help others in their suffering, offering the salve of the God of all comfort.

It's more than that, though. There are two commands implied in Matthew 16:24—the first: Take up your cross. And the second: Follow Him. In this season of Lent, we grasp the nature of accepting, even welcoming the kind of suffering a cross symbolizes. It's really what Lent is all about. But that cross-carrying isn't to be done in isolation. "Take up (your) cross," He says, "AND follow me." We are not carrying our crosses alone, left to struggle and bleed in an aimless and endless pursuit, shoulders and lips scarred. We are carrying our crosses and following Him, right behind, safe within His shadow, going where He is going, led by His hand.

"Do Whatever He Tells You" | Deirdra Jones

"But his mother told the servants, 'Do whatever he tells you.'" –John 2:5

Scripture doesn't give us many details about the thoughts, understandings, revelations, or deep ponderings, prayers, worries, etc., of Jesus' mother, Mary. The few glimpses that we get communicate her awe, fear, faith, and total trust in the Father. Could she have possibly even begun to grasp what her role meant and what it would require of her? We don't read about the uncertainties that could have plagued her heart and mind. Instead, her questions were few. The angel seemed to have settled any doubt or fear that God had chosen her (in all her particulars) to carry, birth, and raise the Messiah by saying, "For nothing is impossible with God" (Luke 1:37).

Fast forward to the wedding in Cana. I don't believe that Mary was asking for a miracle; I believe she was asking for Jesus' help in figuring out how to prevent a major social embarrassment for the wedding couple that had just run out of wine. Jesus provided more than she could ask or imagine, and as a result, we have the first miracle Jesus performed recorded in Scripture.

In my own life and walk with Jesus, I have had and wrestled with many thoughts, understandings, revelations, deep ponderings, prayers, worries, inner arguing, questions, fears, doubts, un-ending "what ifs," etc. that have stalled my faith and walk. Sometimes I have run in the complete opposite direction of His will for me. How much sooner God could have accomplished His will through me, and how much sooner I could have discovered and received His blessings, if I had just trusted and believed like Mary and acted like the servants!

Friend, it's not too late to trust and believe like Mary and act like the servants. The greater joy and blessings lie just ahead of our obedience to trust, believe, and act. Just do whatever He tells you...for nothing is impossible with God. "Now to him who is able to do immeasurably more than all we ask or imagine, according to his power that is at work within us, to him be glory in the church and in Christ Jesus throughout all generations, for ever and ever! Amen" (Ephesians 3:20-21).

A Dip in the Water | Reenie Peppers

"Sir, if the prophet had told you to do something very difficult, wouldn't you have done it? So you should certainly obey when he says simply, 'Go wash and be cured!'" –II Kings 5:13

Several years back there was a popular acronym that was making the rounds: K.I.S.S.: Keep it Simple Stupid (I prefer "Sweetie" to "Stupid"). I find that this acronym is still apropos today, and even more so all the time. We live in a society that thrives on making things as complicated as possible.

Communication, for example, could use a good K.I.S.S. in the pants. We sometimes seem to assume that texting and Instagram and emojis have improved our communication; however, these have only complicated and muddied the waters. Let's say I get a response from a friend to a post or text I sent of a frowning face and a slice of pizza. Does that mean they didn't like my post and they don't like pizza? How many texts or tweets back and forth will be required to understand the message? Things would be simpler if we were actually talking to each other.

Whenever I think about how complicated we like to make things, I am reminded of the story of Naaman in the Old Testament book of II Kings. The mighty warrior Naaman suffered from leprosy. When Naaman went to see Elisha for healing, Elisha sent his servant out with this message, "Go and wash yourself seven times in the Jordan River. Then your skin will be restored, and you will be healed of your leprosy" (2 Kings 5:10). Naaman became indignant over the simple instructions given him. How could mere washing in the river cure his leprosy? Certainly he should be required to do some extraordinary feat to gain his healing. But one of his officers reasoned with him. So Naaman obeyed and was healed of his leprosy.

Sometimes we make things more complicated to prove our importance or bolster our reputation of being competent. Often, we have a hard time seeing the simple solution because of the confusion and difficulties in which our world revels. However, like Naaman, we need to listen for that simple solution and go with it. Sometimes the solution can be as simple as a dip in the water. Let's bring K.I.S.S. back into play—let's Keep it Simple Sweetie!

The Glorious Furnace | JJ Wyzinski

"Then Nebuchadnezzar was so filled with rage against Shadrach, Meshach, and Abednego that his face was distorted. So the men were bound, still wearing their tunics, their trousers, their hats, and their other garments, and they were thrown into the furnace of blazing fire." –Daniel 3:19, 21

Shadrach, Meshach, and Abednego: These three heroes of faith stood faithful to God while everyone around them bent a knee to Nebuchadnezzar, a king whose anger was so hot, he found no recourse but to burn his enemies.

Shadrach, Meshach, and Abednego stood trial before the judge, jury, executioner, and King Nebuchadnezzar and were faced with a difficult predicament. Serve and worship Nebuchadnezzar and his gods and live, or refuse and pay with their lives. With the threat of a painful death before them, they stood firm and responded by saying, "God will save us, but even if God doesn't save us you're not going to see us serve your gods or worship your statue."

Their confidence lead King Nebuchadnezzar to play a game of chicken. He called for the furnace to be heated up, then for the heat to be cranked up even higher...and higher...and higher, until it was seven times hotter than normal. Nebuchadnezzar then asked for the three men to be tied up by the strongest men he knew. Still, no fight broke out and eventually, the three men Shadrach, Meschach, and Abednego were thrown into the furnace.

Here the story finds its peak: God didn't save these men from the fiery furnace, but walked with them in it. God dove into their predicament saying, "I'm here with you, it will be ok." I can only imagine what it was like to walk in the flames with God. Just think, they would have missed this opportunity to know what they could find only in the flames if they were concerned with fighting for their lives rather than resolutely obeying God. That furnace became an opportunity for Shadrach, Meshach, and Abednego—an opportunity to be so close to their God that they were walking together in the flames with Him. With God in their midst, there's no wonder they had no fear in that glorious furnace.

Prayer: Lord, thank you for meeting with us in the fire. Amen.

And Yet I Will Praise You, O Lord! | Bruce Gardner

"For the Lord is good. His unfailing love continues forever, and his faithfulness continues to each generation." –Psalm 100:5

When I was young boy, maybe seven or eight years old, I can remember seeing these older adults fervently praising God in our church services. I found it odd that they would be doing so, because it appeared to me that they lived difficult lives. I wondered how they could have such joy in what seemed to be frustrating and challenging situations.

What I hadn't yet learned was how one could live in the joy of the Lord through the woes of life, facing challenging times and choosing to surrender what one wants for the purpose of what God wants.

As I have now reached the latter half of my life and have experienced many of those same challenges through the years, I am beginning to understand the peace and joy those dear saints from my childhood expressed so well through the way they lived their lives surrendered to Jesus. It isn't dependent upon the circumstances of life. It comes from your response to those circumstances, and it provides a witness to those around you of whom you believe in and base your existence.

I love the Psalms because you can find a response to the human condition—good, bad, or even indifferent—in every one. Psalm 100 gives us a wonderful direction for what our response should and can be to whatever it is that we are experiencing. Because we are His, the sheep of His pasture, we can be thankful and give Him praise because He is good, and He is God!

No matter what else is happening to you in your life that truth will never change. You can be like those saints from my childhood and praise God in the wake of all circumstances because of the truth of this witness that closes Psalm 100 in verse 5: He is good! His love is forever! He is always faithful!

That message includes you today, wherever you may be. My Mom used to say to me, "It doesn't matter what happens to you in life; it is how you respond that matters."

Make your response be praise!

SABBATH

A RHYTHM OF REST

"8 Remember the Sabbath day by keeping it holy.

9 Six days you shall labor and do all your work,

10 but the seventh day is a sabbath to the Lord

your God. On it you shall not do any work, neither

you, nor your son or daughter, nor your male or

female servant, nor your animals, nor any foreigner

residing in your towns. 11 For in six days the Lord

made the heavens and the earth, the sea, and all

that is in them, but he rested on the seventh day.

Therefore the Lord blessed the Sabbath day and

made it holy."

Exodus 20:8-11

Contentment | Bobbie Gardner

"But seek ye first his kingdom and his righteousness, and all these things will be given to you as well." –Matthew 6:33

I spend my free time looking through decorating magazines. I browse and just imagine how wonderful it would be to decorate my home like the pictures. If only I had the money! And I enjoy those H.G.T.V. shows where they come in and totally remodel a house—beautiful new floors, cabinets, bathrooms, appliances, and sometimes even furniture in an hour!

I love those cooking shows where the food budget seems to be no problem and every recipe comes together, leaving everyone full and happy. And how I enjoy those Hallmark movies! All the girls are beautiful, the men are handsome, and they all end up happily ever after while snow is gently falling with Christmas lights in the background. And then it happens...

I begin to look around at my own house and think, "Surely there's something I can do to just spruce things up a bit. I'm sure we deserve new furniture. I had this bedroom set before we got married and I bought it used!" My kitchen cabinets are old. I wish we had a bigger house. I want a screened-in porch. That man in the movie treats his wife like a queen, and my spouse is snoring. I'm bored! I wish we had nice things. We never go out. He never compliments my cooking. Are we even happy?

And then I remember a simple little song I learned as a child:
Oh, be careful little eyes what you see
Oh, be careful little eyes what you see
For the Father up above is looking down in love,
So be careful little eyes what you see.

If we watch TV too long, we'll become discontent with our home, or maybe even our spouse. If we stay focused on social media too long, we'll become dissatisfied with everyone around us and start to believe everyone has a better life than we do. If we even watch the news too much, we might be disappointed with just about everything and everyone in the world.

Our minds are so easily influenced. We need to focus on the things of God and not the things of the world—our families, our church, the Word of God, and reaching the lost. We must choose to seek first His kingdom.

Looking but Not Seeing | Lynne Goodwin

"He is the image of the invisible God, the firstborn of all creation. For by him all things were created, in heaven and on earth, visible and invisible, whether thrones or dominions or rulers or authorities—all things were created through him and for him. And he is before all things, and in him all things hold together." –Colossians 1:15-17

My dad was a photographer in the days before digital photography. Most weekends he put on a suit, took his cameras, and went to a wedding. Little piles of his wedding pictures sat around our living room waiting to be approved by newlyweds.

As a small child, I liked those pictures a lot. All the dressed-up people in pretty places with cakes and decorations—I could look through those photos for hours.

One day, my big brother asked me what I was looking at in a set of pictures. I told him, "I cannot see my dad in any of these." Five years older and so much wiser than me, he said, "You can't see him because he's holding the camera. He's the one making the picture." I had to think about it, but I believed him, and it changed the way I looked at pictures.

This memory surfaced recently as I was talking with a friend about how we miss the evidence of God in the world because we are looking for the miraculous.

While looking for something more amazing, I overlook the gift of my own existence...the beauty of the created world...the experience of delight. I keep thinking I need something extra when I've already been given everything.

When I consider the scope of God's creativity and the invitation to know Him in this life, I see that is miraculous! Because of Him, I have the opportunity to experience this mystery. He made the picture that declares His identity, the goodness of creation and the place I have in it.

The hymn in Colossians calls Jesus "the image of the invisible God." I liked thinking about my brother's explanation and how the one we cannot see is the reason we can see at all.

I am trying to think differently. When I get discouraged and I cannot find the miracle, I think about my brother's words and try looking again for the one I cannot see.

Come, Follow Me | Matthew S.E. Waggoner

"Look, Jesus says, 'Come, follow me, and I will show you how to fish for people!'"
–Matthew 4:19

In January of 2003, I returned to college after some time off as a missionary in Tennessee. I met a young woman online through a friend, and since we lived six hours away from each other, we began calling one another. Our conversations were rich in dreams and hopes. We shared with one another our desire for marriage and love. I shared with her my calling into ministry to be a pastor, and she shared with me the desire to be a wife and mother. Over the course of the first three months that we began this conversation, I wanted to take the conversation a little further; I desired a relationship, and she did too.

I saved up some cash to rent a Pontiac Sunfire and made my way to Alicia's college in Lock Haven, PA, to meet her face-to-face for the first time. I still remember seeing her ascend the stairs from the basement of the dormitory wearing jeans and a pink halter top with open-toed heels. Whew! It was love at first sight and over the course of spending the evening together, I asked her to be my girlfriend. Eighteen years, three kids, and two dogs later, here we are living out my calling as a pastor and her dreams of being a mother and wife in a small town called Montoursville, PA. You see, invitations are more than just an offer; they are a recognition of value and a call into intimacy. I can't imagine doing life without her, and our love has only deepened because we both desire to stay in conversation with one another for as many years as we have. And it all began with a simple invitation—asking her if she would be willing to come and follow me.

Jesus asked Peter the same thing. Peter, would you consider leaving all of this behind to simply come and follow me to fish for people? Where relationship matters? Peter and the other disciples learned that no real relationship grows without a meaningful invitation to be in conversation with one another in the first place.

Abba Father, help us today to take that first step of invitation by being willing to be in the conversation. Amen.

Come and See | Matthew S.E. Waggoner

"He is not here; he has risen, just as he said. Come and see the place where he lay."
–Matthew 28:7

When was the last time you received an invitation to something? How did it make you feel? Did you go? My youngest daughter Abbagail came home one day with an invitation in her hand from a classmate who was having a birthday party at our local theatre to watch the new Mario movie. She was excited about going to celebrate her friend's birthday but just as excited to go watch a movie that would leave the song "Peaches" in our heads for months. It was fun for both of us, and it was also a moment where we together got to spend some amazing time with people we didn't really know.

Invitations are generally moments where others are requesting for us to go somewhere or do something, but often an invitation doesn't call for us to experience something alone. When we receive an invitation, we're being recognized and chosen by someone who sees value in us, even if the invitation is to help them move—they value our strong biceps and back! We all want to be part of something bigger than ourselves, of course, but sometimes we don't know how or we don't feel included. Maybe sometimes we just don't feel appreciated or wanted. I can't tell you how many times I wished someone would just invite me to something but they never did. Those moments often felt lonely, and I felt left out. But one thing I do know is that's not Christianity.

The most fulfilling journey—the journey with Jesus—begins with a simple invitation to come and see. We are like Mary and Mary at the tomb, who had the courage and curiosity to come and see for themselves that Jesus was truly not there. They heard the invitation, and they took a chance to witness something amazing. Faith is simply hearing the invitation to trust in Jesus and then walking in His presence. Where has God invited you to participate, but you've not yet made the decision to simply come and see?

Abba Father, help us today to take that first step of responding to your invitation. Amen.

Come | Matthew S.E. Waggoner

"'Come,' he said. Then Peter got down out of the boat, walked on the water and came toward Jesus." –Matthew 14:29

Peter had decided to go and follow Jesus, and now his faith was being tested. The storm was raging all around him and he saw a silhouette coming towards him. Peter simply yelled out, "Lord, if it's you, tell me to come to you on the water." So Jesus said, "Come."

Many times in our faith, we've heard the invitation to "come and follow" and we've taken that step of faith. But following is easy when we're not required to do anything serious. In this moment, however, Jesus was leading Peter from a time of following into a time of participating. Jesus invited Peter to come out of the boat and walk on water with Him, and Peter responded in faith by stepping out of his comfort zone and onto the raging waves. This is the moment where faith meets trust. This is a moment of testing and courage. This is a moment where the ongoing conversation calls Peter beyond what he can understand.

Moses, leading people into the wilderness, had plenty of moments to go beyond what he understood. Noah building a boat in the desert while being mocked and ridiculed by others had to step out into the unimaginable. And now, Peter stepping out of the boat to walk on water displays yet another instance of great faith. Just as our initial decision to come and follow Jesus requires a commitment to growth and obedience, so our ongoing journey of faith presents us with opportunities to step out of our comfort zones and deepen our trust in Him. Yet oftens, we find many Christians afraid to take that next step into participation.

Did you ever notice that even though Peter was the one to step out, he wasn't alone? The disciples were there with him. Deep, radical faith isn't a solitary journey, and sometimes not everyone steps out of the boat. But I guarantee you that when one person has that kind of faith, it can be used to strengthen the faith of others.

Abba Father, guide our often frightened hearts to accept the invitation to step out into faithful moments of participation. Amen.

Come and Have Breakfast | Matthew S.E. Waggoner

"Jesus said to them, 'Come and have breakfast.'" –John 21:12

No one that I know of would say that living this life of faith is easy. And we also know that any time we step out to follow and participate, there can be moments where we are ridiculed or even falter. I make mistakes, and I've made many of them in my life.

Peter did too; we know this. He said he wouldn't let Jesus die. But Jesus did die. Peter said he would go to the death to protect Jesus, but instead, when the moment came, he denied Jesus and ran away. Once confident Peter, in front of all of his friends, turned out to be a fraud who didn't keep his word. How embarrassing and what a failure! In all of these moments, Peter faltered in his faith, and I believe he felt that his relationship with Jesus was broken because he had failed to live up to the kind of faith he boasted about having in front of the other disciples.

We do that in church, don't we? We try to dress "Christian." We speak the lingo, using words like "blessed" and "holy." We act holy and loving around others, but in our homes we live unclean lives. I'm sure we are aware of Christians in churches today who once boasted of holy, Christ-driven lives—but when others found out they weren't living those lives, they were ashamed. How, when this happens, should we respond to their faltering? Should we make fun of them? Should we drive them out and away from the church? No! We invite them back into the conversation to seek out reconciliation. We bring them back into community through Christ.

I love how Jesus uses a simple breakfast table to reconcile people back into the conversation. He doesn't force people, but He invites them to come and sit and eat—an intimate sort of fellowship. A breakfast of fish gave them the opportunity to be near Jesus! Jesus restored fellowship with Peter and the disciples by calling them to be near Him, and others as well.

Abba Father, reconcile our broken relationship with moments of being near you. Amen.

SABBATH

A RHYTHM
OF REST

"Come to me, all you who are weary

and burdened, and I will give you rest.

Matthew 11:28

Reconciliation Invitation | Camelot Shuff

"For the Love of Christ compels us, because we are convinced that one died for all, and therefore all died...We are therefore Christ's ambassadors, as though God were making His appeal through us. We implore you on Christ's behalf: Be reconciled to God."
–II Corinthians 5:14, 20

Discipleship is not supposed to be overwhelming, but sometimes we make it that way. From membership classes to theology classes to mission trips to mentorship, our minds get overloaded with the "doing" part of being a disciple.

Paul reminds us that as disciples, we must begin with the love of Christ, the love that He Himself has placed in us. It doesn't begin with doing—it begins with receiving what He offers. This love surrounds us through the whole process of becoming more Christlike, and it defines how we relate to God and to the world. It extends back to God as we obey and surrender to Him. And it also reaches out to those around us as we live out a humble invitation to the lost to be reconciled to God. With love—not duty and not a to-do list—we invite our fellow believers to surrender their will to God. For us, this looks a lot less like working ourselves to the bone and more like resting in God's love, letting Him use us as His invitation, and being ambassadors of reconciliation.

To be a disciple is to be a follower, so to be reconciled to God means that all of me—even the smallest part—is reconciled to Him, resting securely in His love. May we not be satisfied with "almost"; may the "almost"—once we recognize it—push us not to work harder or to do more, but to be nearer to Him.

"Oh, My Black Soul!" | Emily Heady

"Though your sins are like scarlet, they shall be white as snow; though they are red as crimson, they shall be like wool." –Isaiah 1:18

John Donne's fourth Holy Sonnet shows us the poet speaking to his own soul—a soul that he wants to persuade to repent and return to the God that he has betrayed.

Donne begins by telling us that he has fallen ill, a reminder of his mortality (lines 1-2). Merely imagining his own death causes Donne to take state of his conscience, and he finds that it is black—dirty from all the wrong, the "treason" he has committed while he was away from God. He fears returning to God precisely because he is so black with sin (lines 1-4).

Donne pauses in that moment of fear to tell us what it is like: He says that he feels like he is a man in prison, doomed to death. He wants to be released, but he knows that if he is released, it will be for his own execution—so he finds himself choosing his own imprisonment again and again (lines 5-8).

The turn in Donne's thinking comes when he recalls that if he repents, God's grace will cover his sin. Donne joyously, then, mourns the blackness of his sin, feeling his red-faced shame and horror, only to see his black heart turn pure and white again when it is washed with the blood of Christ. Here is the poem:

Oh my black Soul! now thou art summoned
By sickness, death's herald, and champion;
Thou art like a pilgrim, which abroad hath done
Treason, and durst not turn to whence he is fled,
Or like a thief, which till death's doom be read,
Wisheth himself delivered from prison;
But damn'd and hal'd to execution,
Wisheth that still he might be imprisoned.
Yet grace, if thou repent, thou canst not lack;
But who shall give thee that grace to begin?
Oh make thy self with holy mourning black,
And red with blushing, as thou art with sin;
Or wash thee in Christ's blood, which hath this might
That being red, it dyes red souls to white.

Following God When We're Stubborn | Torrie Slaughter

"You have disobeyed me. Why have you done this?" –Judges 2:2

I can see myself in stubbornness, fear, and rebellion in Israel's story through disobedience, oppression, repentance, and deliverance.

In Judges 2, I discover a poignant reminder from God about the dire consequences of turning away from Him. Despite His warning, the Israelites, much like myself, still stumble down the path of disobedience.

Allow me to share with you three key insights from the story:

The Consequences of Disobedience: God's voice thunders, painting a vivid picture of the repercussions awaiting those who turn away from Him. Destruction and oppression loom on the horizon for the Israelites, a solemn reminder that disobedience always leads to darkness and sorrow.

The Dangers of Stubbornness: The Israelites remain stubborn, refusing to return to God's embrace. Their obstinacy only deepens their troubles, blinding them to the truth, isolating them from seeking help, and entangling them in a cycle of self-destruction.

The Importance of God's Grace: Despite the Israelites' repeated failures, God's grace shines through. In love, He sends judges to lead His people back to Him. We see that no matter how far we wander or how stubbornly we resist, God's grace and mercy beckon us to return.

As I reflect on the story of Judges 2, I recognize that my journey mirrors that of the Israelites. My stubbornness sometimes blinds me, leading me down treacherous paths. Yet, within the pages of this ancient narrative, I discover a profound truth—I am not alone.

It is within our human nature to crave satisfaction, fulfillment, and purpose. We are wired to seek something greater than ourselves. Yet, we often fall into the trap of worshiping temporary idols that leave us empty and unfulfilled. Only by prioritizing our relationship with God can we find lasting joy and contentment.

What God Has Made Holy | Jennifer Burgett

"So God blessed the seventh day and made it holy, because on it God rested from all His work that He had done in creation." -Genesis 2:3

Out of everything God created—man, mountains, animals, possessions—the first thing He made holy was time. And when He led his people out of Egypt, one of the first lessons He wanted them to understand was Sabbath. He wanted them to know that their value was not found in how much work they could do, but it was to be found in Him.

Just as with the discipline of tithing, God does not demand everything from us, but He does demand a portion. He does want our best—even the best of our time. For most of us, how we use our time gives a clear indication of what we value most. Do we use our time pursuing money? We probably value it a great deal. The same goes for our possessions. If we spend all our time working on our homes, then we know that's where our hearts are. Similarly, if we spend a great deal of time making sure we appear right—perfect clothing, perfect face, perfect reputation—then we know what we care the most about.

So what does giving God a portion of our time look like?

I believe it's spending time in His word, in study, and in prayer. It involves going to church every Sunday and volunteering your time there. It involves—more deeply—finding your value in Him and allowing Him to give you the gift of rest instead of defining yourself by your busyness.

Perhaps we might take time this Lent, 40 days out of your year, to give a gift back to Him. We can choose to use this season to let go of the things on this Earth that we love too much or that control us. Let us practice pouring our precious time into our relationship with God, allowing Him to bring us one step closer to the people He wants us to be.

Onion Milk | Marc Price

"You have wearied Me with your words." –Malachi 2:17

In the book of Malachi (God's last message to His people before 400 years of silence), the prophet brings God's message in a series of "You've fallen woefully short of My plan for you!" and "You've had ample opportunity to change that!" statements. Even in this last book of the Old Testament, God still offers His grace if the Israelites will repent, but they respond over and over again throughout the book with cynical innocence: "Who, us?! – When did we do that? – We would never!"

In Malachi 2:17, God says to His people, "You have wearied Me with your words." When I was a kid growing up on a farm in Kentucky, we had a milk cow named Eloise. Every now and then she'd get into a patch of wild onions. I remember the horrible onion-flavored milk. It had a green tint and it was awful! We worked hard to keep her from grazing in that area.

As disciples of Jesus, we can sometimes weary God. And our response is as the Israelites': "How have we wearied Him?" The truth is, we can become so accustomed to grazing in some field of sin that we convince ourselves it's either "not that bad" or not sin at all. So, we live life with the stench of sin following us wherever we go. We graze on onions, and what we produce stinks.

When God's people arrogantly responded to God's accusations, they already knew God's expectations. And so do we—yet we still act as if we were never in the field of wild onions on purpose. But if your witness to the lost world smells bad and has an off-color tint, it makes sense that a holy God wants to spew you out of His mouth (Rev. 3:16). Your life, like Eloise's onion milk, is lukewarm and it's sickening.

As a Christian enters any season of repentance, inner reflection is paramount to an honest heart before the Lord. Pray, asking the Lord to reveal your field of wild onions and seek His power daily to keep you grazing in the good pastures He's set aside just for you.

Slavery Melons | Caleb Atkins

"...and again the Israelites started wailing and said, 'If only we had meat to eat! We remember the fish we ate in Egypt at no cost—also the cucumbers, melons, leeks, onions and garlic. But now we have lost our appetite; we never see anything but this manna!'" –Numbers 11:4-6

The story of the people of God has strong roots in the desert. All throughout Scripture, we see God's people, even Jesus Himself, enduring seasons of wasteland wandering.

It's in this setting where we find the people of God complaining about the very life-giving blessing they received from Yahweh. Not only did He provide a way out of Egypt, but He also rained down food from the sky—and they complained about it.

It's not just that the Israelites weren't satisfied. Instead, they chose to look back to their former lives of slavery as they yearned for fresh produce. What's more, they even mentioned eating fish without cost, as if the very life of oppression they lived was a worthy exchange for meat on the table.

How quickly a triumphant exit from Egypt leads to complaint! Is there any hope for the desert dwellers? Spoiler alert. His name is Jesus, and He is well familiar with the wilderness.

Remember His forty days following His baptism in Luke 4. He finds Himself led into the same desert. He's tired. He's dusty. He's hot. He's no doubt longing for sustenance—maybe even a big plate of flatbread with olives and hummus. As hunger pains clawed at Jesus' stomach, He was tempted to take matters into His own hands and make food for Himself. He could have done it—but Jesus responds by recognizing the Hebrew story and instead quotes Deuteronomy 8:4: "Man shall not live by bread alone."

And just like that, the very one who spoke the world into existence shows us that surrender is the road through the desert.

It's as if the desert sand is a canvas for choice. What picture will I paint with this bleak landscape? Will it be one of trust and contentment in the Lord? Will it be one of desire for an easier way of life? Out of the bleak landscape comes the whispers of hope.

SABBATH

A RHYTHM OF REST

My heart is not proud, Lord,

my eyes are not haughty;

I do not concern myself with great matters

or things too wonderful for me.

But I have calmed and quieted myself,

I am like a weaned child with its mother;

like a weaned child I am content.

Israel, put your hope in the Lord both now

and forevermore.

Psalm 131

Emotional Swings | Chad Moler

"'It is finished!' Then he bowed his head and gave up his spirit." –John 19:30

"He isn't here! He is risen from the dead!..." –Luke 24:6

Because technology is so advanced, information travels to us at what seems to be an exponential speed. Sometimes that can help us in our jobs or with our families, but other times it can have detrimental effects on our overall mood. We can hit some really high points emotionally, and with a text or a news update, we can be brought down to the deepest of lows.

But—if we're honest—we'll see that has really always been the case, and part of life is learning to navigate these emotional swings in our day-to-day lives. As we walk through the Lenten season in the Church calendar, we do so in anticipation of seeing the cross. We see the miracles performed, those Jesus touched and reached along the way, and cannot help but be filled with joy. Yet we know what happens when He is betrayed, taken before Pilate, and sentenced to a death He doesn't deserve.

E. Stanley Jones reminds us that "Earth's blackest and earth's brightest days are only three days apart."[1]

For as much pain and sorrow that occurred on what we call Good Friday, there was ecstatic rejoicing three days later. What is interesting is that the rejoicing wasn't a one-time event. Instead, it is a continual rejoicing that each person who believes in Jesus has because of His victory over sin and death. We are no longer slaves to sin, but we can rejoice that the grave could not hold Him and that He has risen!

Father, we are thankful for the gift of salvation that you have provided through your son. Let us always remember that the penalty for our sin has been paid and we are free because of His victory! Amen.

---

1 Jones, E. Stanley. *The Way: 364 Daily Devotions*. Nashville: Abingdon P, 2015.

The Dangers of Being Foolish | Torrie Slaughter

"The simple believe anything, but the prudent give thought to their steps. The wise fear the Lord and shun evil, but a fool is hotheaded and yet feels secure." –Proverbs 14:15-16

As human beings, it's natural for us to rely on our feelings to guide us through life. However, Proverbs 14:15-16 warns us of the dangers of being foolish based on our emotions. The passage tells us that the simple believe everything, while the wise think about their steps. The wise person is cautious and turns away from evil, while the fool is reckless and careless. Making decisions based solely on our emotions can cause us to make poor choices resulting in negative consequences. We may end up trusting the wrong people, getting into harmful situations, or making impulsive decisions that we later regret.

To avoid these dangers, we must be aware of the risks involved in being foolish based on our feelings. We should consider our options and weigh the potential outcomes before making decisions.

We can learn from the example of the prudent person mentioned in Proverbs 14:15-16. This person is cautious and thoughtful, taking the time to consider their options before making a decision. By following this example, we can make wiser choices that are less likely to lead to negative consequences.

In conclusion, Proverbs 14:15-16 reminds us of the dangers of being foolish based on our feelings. By being cautious and thoughtful, we can avoid making impulsive decisions and instead make wise choices that lead to a fulfilling and successful life. Let us seek God's guidance and wisdom as we navigate the complexities of life and make decisions that honor Him.

At His Feet | Stephen Willis

"Then Mary took about a pint of pure nard, an expensive perfume; she poured it on Jesus' feet and wiped his feet with her hair. And the house was filled with the fragrance of the perfume." –John 12:3

Mary (the sister of Martha and Lazarus) has always inspired me. She was a woman who lived in a male-dominated religious system and culture and yet she was spiritually lightyears ahead of the men who were supposed to be above her. Charles Erdman proclaims, "The life of Mary is painted for us, in three memorable pictures, in each of which she is at the feet of Jesus."[1] As you look at the three examples Erdman mentions, you discover a life that is devoted to growth and discipleship.

In Luke 10:39, we see Mary learning at the feet of Jesus while her sister served and complained that she didn't have help. Jesus responded to Martha's complaining, "Martha, Martha, you are anxious and troubled about many things, but one thing is necessary. Mary has chosen the good portion, which will not be taken away from her" (Luke 10:41). The "good portion" was her desire to learn and grow.

In John 11:32, we see Mary surrendering at the feet of Jesus. In this snapshot of Mary's life, she is at the end of herself. She is mourning the death of her brother, and she simply can't understand why her Lord didn't return in time to save him. Yet in her despair she surrendered herself to Him, fully proclaiming, "Yes, Lord, I believe that you are the Christ, the Son of God" (John 11:37).

In John 12:3, we see Mary worshiping at the feet of Jesus. Mary approaches Jesus with a heart of humility and a very expensive jar of perfume. This extravagant offering of praise makes many in the room uncomfortable. But Mary isn't concerned about anyone else's opinion at a dinner designed to honor Jesus. The opinion of Jesus is all that matters.

We look at Mary's life and can conclude for ourselves, as Spurgeon says, that "[we] must sit at his feet, or [we] will never anoint them; [we] must pour his divine teaching into [ourselves], or [we] will never pour out a precious ointment upon him."[2]

Pray: Jesus, help us to learn from, surrender to, and truly worship you.

1 Erdman, Charles R. *The Gospel of John: An Exposition* (Philadelphia: The Westminster Press, 1917).
2 Spurgeon, Charles Haddon. *The Metropolitan Tabernacle Pulpit*, Vols. VII-LXXIII. Pasadena: Pilgrim P, 1990.
———. *The New Park Street Pulpit.* Vols. I-VI. Pasadena: Pilgrim P, 1990.

Sacrificial Worship | Stephen Willis

"Then Mary took about a pint of pure nard, an expensive perfume; she poured it on Jesus' feet and wiped his feet with her hair." –John 12:3

If you take time to read John 12:1-16, you'll find a whole host of people who encountered Jesus but completely missed it. You have Martha (v. 2), all the disciples including Judas Iscariot (v. 4), a large crowd of Jews with bad intentions (v. 9), and a crowd of worshipers who welcomed Him into Jerusalem (v. 12). All of them had encountered Jesus and all had misconceptions about Him.

If you study the text closely, you would realize that I left one individual out of my list. I did this on purpose. I left out Mary. I left her out because she doesn't deserve to be mixed in with the others. Why? She is the one who saw Jesus correctly. She had the proper posture of worship. She humbled herself and offered her only possession of worth as the tangible expression of a sacrificial heart. But didn't the disciples and the crowd do that when Jesus entered the city of Jerusalem? The short answer is no. They arrived in the city worshiping a Messiah that they thought would use His power and strength to overthrow the Romans. When that didn't happen, the crowd quickly turned from people of praise to people of persecution as they chanted, "Crucify Him! Crucify Him!"

The disciples were in the midst of the crowd that day. It is obvious that they got it wrong as well. John himself confesses this fact in John 12:16: "His disciples did not understand these things at first, but when Jesus was glorified, then they remembered that these things had been written about him."

As I examine my own heart and life, I often identify with the crowd. I catch myself wanting God to fit into my plans, or answer my prayers based upon my desires. I "come to Him" in order to "get from Him." This text challenges me to take on the posture of Mary. As I write, I long to bow before Him and offer a heart of sacrificial worship—a heart that looks to give instead of receive.

Prayer: Lord Jesus, "May the words of my mouth and the meditations of my heart be pleasing in your sight."

The Fragrance Filled the House | John C. Bowling

"Then Mary took about a pint of pure nard, an expensive perfume; she poured it on Jesus' feet and wiped his feet with her hair. And the house was filled with the fragrance of the perfume." –John 12:3

The story is told of a village in the south of France where many of the townsfolk worked in a small factory in which lavender perfume was produced. In the late afternoon, when the whistle blew signaling the end of the workday, each worker would gather his or her personal belongs and begin walking home through the village, stopping at shops, markets, or a café. Each evening then, little by little, through the presence of these workers, the entire village was scented with the sweet fragrance of lavender which lingered on the workers' clothing.

Similarly, there is an intriguing and multi-layered story from John's gospel telling of a house filled not only with the fragrance of an expensive perfume, but also with the essence of an extravagant love. John 12:1-8 relates a story filled with character sketches: Martha serving, Lazarus reclining, Judas scheming, Jews observing, and Mary carrying out a very personal but obvious expression of love and devotion. "Then Mary took about a pint of pure nard, an expensive perfume; she poured it on Jesus' feet and wiped his feet with her hair. And the house was filled with the fragrance of the perfume" (John 12:3).

Here is a moment which calls for humility and service revealing a glimpse of the kingdom. Rather than waiting until after His death, Mary expresses her love, devotion, and sacrifice while Jesus is still with them. By anointing Jesus now, Mary is giving the very best that she has to the living Jesus as an outpouring of her love.

Mary's devotion gives evidence that love is not love if it counts the cost—love gives its all. This story is filled with giving. Martha is giving: She makes and serves the dinner. Lazarus gives his witness by showing himself to the guests as proof of Jesus' power. Mary gives a very expensive, sacrificial gift. All of that is set against the backdrop of John's gospel, which so eloquently reduces the whole gospel to a single sentence that begins with the words, "For God so loved . . . he gave . . ."

Surrendering Everything to the King | Torrie Slaughter

"They brought [the colt] to Jesus, threw their cloaks on the colt and put Jesus on it. As he went along, people spread their cloaks on the road." –Luke 19:35-36

Dear friends, I am sharing the powerful spiritual significance of laying down our clothes for Jesus. This practice has been around for centuries, and it goes beyond just a gesture of honor and respect. It is a symbol of surrender, sacrifice, and devotion.

In the gospel of Mark, we read about Jesus' triumphant entry into Jerusalem, where a large crowd gathered, spreading their cloaks on the road before Him. This act of laying down their clothes was a sign of honor and respect, a way of welcoming a king or a conqueror. But it was also a powerful statement of surrender and sacrifice. When we lay down our clothes, we say to Jesus, "I give you everything. I surrender my life to you. I am willing to lay down my desires, plans, dreams, and possessions at your feet." This act of surrender is a reminder that Jesus is the Lord of our lives, and we need His guidance and direction. Laying down our clothes is also a way of expressing our love and devotion to Jesus. It means "Jesus, you are worth everything to me. I will give you my all because you have given me everything." It is a way of showing gratitude for His sacrifice on the cross and His unconditional love for us.

So, my dear friends, I encourage you to consider laying down your clothes for Jesus, whether it is a physical or symbolic act of surrendering your lives to Him. Let us honor Him as the King of our lives and lay down our desires, plans, and possessions at His feet.

May we be like the crowd in Jerusalem who welcomed Jesus with open hearts and laid down their cloaks for Him. May we surrender everything to Him and follow Him with wholehearted devotion. Let us remember that Jesus is worth everything and He deserves nothing less than our all.

SABBATH

A RHYTHM OF REST

Restore us, O God; make your face shine on us,

that we may be saved.

Psalm 80:3

To Calvary | Kerry Willis

"When they came to a place called The Skull, they nailed him to the cross. And the criminals were also crucified—one on his right and one on his left." –Luke 23:33

For as long as I can remember, my Aunt Edith (my Dad's only sister and only sibling) was the organist at the church where I was raised—Free Grace Wesleyan Church. She was not a flashy musician, but she was talented and dependable, and her love for the Lord invited breathless souls to breathe again.

Aunt Edith was always content to let the pianist choose the selections for praise and worship. I only remember once when she requested we learn a new hymn. Well, it was written in 1921 by Jennie Hussey, so it wasn't exactly "new" but you know what I mean. It was new to us. As Aunt Edith passionately shared, it was obvious that this new hymn was a personal prayer from her very alive soul.

It must have been the season leading up to Easter when Aunt Edith brought this hymn to our attention. The title? "Lead Me to Calvary." To this day, whenever I think of the wonderful words of "Lead Me to Calvary," I am inspired to consider each word carefully and prayerfully.

Let's remember that before we can breathe again on Easter Resurrection Sunday, the Lord must first "Lead Us to Calvary." Here are the passionate lyrics. Let's pray:

(1) King of my life, I crown Thee now, Thine shall the glory be; Lest I forget Thy thorn-crowned brow, Lead Me to Calvary.

(Chorus) Lest I forget Gethsemane, Lest I forget Thine agony; Lest I forget Thy love for me, Lead me to Calvary.

(2) Show me the tomb where Thou wast laid, Tenderly mourned and wept; Angels in robes of light arrayed Guarded Thee whilst Thou slept.

(3) Let me like Mary, through the gloom, Come with a gift to Thee; Show to me now the empty tomb, Lead me to Calvary.

(4) May I be willing, Lord, to bear Daily my cross for Thee; Even Thy cup of grief to share, Thou hast borne all for me. Amen and Amen.

Take Shelter | Bill Willis

"Whoever dwells in the Shelter of The Most High will rest in The Shadow of The Almighty." -Psalm 91:1

The Spirit of God often transports me back to Free Grace Church, the house of faith where my parents raised their three sons. Often it's like I am there, worshiping God and singing the hymns of old, songs like "At the Cross."

How well I remember the words of this great hymn, which is all about HIM! Embedded deep in my heart and soul are the words: "Alas, and did my Savior bleed and did my Sovereign die. Would He devote that Sacred Head, for sinners such as I? At the Cross, at the Cross, where I first saw the light, and the burden of my heart rolled away. It was there by faith I received my sight, and now I am happy all the day."

The "Shelter of the Most High" the psalmist wrote about recently came full circle for me, as I humbly considered how Christ and His cross are the shelter of our salvation and lives. The Holy Spirit made this connection in my soul as I ministered to some precious seniors at a nursing home.

Mrs. B., who is 100 years old, is one of these people. Part of a mainline denomination for many years, she received Christ in her heart last year. This intelligent, nearly blind lady asked Jesus to forgive her sins and move in. As I shared the wonderful truth that God is our shelter, Mrs. B. smiled and testified: "I guess I was late coming to The Shelter!"

Led by the Spirit, I reminded her God was not concerned with the first 99 years of her life, for she had knelt before His Son's cross. In essence, she had taken shelter in Jesus Christ, who had imparted His rest and peace to her heart for the rest of her days here, followed by endless days in heaven.

At the end, we sang a hymn for all who take shelter in Him:

"Amazing Grace, how sweet the sound that saved a wretch like me. I once was lost, but now I'm found, was blind but now I see. When we've been there 10,000 years, bright shining as the sun. We've no less days to sing God's Praise, than when we've first begun."

Disciples of the Cross | Bill Willis

"The Roman soldiers compelled a certain man, Simon of Cyrene, the father of Alexander and Rufus, as he was coming out of the country and passing by, to bear Jesus' cross. And they brought Him to the place called Golgotha, which is translated, Place of a Skull." –Mark 15:21-22

Those who follow Jesus the Nazarene are familiar with His call to discipleship, which is a call to carry the cross of Christ, as well as our own.

Simon was the first to pick up the cross and follow Jesus, the first who desired to love and follow Him more than anything. May all who claim the Nazarene cling to "The Light and Life of the Cross!"

There's a Friday on the calendar many call "Good," the day Jesus was nailed to a cruel piece of wood.

At His Birth angels proclaimed Him "Savior," at thirty-three He hung for our sins, refusing to waver.

Many have sung of "The Old Rugged Cross," how Jesus died for all, unconcerned with the cost.

For the joy set before Him He endured the Tree, He hung there six hours, for you and for me.

Jesus died on a Cross, on a hill far away, but to live in Its Power we must embrace It in a personal way.

His Cross must become more than a symbol or sign, He asks us to carry It daily, and own it as mine.

Paul embraced Jesus and His Cross, accepted His Invite: "Follow Me, no matter the loss!" The Cross has all Power over our sin, and by Grace we always prevail and find victory in Him.

Focus on the Suffering Christ on the middle tree, You'll find peace, hope, love, for all eternity.

Our hearts are broken at the horror of Black Friday, But on Sunday Jesus defeated death; He made the way.

As we look to The Hill of Compassion and Care, The Light and Love of The Cross reminds us nothing can compare.

May we live in The Shadow of The Cross day and night, And forsake sin and self, and give up the fight.

Let's embrace the Cross—Its Power over sin and self, And ask Jesus to live as Lord, not just on a shelf.

If 'yes' is always our response to the Savior, we'll live life filled with His joy and all of God's favor!

"Do You?" | Gary O'Shell

"Then Jesus said to her, 'I am the resurrection and the life; he who believes in me shall live even if he dies, and everyone who lives and believes in Me shall never die. Do you believe this?'" –John 11:25-26

In my prayer journal I've written, "What will I believe today?" That's a question He asks each of us every day. What is it that we'll believe today? What will we believe about Him, His Words, His promises, His call? What will we believe about what the Father has revealed about Himself both through His Word and through our experiences of Him? What will we believe about His promised peace, joy, strength, and faithfulness to us? What will we believe about what He calls good and what He identifies as evil? What will we believe about the life He created us for and the ministry He's called us to? In short, there is little or nothing about which our belief will not be tested.

Jesus asked a question of Martha that stretched her faith and belief system beyond anything she had previously experienced with Him. She believed Jesus was indeed the resurrection and the life, but her belief was pointing to some future point. Jesus asked her if she could believe that He was the resurrection and the life right now—right now as she stood before the tomb of her brother Lazarus. Death was very real in that culture and time. Few people lived past 40. Death may have seemed more real than life. Jesus told her He and His life were greater than all the power of death, and He asked if she could believe that. It was a mind-boggling statement to her. Jesus doesn't shy away from making such statements to us, and He asks if we will believe Him as well. Will we? That's why, even before He does speak what appears impossible, we need to decide what it is we will believe of Him this day, and every day. What will we believe?

Who knows what you'll face as you go through this day? What will you believe as you do? Will you believe the circumstance, need, or threat...or will you believe Him? Jesus asks us. How will we answer?

A New Thing | Janette Berge

"Forget the former things; do not dwell on the past. See, I am doing a new thing! Now it springs up; do you not perceive it?" –Isaiah 43:19

I absolutely adore the summer season! Of course, I appreciate the warmth, but what I truly love is how stunning everything appears during this time. The blossoming flowers are a constant sight, while the vegetable plants that were mere seedlings in the spring now show signs of growth. It's mesmerizing to witness the birds that had flown south make their way back north, singing a new melody.

To me, summer signifies happiness and joy. As the night begins to cool down, my husband, Brian, and I often sit outside on our porch, sipping coffee and relishing the beauty of God's creation. During one such evening, God reminded me of the previous season's ugliness. The same trees that now rustle in the breeze were once bare, and the vibrant day lilies that had recently bloomed were dry and lifeless. This made me realize that the new life I was experiencing through God's artwork in nature hadn't always been: There was a time when it wasn't very beautiful and vibrant. In winter, the flowers are non-existent, yet God is working underground, preparing them for their next season of bloom.

Isaiah 43:19 reminds us to look around and see the new thing God is doing—even when it seems dreary outside. Perennials, plants that grow yearly, require pruning in winter to prevent disease. Good gardeners tend to their beds in fall and winter to ensure they thrive in spring and summer.

Our life's seasons may not align with the earth's seasons. There are times in our lives when it seems like God is silent and not much is happening. We may feel stagnant, even as everything around us is blossoming. During such seasons, it's essential to take care of ourselves. How we prepare during the "downtime" determines how well we'll thrive during growth and renewal. Perhaps God is "pruning" us to prevent heart disease or burnout. Regardless of our season, we must be content and know that God is diligently working and preparing our hearts and minds for His will to be accomplished.

I Am Worthy? | Brian Charette

"Whoever does not take up their cross and follow me is not worthy of me." –Matthew 10:38

"I am worthy of Jesus."

I have to admit, I cringe even writing those words, checking the window to see if there is lightening on the horizon. There is something about us—something very healthy, I think—that holds the Lord with sufficient awe that we always have a deep sense of understanding that we are not Him. We didn't speak the universe into being with a word. We didn't create mankind from a heart of love. We don't offer redemption to all who will believe. We didn't carry the sin of the world to the cross in the ultimate majestic act of mercy.

He is God and we are sod, as they say. And something in us cries, "We're not worthy!"

Yet...

To consider the implication of Matthew 10:38 is to acknowledge this possibility. It is not improper theology or exegesis to read from Matthew 10:38 in converse. "Whoever does not take up their cross and follow me is not worthy of me" may instead become "Whoever takes up their cross and follows me is worthy of me." (Are you squirming yet?)

As scary as it is to think of not being worthy of Him, it is equally hopeful to think of the opposite. And maybe that's what the writer of Hebrews was implying toward the conclusion of the faith dialogue in chapter 11 when he wrote, "The world was not worthy of them..." Perhaps if it can be said of us that the world is not worthy of us, it can be said that we may be worthy of Jesus.

But the cost is steep—it requires the taking up of our cross. If we refuse the level of daily self-sacrifice required by that cross, we will not and cannot be worthy to be called His disciple—His friend.

SABBATH

A RHYTHM
OF REST

⁵⁴ *Jesus replied, "If I glorify myself, my glory means nothing. My Father, whom you claim as your God, is the one who glorifies me.* ⁵⁵*Though you do not know him, I know him. If I said I did not, I would be a liar like you, but I do know him and obey his word.* 56 *Your father Abraham rejoiced at the thought of seeing my day; he saw it and was glad."*

⁵⁷ *"You are not yet fifty years old," they said to him, "and you have seen Abraham!"*

⁵⁸ *"Very truly I tell you," Jesus answered, "before Abraham was born, I am!"*

John 8:54-58

Jo Ann's Ugly Hat | Deb Huff

"... if you confess with your mouth, 'Jesus is Lord,' and believe in your heart that God raised him from the dead, you will be saved. For it is with your heart that you believe and are justified, and it is with your mouth that you confess and are saved." –Romans 10:9-10

Bonnets and frilly dresses marked the Easter holiday for my generation. Getting to church required lots of extra fussing to "dress for Jesus." The hair had to be done just right. Shoes shined. Crinolines starched. A decorated hat had to set on top of perfectly coiffed curls.

My cousin Jo Ann was eight and I was seven. That Easter Sunday, our mothers prepared us to go to the small country church where our grandmother attended.

My hat was a sweet combination of a small brim with a row of flowers and ribbon around the crown. It matched my ringlet curls and the flowers on my dress. Jo Ann's hat looked like a frisbee sitting flat atop her pixie cut hair. She didn't like her dress and her shoes hurt. She was not happy. "Why do we have to wear this?" she demanded.

My grandmother's response was the same as it had been on many Sunday mornings. "We are dressing in our best to honor Jesus." Jo Ann grumbled all the way to church.

That Easter Sunday was special because the pastor spoke a message that was clear enough for my seven-year-old mind and heart to accept. From that day forward, I knew that Jesus had died on the cross for me, He was buried and rose from the grave, and all I had to do was confess my sins and believe and I would have eternal life. It was so simple, so wonderful.

Jo Ann and I were both baptized a few years later, but on that Sunday morning, we sat with Grandma wearing our best to honor Jesus. As soon as the service was over, Jo Ann dashed outside to throw her hat in the neighboring field, never to be seen again.

Today's children don't have to go through the process of primping and preparing like my generation. And that's a good thing. What really matters is not clothes but the heart. Jesus simply wants us to accept Him as Savior and spend our days living for Him. No ugly hats needed.

The Winter is Past | Emily Heady

"My beloved spoke, and said to me: 'Rise up, my love, my fair one, and come away. For lo, the winter is past, the rain is over and gone. The flowers appear on the earth; the time of singing has come, and the voice of the turtledove is heard in our land.'" –Song of Solomon 2:10-12

Having grown up in Ohio, I have a keen appreciation for the first hint of spring in the air. Winters there were long—steel-grey stretches of damp and chill that did not relent until March was well advanced. Typically, by the time the end of winter rolled around, my mood matched the sky. I was just done.

More often than not, the hardest stretch of winter fell during Lent, and Easter just as often coincided with the green of the first tulips poking through the hard Midwestern soil. It all seemed right in a cosmic kind of way, and for sure, that first breath of spring gave me new hope, new energy—the urge to go do something, anything! In the Jewish calendar, fittingly, Passover falls midway during the month of Nisan, which is actually the first month of their year. New beginnings were in season right as Jesus was preparing for His crucifixion and resurrection; no wonder He longed to eat the Passover with His disciples. It was the start of a new story. Like us, I imagine that Jesus was ready for new life.

Easter is an invitation to rise up, to be on our way. Jesus, the firstfruits of a new creation, fell to the ground as a kernel of wheat and died. But, rising again, He showed us what the harvest will look like. The invitation in Song of Solomon prefigures the invitation that Jesus gave to Mary Magdalene, the first to see Him in the flesh, at the tomb. Mary was clinging to Jesus—bowed down, no doubt, and overcome with joy once she recognized her Rabboni. He tells her, though, not to hold onto Him but rather to go and tell what she has seen (John 20). She does just this. She rises up and goes away, sharing with the disciples that she has seen the Lord.

Jesus, as we celebrate the new life you bring, let us also take seriously your words to rise and tell others that we have seen you.

When God is Silent | Jonny Bailey

"You will seek me and find me when you seek me with all your heart." –Jeremiah 29:13

The day between Good Friday and Easter is a day characterized by a series of lack, or empty things: the unknown, the downcast, the silence. The mood of these few days recalls the times in our relationship with God where we go through a "season of silence," or what has also been called the "dark night of the soul."

I want to make it clear that I am not talking about a time of silence when we are living in disobedience to Christ, but rather, seeking Him daily yet hearing nothing—the days when we feel like we just can't connect with God. Many of us know that we have God's direction or calling in our lives. The times when we feel this the most acutely are glorious times. Yet even those of us who pursue God with our whole hearts will find that sometimes a day comes when there is nothing. Complete and utter silence.

Thoughts run through our minds: "Am I disappointing God, am I refusing a calling?" When you go through this time, don't wander. Lean in. What we may not realize at first is that God is silent to show love to us.

Saint Ignatius of Antioch, who was a disciple of the apostle John, wrote, "Whoever has understood our Lord's words, understands his silence, because God is known in his silence." God restrains His voice at times in a Christian's heart to grow closer to us. Often, we can get caught up in the ways God has found us—so much so that sometimes we forget that we need to seek Him in wild pursuit as well. He tells us in Jeremiah 29:13, "You will seek me and find me when you seek me with all your heart." We must hold fast to the truth that even when God is silent, He is still present! Even when you think He is nowhere to be found, He is closer than the air we breathe.

So how does God use this silence to deepen our relationship with Him? I believe that He matures us during this time. When we continue in faith to seek and serve Him even in the times when we don't feel His direction, it is as if He is trusting us to live as He taught us and is giving us an opportunity to persevere in His calling on our lives. This time truly refines our faith. Let us grow out of our infancy of only praising Him when we feel He is near and realize that we must seek God with all of our heart because He is always with us!

Different Hostilities | Stephen Willis

"For he himself is our peace, who has made us both one and has broken down in his flesh the dividing wall of hostility by abolishing the law of commandments expressed in ordinances, that he might create in himself one new man in place of the two, so making peace, and might reconcile us both to God in one body through the cross, thereby killing the hostility." –Ephesians 2:14-16

There have been countless scientific studies that have proven that feelings of hostility lead to changes in heart rate and blood pressure, as well as weakened immune response, all of which increase the likelihood of depression, heart disease, and diabetes.

In Ephesians 2, we see the word "hostility" twice in a matter of just three verses, each time with a different meaning.

In verse fourteen, the text is speaking about the hostility between groups of people—the Jews and Gentiles specifically. The Jews had first been given the truth of the gospel, and a vast majority of them had no desire to share it with the Gentiles. In return, the Gentile people hated the Jews simply because they were Jews.

When Paul gets to verse sixteen, he refers to a different hostility: one between a Holy God and sinful humanity. This hostility is in the fabric of the sin-soaked world that we live in; it is the reason for the chasm that lies between God and man. As Paul proclaims in Colossians, "Once you were alienated from God and were enemies in your minds because of your evil behavior" (Colossians 1:21).

If the story of hostility were simply presented with no resolution, we would all be in serious trouble. However, Paul's initial words in our selected text makes all the difference. "For [Jesus Christ] himself is our peace" (v. 14). Yes, two different hostilities are presented to us, and yet one person is the answer to both. His name is Jesus.

In view of what Christ has done for us, we must know that God longs for us to be people who pursue forgiveness and long to forgive others. This, my friends, is the essence of the gospel. May our lives and the relationships that we form be testimonies not of the hostility in the world, but of the good news.

Blessed to Bless Others | Chene Heady

"The LORD said to Abram: 'Go forth from your land, your relatives, and from your father's house to a land that I will show you. I will make of you a great nation, and I will bless you . . . All the families of the earth will find blessing in you.'" –Genesis 12:1-3

Most of us are willing to believe that God desires to bless us. "I'd like to thank God for my accomplishments," with the obligatory finger pointing toward heaven, says the celebrity at many an awards show. If our lives have gone reasonably well, we believe in God's benevolence—for us. Because, after all, He's a good Father and what Father wouldn't give His children good gifts (Matt. 7:11)? One couple I knew used to spend hours drafting the floor plan and arranging the furniture of the giant house God was going to give them for being such good servants. If the Father has prepared many mansions in heaven, they seemed to reason, why not one for us, right now?

Yet when God calls Abraham to abandon the life he has known and to set perilously into the unknown, it isn't ultimately for his own personal benefit. It's so his descendants will become "a great nation"—not him. And even his descendants can't just kick back, enjoy God's bounty, and bask in the greatness of their nation. They are to become a great nation for the benefit of "all the communities of the earth." So, if we are Abraham's spiritual descendants, we also do not get to live for ourselves. Our blessings, too, are for the benefit of "all the communities of the earth."

Abraham knows that whatever we have been given isn't simply for our pleasure, but is to be held in trust. Possibly for people who haven't yet even crossed our minds. Maybe that's why when two strangers show up at his tent, he so easily upsets the order of the whole household to show them hospitality. Or why when he finally reaches the Promised Land, he almost immediately gives the better part of it up to his nephew Lot. Abraham never really saw it as his anyway. He clings to nothing, and so has everything (2 Cor. 6:10).

Dear God, may our eyes be open this day to your blessings and the ways we might bless others.

The Challenge | Gary O'Shell

"Jesus said to her, 'I am the resurrection and the life. The one who believes in me will live, even though they die.'" –John 11:25

In my prayer journal, I have a great proclamation from Oswald Chambers. He says, "The great challenge is, Do I know my risen Lord? Do I know the power of His indwelling Spirit? Am I wise enough in His sight and foolish enough according to the world to bank on what Christ has said? Or am I abandoning the supernatural position, which is boundless confidence in Christ?"

Jesus spoke the words of John 11:25 to Martha after the death and burial of her brother Lazarus. He then added, "Do you believe this, Martha?" She did, to an extent. She believed it as a future hope, but not as a present possibility. We have much the same problem. We believe in the resurrection as a fact. We hold it as a hope. But we struggle to believe that the resurrection power of Christ can be experienced in the here and now. That's why Chambers' proclamation/question pierces us to the marrow of our being. What do we really believe about the resurrection life of Christ as it pertains to our daily life experience? Do we live in the power of a risen life?

When Jesus rose, He gave the power to do the same to all of us who are His. When His Spirit takes residence in our heart and life, He does so in the power of His risen life; we are meant to experience the wonder and victory of the resurrection life. We are to live in "boundless confidence" in that life, as Chambers says.

To base all of our hope in the risen Christ is beyond foolish in the eyes of the world. Does it seem foolish to you? We seem to easily drift into that place of abandoning our supernatural position. Where might it have happened in you and me?

If you confess Him as your Lord and Savior today, He has called you forth from your tomb of death, just as He did Lazarus. He calls you into the fullness of His risen life—all of His risen life. He calls us to bank everything on His promise of life. To live in that boundless, endless confidence in Him. May we come forth and enter in.

SABBATH

A RHYTHM
OF REST

Jesus said to her, "I am the resurrection
and the life. The one who believes in me
will live, even though they die."

John 11:25

Fear to Peace | Bobbie Gardner

"But you, Lord, are a shield around me, my glory, the One who lifts my head high. I call out to the Lord, and he answers me from his holy mountain." –Psalm 3:3-4

"In peace I will lie down and sleep, for you alone, Lord, make me dwell in safety." –Psalm 4:8

I've never written nor talked publicly about this prior to writing this devotional. Many people know my story, but I'm not sure I've shared this part with anyone before.

I was married to my first husband for sixteen years. Two months into our marriage, I began a life filled with major fears! I discovered I had married a man with a serious mental illness. I feared for his life, I feared for my life, and eventually I feared for the life of our child. He controlled absolutely everything in our home and about our life together. My once happy, easy-going personality changed. I never knew what to expect. Life was a roller-coaster and I hated the ride.

My husband needed professional help, which he refused. He suffered greatly with depression. He had childhood trauma that he never dealt with or even discussed. He made comments that he really didn't want to live into his 40s, and at the age of 39 my husband took his own life, leaving me to raise our 15-year-old daughter alone. When we found out that he had passed, my mom's first reaction was, "I always feared he would take you and [our daughter] with him."

I lived with great fears after that event in my life. I was afraid at night.

Everything out of the normal routine at school where I taught—fire drills, for example—rattled me. One day our principal made an announcement asking the teachers to meet briefly after dismissal. I just knew something terrible had happened. I headed to her office crying uncontrollably, thinking someone had died. She very lovingly hugged me and told me she just wanted to ask everyone to park in the back parking lot the next day because they needed the front parking lot for an event.

My peace came through God's beautiful Word, which reminds me that God is my shield, my peace, and my safety.

Risen and Scarred | JJ Wyzinski

"But Thomas, one of the twelve, was not with them when Jesus came. So the other disciples told him, 'We have seen the Lord.' But he said to them, 'Unless I see the mark of the nails in his hands, and put my finger in the mark of the nails and my hand in his side, I will not believe.'" –John 20:24–25

If you were to imagine your resurrected body, I'm sure you would go back to your finest moments of physical health: the full head of hair, ache-less back, and smooth, clear skin would probably be near the top of your list. I doubt that "mark of the nails" would even be an option. Jesus walking out of the tomb with holes in his hands is an odd thought on its own, but for Thomas to ask for this kind of proof is even more odd. "Unless I see the mark of the nails..."—Why would the marks of crucifixion be a part of the resurrected Jesus?

It seems Thomas recognized something we often forget. The display of love represented by the marks was exactly what the world needed. They didn't need a savior without wounds. They needed Jesus—the blood, the nails, the holes, and the lot.

Maybe this risen and scarred Jesus is what the world is waiting on the Church to reveal today. So many people like Thomas are hurting, closed in a room and struggling with doubt, and they don't need a church without scars. They need a church bearing the "mark of the nails." This kind of church shows them how far God went and will always go for their healing. Maybe we should stop hiding our scars from hurting people and let them see what God has done. Maybe Jesus appeared to Thomas exactly how He needed to, showing exactly what God brought Him through. Bearing the mark of healing. If we were willing to show what God has done in our own lives instead of presenting a flawless, unscarred image, maybe the world would believe like Thomas.

Prayer: Lord, help me be a real representation of your healing and love, to not portray a flawless life, but a life marked by what you've done for me and the healing you've brought. Amen.

The Church as Physical | Mike Lyle

"That which was from the beginning, which we have heard, which we have seen with our eyes, which we have looked at and our hands have touched—this we proclaim concerning the Word of life. The life appeared; we have seen it and testify to it, and we proclaim to you the eternal life, which was with the Father and has appeared to us. We proclaim to you what we have seen and heard, so that you also may have fellowship with us. And our fellowship is with the Father and with his Son, Jesus Christ. We write this to make our joy complete." –I John 1:1-4

What is the Church? John speaks about three things: 1) a physicality, 2) a proclamation, and 3) a fellowship between God and humanity. Could these ingredients form the foundation of what it means to be the Church in the world today? Let's explore that first one together.

The Church is anything but abstract. It is grounded in reality and anytime it leaves this grounding, it becomes something less. The Greek myth of Antaeus provides some help in understanding this. According to the myth, Antaeus gained strength by touching the earth. Hercules had trouble defeating him because every time he knocked Antaeus to the ground, the beast got stronger. Eventually, Hercules had to find a way to keep Antaeus in the air to defeat him.[1] Like Antaeus, when the Church loses its grounding, it loses a vital aspect of what it means to be the Church; it loses its strength.

John opens his letter with a testimony about a physical reality; that which, "we have heard...seen with our eyes...looked at...our hands have touched." This idea is pointing to the incarnation, and I think applies to the Church as well. "Just as the Son of God, in order to share our humanity, had to take flesh in a particular human body at a given place and time (and culture) within human history, so the Word of God is present only in specific embodiments."[2] It is important to remember that the Church is not an idea. It is an embodiment that includes real people, real names, and real faces. Have you come to think of Church as a show that you can merely attend or watch from home? It isn't. It's a physical body.

---

1 Peterson, Eugene H. *Five Smooth Stones for Pastoral Work*. Grand Rapids: Eerdmans, 1992.
2 Pelzel, Morris. *Ecclesiology: The Church as Communion and Mission*. Chicago: Loyola P, 2001.

The Church and Its Proclamation | Mike Lyle

"That which was from the beginning, which we have heard, which we have seen with our eyes, which we have looked at and our hands have touched—this we proclaim concerning the Word of life. The life appeared; we have seen it and testify to it, and we proclaim to you the eternal life, which was with the Father and has appeared to us. We proclaim to you what we have seen and heard, so that you also may have fellowship with us. And our fellowship is with the Father and with his Son, Jesus Christ. We write this to make our joy complete." –I John 1:1-4

We're exploring the potential of the opening of John's letter in forming a foundation of what it means to be the Church in the world today. Yesterday was about the physical expression of the Church. Today, we will discuss the proclamation.

In verse 2, John speaks of proclaiming the eternal life that came from the Father. This is reminiscent of the words he recorded in another one of his books: "I am the Alpha and the Omega, the First and the Last, the Beginning and the End" (Revelation 22:13). The "eternal" life that comes from the Father is Jesus. He is the eternal life that the Church proclaims. We are not proclaiming a doctrine or a plan for salvation. We are proclaiming a person. It is His eternal kind of life that is lifted up by the Church. It is, in fact, the proclamation of the life of Jesus that makes the Church Christian.

Also, by proclaiming the life of Jesus, the Church is pointing to creation as it was meant to be, as God intends to restore it. In fact, [1]"a number of the fathers of the Church referred to the Church as the 'transfigured world,' meaning that the Church represents what the world is destined to become" (Pelzel 99). The method is not the issue. When we teach the Words of Jesus, we are making the proclamation. When we help the poor and work for justice, we are making the proclamation. When we worship together, forgive one another, and bear each other's burdens, we are also making the proclamation. In this way, the Church becomes a sign of the eternal kind of life. Are you a part of this Church? Are you making the proclamation?

———————

1 Pelzel, Morris. *Ecclesiology: The Church as Communion and Mission.* Chicago: Loyola P, 2001.

The Church in Fellowship | Mike Lyle

"That which was from the beginning, which we have heard, which we have seen with our eyes, which we have looked at and our hands have touched—this we proclaim concerning the Word of life. The life appeared; we have seen it and testify to it, and we proclaim to you the eternal life, which was with the Father and has appeared to us. We proclaim to you what we have seen and heard, so that you also may have fellowship with us. And our fellowship is with the Father and with his Son, Jesus Christ. We write this to make our joy complete." –I John 1:1-4

In this letter, John says that the apostles proclaim the message of eternal life so that other people may have fellowship with them (vs. 3). He then goes on to explain that their fellowship is not only with each other but also with the Trinity. Not only is the Church a physical body made up of real people with all of their problems and idiosyncrasies, but it is also making an eternal proclamation while enjoying communion with the Trinity!

What does it mean to be invited into fellowship with one another and with God? At the very least, it means that the Church is fundamentally relational. In Genesis 2:18, God looks at Adam, who was living at that moment within a completely good creation, and says, "It is not good for the man to be alone." At this moment of creation's history, there was no sin and no curse: only a perfect world where God and Adam were enjoying fellowship with one another. This, in God's eyes, was the only thing about his entire creation that was not good. That surprises me. But, apparently, when God said, "let us make mankind in our image," He meant that humanity would be relational to the core. We were made for communion. That means when it's just you and God, it's not as good as when it's you and God and others.

When you are baptized, you are not only identifying with Jesus. You are joining a family. We forgive one another, eat together, pray for each other, and encourage one another. Have you tried to enjoy fellowship with Jesus apart from the fellowship of the Church? That just won't work. Make John's joy complete and enter into full fellowship.

The Church as Sacrament | Mike Lyle

" *...The Lord Jesus, on the night he was betrayed, took bread, and when he had given thanks, he broke it and said, 'This is my body, which is for you; do this in remembrance of me.' In the same way, after supper he took the cup, saying, 'This cup is the new covenant in my blood; do this, whenever you drink it, in remembrance of me.' For whenever you eat this bread and drink this cup, you proclaim the Lord's death until he comes.*" –I Corinthians 11:23-26

Today's reading is about the Sacrament of Communion. The word for sacrament is derived from the Greek word "mysterion," which means mystery. When we drink from the cup and eat the bread, we participate in the mystery of the Gospel. You might have heard that a sacrament is an outward sign of an inward grace. That's true. But perhaps sacraments are a bit more. They might be "signs that actually bring about what they show"[1] (Pelzel 64).

Theologian Lubac carries this idea further. He says, "If Christ is the sacrament of God, the Church is for us the sacrament of Christ; she represents him, in the full and ancient meaning of the term, she really makes him present..."[2](qtd. in Dulles 56). The Church, therefore, is the ultimate sacrament that seeks to bring about the communion it is proclaiming.

The physical symbols of ordinary bread and wine remind the Church that the Christian life demands physical expression in normal, ordinary life. This impacts how the Church exists in the world. The Church proclaims that it is better to forgive enemies than to hold grudges, and it does this by actually forgiving enemies. It proclaims that there is love for the outcast by showing love for all people and practicing radical inclusivism. The Church proclaims communion with God, fellow mankind, and the earth by actually living in this communion. Too often, the communion supper has been reduced to remembering that we go to heaven when we die. However, Jurgon Moltmann declares, "If Christian hope is reduced to the salvation of the soul in a heaven beyond death, it loses its power to renew life and change the world..."[3] (qtd. in Rausch xiii).

Come, do this in remembrance of Jesus: Proclaim His death until He returns. In this way, we help to actualize the reality we point towards.

---

1 Pelzel, Morris. *Ecclesiology: The Church as Communion and Mission.* Chicago: Loyola P, 2001.
2 Dulles, Avery. *Models of the Church.* New York: Image, 2002.
3 Rausch, Thomas P. *Eschatology, Liturgy, and Christology: Toward Recovering an Eschatological Imagination.* Collegeville, MN: Liturgical P, 2010.

SABBATH

A RHYTHM
OF REST

Dear children, let us not love with words or speech

but with actions and in truth.

This is how we know that we belong to the truth

and how we set our hearts at rest in his presence: If

our hearts condemn us, we know that God is greater

than our hearts, and he knows everything.

1 John 3:18-20

Just Tell Them | Deirdra Jones

"Jesus called his twelve disciples together and gave them authority to cast out evil spirits and to heal every kind of disease and illness." –Matthew 10:1

"A spiritual gift is given to each of us so we can help each other." –I Corinthians 12:7

Season 3, episode 2 of the series The Chosen is based on Matthew 10:1-15. Here, we find Jesus seated at the table in Simon's house with the twelve disciples. In so many words, He explains to them that it is unsustainable for Him to do the work of ministry all by Himself...so, He is sending them out, two by two, in different directions to do His work. The disciples show signs of worry and speak words of fear. They cannot imagine going out without Jesus to do what they have seen Jesus do. They are worried that they don't know enough to go out on their own, and they are worried they won't know what to say. Jesus responds by saying, "Just tell them what you know."

This sentiment remains in the Church today. It is unsustainable for the pastor and leaders of a church to do all of the work of ministry. We are all called not only to BE disciples, but also to GO AND MAKE disciples.

One thing to remember is that we cannot, nor are we expected to, carry out this command in our own power. Also like the disciples, we are not expected to be scholars and theologians. Jesus gave the disciples the authority to do what He was asking of them. The Holy Spirit does the work in and through us. Our responsibility is to yield obediently to His leading and "just tell them what [we] know."

God has gifted each person to participate in the work of ministry in some capacity. We are all needed, and we all need each other.

Take some time to read 1 Corinthians 12. Reflect on how you are participating in the work of ministry.

Father, it can be easy to sit and receive your Word, but you didn't intend for me to keep it all to myself. Help me to have the courage to share your Word with others, and remind me that I don't have to have all of the answers. I just need to tell them what I know. Amen.

Humility | Matthew S.E. Waggoner

"...in humility value others above yourselves, not looking to your own interests but each of you to the interests of the others." –Philippians 2:3-4

When our family lived in Colorado, I took a Serve-Safe course for the job I had at the hospital. The requirements back home in West Virginia were modest: Show up at the local health department, get a TB test, and watch a video with a short quiz. Serve-Safe was the same but on steroids. It was a week-long class teaching us all the ins and outs of food prep, storage, and care. Within this course was a hand-washing seminar. The teacher took this white powder that looked like baby powder, sprinkled it on both sides of our hands, and told all of us to head to the bathroom to wash it off. We all scurried into the bathroom, and I knew in my heart I had the desire to be the best.

It's a competitive string in my heart, and I was plucking it. I scrubbed and scrubbed and washed those hands, for which I believed I was ready for surgery. I ran back into the room, and waiting there was the instructor with a special black light to see how well I had done. I stuck my hands into that light to be appalled at the evidence. My entire back of my hand on my right hand was untouched.

Literally, the right hand wasn't that clean at all; only the palm of my right hand which had vigorously scrubbed at my left hand until it was clean. I learned a valuable lesson that day. When it came to washing my hands, my dominant hand did most of the work, and I never allowed the servant hand to reciprocate and do its part. What I also learned was that just because something dominates my life doesn't mean it's the best. All the parts are needed. Take Jesus, for instance. Jesus had countless kingly, priestly, and prophetic traits, but with humility, he chose to serve. Maybe in our lives we should learn that the least of these can do what the dominant can, if only we would remember them and let them. Isn't it much better to walk side by side with others?

Abba Father, remind me it's not all about me, but about thee. Amen.

Humility and Holiness | Kerry Willis

"He must increase, but I must decrease." –John 3:30

A few years ago while preaching a series on humility and holiness, I wrote these words to this simple yet sincere personal song of prayer:

A PRAYER SONG FOR HUMILITY AND HOLINESS

Verse 1
Lord, I seek You and Your humility.
Destroy self-centeredness that has blinded me.
Pardon my inconsistencies.
And let Your Spirit be my purity.

CHORUS
Oh, I adore You, in my days and nights.
Let my devotion lift you up on high.
You sacrificed Your Life for me.
Now, give me Vision that I might see.

Verse 2
Lord have mercy, reveal my need for You.
I must decrease, it's what I want to do.
Keep me from all wickedness.
Oh, how I want to be Your friend.

BRIDGE:
I desire You to Breathe in me.
I want to know You,
Know Your Holiness, completely.
I desire You to Breathe in me.
I want to know You,
Know Your Holiness, completely.
I desire You to Breathe in me.
I want to know You,
Know Your Holiness, completely.
It's my prayer. It's my praise.
To Love You with all of me.

Being Extraordinary | Reenie Peppers

"So here's what I want you to do, God helping you: Take your everyday, ordinary life—your sleeping, eating, going-to-work, and walking-around life—and place it before God as an offering. Embracing what God does for you is the best thing you can do for Him . . . God brings the best out of you, develops well-formed maturity in you."
–Romans 12:1-2 (The Message)

I am a big fan of biographies. I am fascinated with people who took an idea, ran with it, and created something extraordinary. For example, how did Walt Disney take a little black-and-white drawing of a mouse and turn it into Disneyland, the happiest place on Earth? Or take the Wright brothers. How did working in a bicycle shop translate in their minds to the first flying machine? And what goes on in the mind of someone who successfully creates a whole world with its own map and languages and fantastical beings as did J.R.R. Tolkien with his Lord of the Rings chronicles? As far as I know, none of these people had superpowers. They were all ordinary men going about their ordinary lives, whose efforts produced something extraordinary.

I guess the reason I am so captivated with people like this is that I want to be an ordinary person with an ordinary idea that I turn into something extraordinary. So, where do I begin? I believe that Romans 12:1-2 points me toward the starting line. "So here's what I want you to do, God helping you: Take your everyday, ordinary life—your sleeping, eating, going-to-work, and walking-around life— and place it before God as an offering. Embracing what God does for you is the best thing you can do for Him . . . God brings the best out of you, develops well-formed maturity in you."

The first step is to commit my every-day, ordinary life to God. He's the one who gave me my mind, my talents, and my aspirations. I start with what I have been given and work from there. God is the one who takes what the world classifies as ordinary and transforms it into something extraordinary. That spark of creativity and innovation comes out of the ordinary, everyday life we have been given.

Remember, the idea for the first flying machine came from two ordinary brothers working their everyday jobs in an un-extraordinary bicycle shop.

More Room for God | Jim Chapman

"He brought in the priests and the Levites, assembled them in the square on the east side..." –II Chronicles 29:4

"My sons, do not be negligent now, for the Lord has chosen you to stand before him and serve him, to minister before him and to burn incense." –II Chronicles 29:11

"When they had assembled their fellow Levites and consecrated themselves, they went in to purify the temple of the Lord, as the king had ordered, following the word of the Lord." –II Chronicles 29:15

It is no secret that I love to clean. I have a special day during the week to clean the bathrooms: "Toilet Tuesdays." I also enjoy getting rid of things that have lost their use. I desire to make more room in our house.

Purging is not easy for everyone. And yet purging can be helpful not only with clutter in our houses, but also in our lives and our churches.

Hezekiah, a good Old Testament king, comes along after several evil ones. His predecessors had destroyed the temple and had begun to worship other gods. Hezekiah began the purge. He began to make more room for God. There were several areas God called Hezekiah to clean out. I believe those are the same areas God calls His Church to make more room for Him.

I want to focus on the first area God instructed Hezekiah to start with: the leaders of the Church, the Priests. Hezekiah called the leaders and asked them to return to what they were called to do—to be Godly leaders, to help lead the people in worship and service to God. The Priests were to remove those things in the temple that had nothing to do with God or worshiping the one true God.

Today, the leadership of the Church needs to make more room for God. A real move of God begins with leadership. Our responsibility is to remove the stuff that distracts our churches from worshiping and serving God. Every Church leader could stand to make more room for God.

Prayer: Father God, I permit you to purge things in my life and church that distract and take away from genuinely serving and worshiping you. Please help me make more room for you and help others I lead to do the same.

God Made You Special for His Special Work with His Special People | Steve Dillman

"For we are what He has made us, created in Christ Jesus for good works, which God prepared beforehand to be our way of life." –Ephesians 2:10

We are what He has made us—created in His image to be like Christ to do what God has called us to do. We often think of ourselves as having strengths and weaknesses, but what if I told you that you don't have any weaknesses because God, in whose image you are created, doesn't have any weaknesses? What we call weaknesses may simply be immaturities or undeveloped strengths.

The Gallup organization developed an assessment tool called Strengths Finder. It is based on the concept that you have 34 strength themes in a ranked order. These strengths identify how you are designed to accomplish things. For each of you, some strengths are dominant. Some are moderately evidenced in your life. And some are just non-existent. Similarly, you didn't get all of the aspects of God's character; you received the aspects of His nature that were needed to accomplish His will through your life.

Gallup also determined that there is no one who has lived or is living now that has your strengths in the same ranked order as you. That's why I can tell you that God made you special. And He has made you special for a reason. He has called you to do something that only someone with your strengths can do. As you recognize the strengths of God's image in your life, you will also start to see the strengths that God has put in the people around you. The work of His kingdom is bigger than what any one of us can accomplish and as such, we need each other. We work in community and in concert with each other to accomplish together what none of us can accomplish alone.

So, rejoice today! God made you special for His special work with His special people.

Prayer: Thank you, Father, for creating us in your image and calling us to do work in your kingdom that only we can do with the strengths you give us. Thank you for the people who join us in your mission. We look forward to what you will accomplish through us all. Amen.

SABBATH

A RHYTHM
OF REST

*² By the seventh day God had finished the work he
had been doing; so on the seventh day he rested from
all his work. ³ Then God blessed the seventh day and
made it holy, because on it he rested from all the
work of creating that he had done.*

Genesis 2:2-3

Witnessing Power | Bobbie Jo King

"But you will receive power when the Holy Spirit comes on you; and you will be my witnesses..." –Acts 1:8a

In preparation for Pentecost Sunday, God has persuaded me to examine my own spiritual life for the presence of Holy Spirit power to witness, in which I have been lacking. I have asked myself, what's happening? Why am I exhausted? Where is the fruit I'm expecting? My Father whispered, "Because you are doing it in your own strength. You've become unaware that you need me." I was depending on my own strength, ability, and personality without even realizing it! As I began to lay it all down, He said, "Do not quench the Holy Spirit" (I Thessalonians 5:19; Ephesians 4:30). I realized the reason I was not experiencing a fresh anointing and outpouring of His power was because I had been quenching the Holy Spirit living within me with my own desires, thoughts, and will. My selfishness had hindered the working of the Holy Spirit!

The Holy Spirit and sin cannot live in the same place. Sin must be eradicated from our lives by repentance and surrendering our will to His. We are empowered by the Spirit to be His witnesses by totally depending on Him, giving Him complete control of our lives, marriages, families, churches, and communities. We are to be entirely sanctified: completely surrendered, devoted, and loving toward God and one another.

The God we serve today is the same God in the book of Acts. The Holy Spirit will empower us today, just as He did the disciples, because God is absolute and unchanging. His desire is to redeem, reconcile, and empower all who believe and call upon the name of Jesus. There is so much yet to be done and we cannot do it in our own strength and power. We must be filled with the Holy Spirit to accomplish such a great and glorious task. Help us, Lord!

Prayer: Holy Spirit, I need you. Holy Spirit you are here. Please forgive me for the times I've quenched you with my own desires, my own thoughts, my own will. Help me to rise above myself to the love of Christ above all else. Purify my heart. Help me to see any hidden parts and to forgive the sin and pain and stop the blame in Jesus' name.

Follow the Nudges | Bobbie Gardner

"My sheep hear my voice, and I know them, and they follow me." –John 10:37

"Whether you turn to the right or to the left, your ears will hear a voice behind you, saying, 'This is the way; walk in it.'" –Isaiah 30:21

I often say I failed at retirement. After 30 years in education, I retired and found joy in less structure and home canning. If it grows, I will can it. Chances are if you spend any time with me, you will likely end up with pickles, jam, or salsa!

This spring, I had the opportunity to become part of the Chick-fil-A team. I decided I wanted to be the "lady in the dining room."

Often while working I am impressed to pray for many of these precious people with whom God has so graciously put in my path, both fellow employees and customers.

Sometimes when I see someone who is eating alone, I get a little nudge from the Lord to spend a few extra moments with them. Recently, I met a very distinguished gentleman. As we talked, I learned he had just lost his wife of 62 years. After a brief but meaningful conversation, he thanked me several times for taking the time to sit with him and talk. His demeanor noticeably brightened because I followed God's gentle nudge.

The same week, I had another nudge to sit with a beautiful lady who had been a caregiver for her now deceased husband. She is currently caring for her mother who is dying of lung cancer. She was able to have only a brief outing because of a necessary appointment. While knowing it's an honor to care for both, she has found herself very lonely.

That ordinary day in Chick-fil-A, God nudged this dining room lady to stop for a few moments to show the love of Jesus. I listened while she talked. She simply needed an ear to listen that day. I'm honored I was there.

I pray for both of them often. They matter in the kingdom. I know the beautiful people I greet and work with each day also matter greatly in the kingdom.

Is there someone who may just need a listening ear today? God, help us to always be sensitive to follow your nudges.

Sacred Smallness | Gary O'Shell

"Call to Me and I will answer you, and I will tell you great and mighty things, which you do not know." –Jeremiah 33:3

"Your life doesn't have to be big to be beautiful in the Lord." –Jenny Papapostalou

I love Jeremiah 33:3 and I know that it's true. He will open our eyes to see wonders and He will share His heart and His thoughts with us. He reveals what's hidden, and He does so with those whose hearts are attuned to His. Still, though I have always believed and experienced this promise, I think for much of my life and ministry in Him, I had a flawed understanding of what He was promising. I thought that if He would tell me of great and mighty things He would also use me to do great and mighty things. But that isn't His promise at all, and my believing that it was led to a lot of frustration in my calling. That's why the quote from Papapostalou is so powerful.

Papapostalou speaks about the "sacred smallness" to which most of us are called—hidden places where the only one who sees is Him. Those of us who covet renown and applause can never be happy in that place. In our quest for a great life, though, we must not miss having a beautiful one. We may not live and minister on a grand and mighty scale, but we do so on a beautiful one. We may not be a fragrance of Christ to thousands, but we are to some who may never have an encounter with Him without us.

You may be in a hidden place right now. Very few know that you're there. He does. All you do for Him, preach for Him, love for Him, and give for Him may be hidden from almost everyone, but it is not hidden from Him. You're His fragrance there: a fragrance that would be absent if you weren't. Your scope of influence and ministry may not be great and wide, but it's beautiful. Eternity will show the wide effects that your life has had . . . all while you thought no one noticed. And the outward ripples of your life, ministry, and service will go on throughout eternity. What could be more beautiful than that?

Community or Family | Stephen Willis

"For through him we both have access in one Spirit to the Father. So then you are no longer strangers and aliens, but you are fellow citizens with the saints and members of the household of God." –Ephesians 2:18-19

My oldest son went through a ten-month interview process to get accepted in the Nuclear Propulsion Program in the US Navy. After much testing and many interviews, acceptance in the program hinged on one final meeting with the Admiral. At the end, he heard these words he had longed to hear: "Candidate Willis, welcome to the United States Navy."

It was a major accomplishment for him to be accepted into such a prestigious community. Here's the truth, though: Any community is a poor substitute for the family of God. Whether it is a travel sports team, a civic organization, a country club, or a military branch, these communities ultimately fall short in comparison to "the household of God." The family of God is made up of imperfect people, as we all know. But we mustn't use our imperfections as an excuse to distance ourselves from the family of God.

Have you ever considered where you would be today without the family of God? Sure, you can spend time picking through all of the short-comings of God's Church, but to me that is like someone who's drowning in the ocean commenting on the poor paint job on the boat that is about to save him. While Jesus Himself is our salvation, the Church is the vehicle that God uses to deliver safely to shore those whom He has saved.

Over the years, I have been a part of many different community groups. What I know is this: I am no longer a part of most of those groups, and in the end they will all pass away. However, the family of God will never pass away. People don't need to take complicated tests or be interviewed by high-ranking officers to join it. They simply have to receive the free gift of salvation through repentance, and then look for their place at the table. Pull up a seat and join me in a meal! We are family.

Prayer: Lord, help me to make your household my priority.

"At the Round Earth's Imagin'd Corners" | Emily Heady

I suspect that I am not the only child who was a little bit traumatized by the books of Daniel and Revelation. I recall sitting in Sunday School, watching our Sunday School superintendent unfurl a wall-sized apocalyptic chart, with angry horses of varying colors, bowls of wrath, plagues, and so on. He found the end of the world riveting; I found it frightening.

If perchance I found myself unexpectedly alone, I feared that the rapture had happened and I had been left. As I grew older, I wondered how much this world mattered. Why plant a garden? Why go to college?

John Donne's seventh Holy Sonnet shows that he too had a vivid imagination—at least when it came to the end times. He imagines the angels blowing their apocalyptic trumpets (lines 1-2) and the souls of the dead collecting their bodies from their various executioners—floods, fires, war, old age, illness, tyrants, despair, justice, and random chance (lines 7). They, together with those still alive, see God face to face (line 8).

But, Donne knows, there is work to be done before that happens. He wants to pause in the present moment, before any of this transpires, to consider his own need for grace. He knows he needs to repent and to ask for God's forgiveness now, before it is too late—and repentance, he knows, seals his pardon.

"At the round earth's imagin'd corners, blow
Your trumpets, Angels, and arise, arise
From death, you numberless infinities
Of souls, and to your scattered bodies go,
All whom the flood did, and fire shall o'erthrow,
All whom war, dearth, age, agues, tyrannies,
Despair, law, chance, hath slain, and you whose eyes,
Shall behold God, and never taste deaths woe.
But let them sleep, Lord, and me mourn a space,
For, if above all these, my sins abound,
'Tis late to aske abundance of thy grace,
When we are there; here on this lowly ground,
Teach me how to repent; for that's as good
As if thou hadst seal'd my pardon, with thy blood."

Prayer: Jesus, help us to remember that now is the day of salvation.

Tombstones | Gary O'Shell

"Early on Sunday morning, while it was still dark, Mary Magdalene came to the tomb and found that the stone had been rolled away from the entrance." –John 20:1

"The blessings of salvation began the day Jesus blew the doors off a tomb." –Chris Tiegreen

I've been thinking a bit recently about the stone that sealed the tomb of Jesus. Tombstones separated life from death. Those who died were placed in a burial tomb and then the tomb was sealed with a large stone. To remove a tombstone was a very difficult thing. The stone was a symbol of the finality of death. Yet, as Tiegreen's above quote shows, Jesus "blew the doors" off His tomb and in doing so conquered the power of sin and in its greatest form, death.

In our own lives, what "tombstones" seek to block His life from ever reaching the areas of death that are found there? Where do we need stones to be rolled away? Stones of unforgiveness, bitterness, resentment. Stones of fear, addiction, confusion. Stones that have formed because of lies we've believed, or forgiveness that we can't really accept. We can even begin to "worship" these stones and not wish to have them removed. Our tombs can become comfortable, familiar; we can grow so used to their darkness that we shun the light that comes with Christ. Charles Wesley wrote in his great hymn that his spiritual dungeon flamed with the light of Jesus Christ, that he rose from his spiritual death and went forth and followed Christ. Jesus stands before every one of these tombs, and with a word those stones, even the most massive, simply roll away. He stands before yours. With one word He'll remove it. Will you have Him speak it?

Whatever your "tombstone," it cannot stay in place when Christ speaks His life and freedom to it. The tomb that held Him is empty and has been for more than 2000 years. May whatever that has entombed you, as well as the stone that seals you in with it, be rolled aside by the one whom no tombstone can withstand. He stands there, whispering your name, calling you forth. Take that step towards that stone...and behold as He rolls it away...and you're free.

SABBATH

A RHYTHM
OF REST

"I am the good shepherd; I know my sheep
and my sheep know me—just as the Father
knows me and I know the Father—and I lay
down my life for the sheep."

John 10:14-15

A Holy Hunger | Cavan Carlton

"And he said to me, 'Son of man, eat what is before you, eat this scroll; then go and speak to the people of Israel.' So I opened my mouth, and he gave me the scroll to eat."
–Ezekiel 3:1-2

Have you ever stopped to consider just how much of our time and energy is spent on satisfying our physical hunger? Grocery shopping, cooking, actually eating, cleaning up. And of course, planning the next meal. When my family gathers around the holidays, it seems that most of our activity revolves around meals. As soon as we finish lunch, someone will ask, "So who's making dinner?" My brother Brett cooked up a massive seafood boil at a family gathering fifteen years ago...the kind where you dump everything out onto tables lined with butcher paper and eat with your hands standing up...and we're still talking about it!

We eat not just for sustenance, but because food is delicious. The average person has 10,000 taste buds in their mouth, and mine say yes to homemade spaghetti, coffee ice cream, and fresh strawberries. They also say a big NO to olives. Our hunger for physical food is hardwired into us from birth. It's the fuel that feeds the furnace of our earthly self.

I believe the hunger for spiritual food is also hardwired into us, but it requires a quickening. God, through His prevenient grace, will provide the quickening in our souls. He will create a holy hunger in us, a deep desire for His presence. For me, this was an awareness of a spiritual void deep inside my soul, a strong desire to fill that void, and a realization that only Jesus Christ was capable of doing so. Everything else that was not Jesus would be like eating air.

How strong is your appetite for the things of God? How badly do you want to fill the void that exists in your soul? Sadly, many people take the posture that once they profess faith in Jesus Christ they're all good spiritually, and they push themselves back from the table. Our great God, the master chef of heaven, has prepared an extravagant banquet for our souls and invited us to come and eat with Him now and forevermore. Are you hungry?

Nothing Else | Stephen Willis

"Blessed is the man who trusts in the Lord, whose trust is the Lord. He is like a tree planted by water, that sends out its roots by the stream, and does not fear when heat comes..." –Jeremiah 17:7-8

I recently went to bed so frustrated that I was concerned that I wouldn't be able to sleep. My frustration centered on an "opportunity lost" simply because I hadn't learned of it until past the deadline to make it happen. I'm intentionally being vague because the "opportunity lost" isn't the point. I slept fine, but I woke up earlier than normal with the "opportunity lost" still dominating my mind. I dragged myself out of bed because lying in bed with the issue before me seemed like torture. I fixed my coffee, grabbed my Bible, and retreated to the basement. I turned my YouTube worship music on low and simply sat quietly in the presence of God. As I sat, I continued to lament about the "opportunity lost" and how frustrated I was to have missed it. I asked God about it and pondered why this opportunity had evaded me. Honestly, I didn't feel like it was fair. As I sat in silence with the worship music on low, the lyrics of the song quickly resonated with my heart and became my own confession.

[1]"I'm sorry when I've come with my agenda
I'm sorry when I forgot that You're enough
Take me back to where we started
I open up my heart to You
I just want You
Nothing else, nothing else
Nothing else will do
I'm coming back to the heart of worship
And it's all about You
It's all about You, Jesus
I'm sorry, Lord, for the thing I've made it
When it's all about You
It's all about You, Jesus"

My confession was necessary that morning. For a number of hours, I had mistakenly come to believe that this "opportunity lost" had been my hope. Look closely at our text today. Jeremiah calls us to trust in the LORD and then immediately calls us to trust in the LORD again. Opportunities will come and go, but our confidence should always remain in our LORD.

---

1 *Nothing Else + The Heart of Worship // Kari Jobe // Take 2

Hungry for the Beauty of His Holiness | Kerry Willis

"Give to the Lord the glory due His name; Bring an offering, and come before Him. Oh, worship the Lord in the beauty of holiness!" –I Chronicles 16:29

"Give unto the LORD the glory due to His name; Worship the LORD in the beauty of holiness." –Psalm 29:2

Indeed, the beauty of God's holiness is what I am hungry for, so I am feeding on these verses from the Holy Scriptures. Also, the lyrics of this song, "Hunger for Holiness" by Carman Licciardellog, make for a powerful prayer:

There's a silent war that's raging deep within me
My lower nature fights to dominate
My spirit man is poised and locked in battle
With the carnal side of me I've grown to hate.
The trumpet of my prayers plays toward Heaven
A voice of desperation in my cry
Lord, strengthen me that I might not yield myself to sin
But keep Your righteous banner lifted high.
Lord, I hunger for holiness
And I thirst for the righteousness that's Yours
That my mind would be cleansed
And my spirit renewed
And this temple that You dwell in would be pure.
The tempter stalks about me as a lion
Searching for the slightest scent of blood
For when the skin of my resistance is broken
He moves in swiftly to deepen the cut.
Oh, Lord of all Creation, hear Your servant
You understand the weaknesses of man.
I'm counting myself crucified with Jesus
Alive to Christ and dead indeed to sin.
Lord, I hunger for holiness
And I thirst for the righteousness that's Yours
That my mind would be cleansed
And my spirit renewed
And this temple that You dwell in would be pure.
Worship the Lord in the beauty of His Holiness! Amen!

"Batter My Heart" | Emily Heady

"For whom the LORD loves, he chastens, and scourges every son whom he receives."
–Hebrews 12:6

John Donne's fourteenth Holy Sonnet offers up an urgent prayer to God for Him not to withhold His necessary discipline. Donne knows himself well—he knows that he needs for God to handle him roughly, to get his attention, or he will continue, again and again, to wander away.

In the first line, he offers the prayer explicitly: "Batter my heart"—or, to put it bluntly, "Beat me up!" But I picture here not the sort of battering that wounds, but the sort that shapes. When I make bread, I have to spend a certain amount of time kneading the dough—and sometimes that looks less like a really relaxing massage than a pummeling. That process of "battering" makes something newer, stronger, and more flexible.

Donne notes that God has, thus far at least, treated him gently—breathing and knocking and shining rather than doing the rough work he knows he needs if he is to rise and stand before God (lines 2-3). Donne asks God outright to "break, blow, burn and make [him] new" (line 4)—all metaphors we recognize as part of the sanctification process God works in all those who are His.

Donne imagines himself as a town that has been taken over by an enemy; he knows better than to let the enemy rule, and he struggles to let reason govern his desires (lines 5-8). Yet he knows he loves God, even as he struggles to surrender. He thus begs God to break the bonds he has made to evil, to conquer him for his own good:

Batter my heart, three person'd God; for, you
As yet but knock, breathe, shine, and seek to mend,
That I may rise, and stand, o'erthrow me, and bend
Your force, to break, blow, burn and make me new
I, like an usurpt town, to another due,
Labor to admit you, but Oh, to no end,
Reason your viceroy in me, me should defend,
But is captiv'd, and proves weak or untrue.
Yet dearly I love you, and would be loved fain,
But am bethroth'd unto your enemy:
Divorce me, untie or break that knot again,
Take me to you, imprison me, for I
Except you enthral me, never shall be free,
Nor ever chaste, except you ravish me.

A Sweet Fragrance | Deb Huff

"Follow God's example, therefore, as dearly loved children and walk in the way of love, just as Christ loved us and gave himself up for us as a fragrant offering and sacrifice to God." –Ephesians 5:1-2

The smell of lilacs floating in the air says spring has pushed winter away. I planted a variety of lilacs in a backyard garden for the sole purpose of taking advantage of that heavenly scent. I sit on my swing, read my Bible, pray, and just breathe. When I am in that swing, I have my most precious times with the Lord.

When I think of the Lord, I don't think of God's ability to smell or His desire to enjoy a fragrance. But He does. Numerous times in the Bible, fragrance is used to trigger a response from God or to purposefully help in praise and worship. Here are a few examples:

After the flood, Noah built an altar and he sacrificed a burnt offering. The Lord smelled the pleasing aroma and said in his heart, "Never again will I curse the ground because of man" (Gen. 8:21).

In the instructions to Aaron about how to consecrate the priests, several references tell him to create "a burnt offering to the Lord, a pleasing aroma, an offering made to the Lord by fire" (Ex. 29:18, 25).

In Exodus 30:34-36, God instructs Moses to "Take for yourself spices. . ., spices with pure frankincense; there shall be an equal part of each. With it you shall make incense, a perfume, the work of a perfumer, salted, pure and holy. Grind some of it to powder and place it in front of the Testimony in the Tent of Meeting, where I will meet with you." No one else could use this exclusive blend, only Moses and only when he met with the Lord.

Fragrance is not required in our worship, but it's a nice addition to our lives and I think the Lord appreciates it too.

Smelling the lilacs as I enjoy time in study and prayer from my swing—there's nothing like it. Sadly, the fall will come and I will have to return to my inside room, where I will have a cinnamon candle burning. While it's not the same as the lilacs, breathing in the time spent with the Lord is still precious.

Pray Now. Understand Later |Kerry Willis

"In the morning, LORD, you hear my voice; in the morning I lay my requests before you and wait expectantly." –Psalm 5:3

Praying is a very peculiar thing. While I would never deny prayer works—it surely does!—I am still at a complete loss as to understanding how prayer works.

Prayer is a real mystery. Yes, though I am indeed drawn to pray non-stop, yet I grasp at words to explain what prayer really means to me; all my attempts fall short and do not even come close to rendering a true expression.

Prayer was an overwhelming idea even to the original disciples of Jesus. Once they said to Him: "Lord, Teach Us to Pray." Though they saw and heard Jesus pray many times, they still could not wrap their human minds around this holy phenomenon.

When it comes to learning about prayer and knowing how to pray, I can only quote an old Englishman, Samuel Chadwick, who said: "We only learn to pray by praying."

Finally, as Vance Havner said: "I cannot comprehend prayer, yet I must pray anyway. I don't understand electricity, but I refuse to sit in the dark until I do. I just turn on the switch and bask in the light."

Let us pray now. Understanding will come later.

"... and I wait." Psalm 5:3 (GWT)

SABBATH

A RHYTHM
OF REST

Satisfy us in the morning with your unfailing love,

that we may sing for joy and be glad all our days.

Psalm 90:14

Bird Feeders | Camelot Shuff

"For since the creation of the world God's invisible qualities—his eternal power and divine nature—have been clearly seen, being understood from what has been made, so that people are without excuse." –Romans 1:20

I love to watch birds, and I love bird feeders. Some feeders are better than others about drawing birds, and some draw only squirrels—but either way, on display from my back windows, I see the imagination and goodness of God at work.

Jesus reminds us to consider the flowers and birds, to call to mind how the Lord cares for them. While considering the birds, I also consider the bird feeders and their impact on the birds. Why do we put them out? It's not because we don't trust God to feed the birds; really, I do. I just want to pull His creation into my view a bit more and delight in seeing God's creation at work. It allows me to consider what that tells me about Him.

When I go on vacation the birds will not starve.

When I am gone, the birds will busy themselves finding other seeds and other bird feeders. Yet while I am here and I lean into participating with God in His good work, I get to participate in what God is already doing, I get to spend my life on what He has already called good, and I get to watch and take delight in the tiny part that God enabled me to play. Creator God who gave me life has placed me here with purpose. My purpose is to love Him and His creation. My purpose is to make disciples as I go. The mission is His, the strength is His, the results are His. May I make no excuses, but simply allow Him to live out His divine nature in and through me.

Kingdom Birds | Caleb Atkins

"Look at the birds of the air; they do not sow or reap or store away in barns, and yet your heavenly Father feeds them. Are you not much more valuable than they?"
–Matthew 6:26

Have you participated in the spiritual discipline of bird watching? Have you seen the effortless flight of a hawk as it floats heavenward? Have you heard the orchestra in the forest at first light? How about the brilliance of a bluebird as it sings for its maker? Can all of this point to our Heavenly Father?

When I was a young boy, I was taught to look and listen, to pause and smile at our feathered friends. It was as if my dad knew that these little creatures were a kiss from heaven. The color, the flight, the song—it was as if we had a constant reminder of a life lived in the hands of our maker.

I love how Jesus prompts His followers to take such cues from the natural world. In this passage, the example of birds can teach us to fly in opposition to worry.

You weren't made to worry; you were made to fly. Remember the time that God captured your heart and arrested your attention? What did that feel like?

You weren't made to worry; you were made to sing. Remember the time that God spoke to you through a song? I bet you were moved to tears in the presence of the divine.

You weren't made to worry; you were made to look to Jesus.

Remember, we walk with a loving savior whose yoke is easy and whose burden is light. So, take a deep breath, look to the sky, and fly with our Father.

Prayer: Father, help me to learn your ways. Help me to put my hope in you and soar like an eagle. Help me to abandon worry and sing heaven's song. Like a baby chick I will rest in the safety of your caring wings. Thank you for your love. Thank you for your creation.

Scared Sick | Brian Charette

"Do not be anxious about anything, but in every situation, by prayer and petition, with thanksgiving, present your requests to God. And the peace of God, which transcends all understanding, will guard your hearts and your minds in Christ Jesus."
–Philippians 4:6-7

Not too long ago, an article in the Journal of Personality and Social Psychology came to an eye-opening conclusion: If the average modern-day child were to be teleported back to the year 1957, he or she would likely have sufficient anxiety levels to be institutionalized as emotionally disturbed. The average child. [1]Another study indicated that either fear, stress, or a combination of the two account for more than three quarters of the appointments family doctors see in a typical week.

We are bathed in fear, fed a steady diet of it from our earliest days. Just turn on a television or click on any online news source. We are prone to wander from the "peace that passes understanding" available in Christ. But you don't have to be afraid. (Read that again, slowly and carefully.) You can choose courage, which isn't the absence of fear, but the presence of godly action in the face of fear.

Today's Philippians text presents two options for us:
1. We can be anxious.
2. We can pray and petition God with thanksgiving.

They are mutually exclusive options available to you right now. Right at this moment. So I invite you to stop and take an account of all your fears. Then, with gratitude in your heart, ask the Lord to help you. Start casting (and re-casting) any and all fear (I Peter 5:7) on Him. I assure you, something will happen. Supernatural sentries will take their positions at the gateway to your heart and peace will come—peace that your heart will welcome even if you mind doesn't understand it. Make your choice.

Fear. Not.

————

1 Twenge, Jean. "The Age of Anxiety? Birth Cohort Change in Anxiety and Neuroticism, 1952-1993." Journal of Personality and Social Psychology 79.6 (2000), 1007-21.

Freely | Matthew S.E. Waggoner

"I will freely love them..." –Hosea 14:4

I couldn't breathe, and every time I tried, I struggled to find the one thing that would keep me alive—air. The day began normally enough for a young boy playing hide and seek with his cousins. I ran around to all the hiding places as my oldest cousin began counting. Behind a door, behind the banister, under a rug—but there was one option that I had thought was the perfect hiding place: an old 1950s refrigerator with a metal latch on the front porch. I said to myself, "I can fit in here."

I opened the door, turned around, and sat on the bottom shelf while the door slammed and locked behind me. Immediately, I realized I couldn't breathe. It was as if the very air inside had been sucked out, and I sat there with all the strength a young six-year-old could muster trying to push open the door. I was stuck, suffocating, until my oldest cousin opened the door, and the air that was so freely available on the outside came rushing in, bringing back the essence of life.

The steady rhythm of our breath is a reminder that we are alive. When we inhale, we feel the air rushing into our lungs, and as we exhale, we feel the release of tension and stress. During times of sadness, we breathe heavy sighs, and when we are happy, our lungs feel as though they may burst with joy. In moments of fear, we hold our breath and must be reminded to breathe slowly to calm our nerves. When we face challenges, we take a deep breath to find our courage.

God's love is like the air we breathe—ever-present, sustaining us even when we may not realize it. It is easy to take our breath for granted, and we may sometimes overlook the ways in which God's love surrounds us. But if we take a moment to stop and breathe, to open our hearts and minds to the world around us, we may begin to see the ways in which God's love is freely given to us every day.

Abba Father, remind us to inhale your grace and exhale your praise today. Amen.

I Know the Plans | Wynne Lankford

"'For I know the plans I have for you,' declares the Lord, 'Plans to prosper you and not to harm you, plans to give you hope and a future.'" –Jeremiah 29:11

Almost every follower of Jesus has heard or seen this verse in their lifetime. We quote it, we place it on plaques, we post it on Instagram, and we may have seen it embroidered on a pillow at our grandmother's house. It is our go-to verse for security and hope as we envision the future.

While this verse has come to seem like a spiritual security blanket, many don't understand its context. These words were delivered by Jeremiah as he prophesied to the Israelites that they were going to be in captivity for 70 years. Jeremiah tells them to work, build, settle down, plant, eat, get married, have children, and increase in number. In other words, prosper where you are planted; be a blessing to the people around you, all while you're living in captivity. Jeremiah gave the bad news, then described how they should live before he gave the good news found in verse 11.

What if God is wanting us to flourish by asking us to bloom where we are planted? What if we are called to become a blessing to our neighborhoods? What if the vision is less about personal prosperity and more about how we can be a blessing to those around us, even in hard times?

God has a plan for us. He has a vision for us in our new season as a church. Let's fulfill His vision and become a blessing regardless of our circumstances! May God give us courage as a unified church to become a blessing to the world around us as we fulfill the plans God has for us.

God, give us a clear understanding of the hope and future you envision for us. Help us take our eyes off our circumstances and become the people you are inspiring us to become. Prosper us where we are planted so we can become a blessing to the people you have surrounded us with in our communities! Amen.

Pied Beauty | Emily Heady

"Then God said, 'Let us make mankind in our image, in our likeness, so that they may rule over the fish in the sea and the birds in the sky, over the livestock and all the wild animals, and over all the creatures that move along the ground.'" –Genesis 1:26

"We have different gifts, according to the grace given to each of us." –Romans 12:6

Gerard Manley Hopkins (1844-1889) understood diversity! Not the political kind that people like to fight about—instead, he appreciated the infinite variety that God baked into creation, and he gave God glory for all the ways in which difference allows us to reflect on the beauty of God Himself.

Hopkins was an Oxford graduate and priest who died young, having contracted typhoid fever while serving in Dublin. His Terrible Sonnets offer honest, gut-wrenching descriptions of depression and spiritual malaise, but his "Pied Beauty" rises to the heights of created glory, as it celebrates the beauty of the world God created. "Pied" means speckled, or diverse, and what Hopkins wants us to notice here is the beauty that we can see in variety:

Glory be to God for dappled things – For skies of couple-colour as a brinded cow; For rose-moles all in stipple upon trout that swim; Fresh-firecoal chestnut-falls; finches' wings; Landscape plotted and pieced – fold, fallow, and plough; And áll trádes, their gear and tackle and trim.

All things counter, original, spare, strange; Whatever is fickle, freckled (who knows how?) With swift, slow; sweet, sour; adazzle, dim; He fathers-forth whose beauty is past change: Praise him.

In the first stanza, Hopkins praises God for the infinite and changeable variety of skies, cows, fish scales, chestnuts in the fall, birds' wings, fields ploughed into a quilt pattern. He praises the many ways humans work, using tools of many types and functions. Hopkins' structure is orderly, though, with every third line rhyming.

In the second stanza, Hopkins merely scratches the surface of the variety of creation—all the ways that opposites combine to make something glorious. But in all this, he never loses sight of the way all this variety points back to our changeless, ever-creative, glorious God. The thought of God—"Praise him"!—stops his rhyme in its tracks. Dear God, may you stop us in our tracks with your

A RHYTHM
OF REST

Then, because so many people were coming and

going that they did not even have a chance to eat, he

said to them, "Come with me by yourselves to a quiet

place and get some rest."

Mark 6:31

Show Me Your Glory | Marlon King

"Then Moses said, 'Please, show me Your glory!'" –Exodus 33:18

"Well, GLORY," said the preacher of the little storefront church, who also happened to be my grandfather. My ears perked up, and I began to look around with anticipation. I had no idea what "glory" meant. How could I since I was only a four-year-old boy? I had heard it used many times before in my short lifespan. I did know, however, that things were about to get interesting. Our little church only had about 35-40 in attendance that night. Many of them appeared to me to be very old, even near death to my four-year-old eyes. In the coming moments, though, they would come to life as if by an unseen, revitalizing power.

One saint began to quote a psalm.

"Bless the LORD, O my soul: and all that is within me, bless his holy name. Bless the LORD, O my soul, and forget not all his benefits: Who forgiveth all thine iniquities; who healeth all thy diseases; Who redeemeth thy life from destruction; who crowneth thee with lovingkindness and tender mercies; Who satisfieth thy mouth with good things; so that thy youth is renewed like the eagle's" (Psalm 103:1-5, KJV).

As these words flowed from her heart and mouth, that little congregation erupted in praise to the most high God. Many of them came to their feet with hands lifted high, shouting, "Hallelujah," "Praise the Lord," and "Glory be to Heaven's King." I watched in awe and amazement as the very God of creation visited with that little congregation of just 40 people as if they were the pinnacle of His creation, and in that moment, the center of His joy. I didn't flinch or shrink back, but rather, I drank it in as something spectacular. Even at the age of four, I knew this moment was special. I didn't know why, but I had tears in my eyes and my little heart was touched by the manifest presence of the Godhead. Nobody had to tell me His Holy Spirit was there. Intuitively, I knew that Papaw King had both sensed His coming and announced His arrival with that one simple phrase, "Well, GLORY!"

My heart cries out today, come Lord Jesus, "Well, GLORY!"

Glory Revealed | Marlon King

"Then the glory of the LORD will be revealed, And all flesh will see it together; For themouth of the LORD has spoken." –Isaiah 40:5

Experiencing the manifestation of God's presence in the worship services of my youth made me curious to understand the word "GLORY." Looking up the Hebrew word "Kabod" H3519 and the Greek word "Dóxa" G1391 gave me a greater understanding of our English use of the word GLORY.

kāb ōd : A masculine singular noun meaning honor, glory, majesty, wealth. This term is commonly used of God; humans; and objects, particularly of the ark of the covenant.

In brief, Dóxa can mean appearance, reputation, glory. The predominant meaning in Scripture is recognition. It may denote form, aspect, or that appearance of a person or thing which catches the eye, attracts attention, or commands recognition. It is thus equivalent to splendor, brilliance, glory attracting the gaze . . . Dóxa embraces all which is excellent in the divine nature, coinciding with God's self-revelation. It comprises all that God will manifest Himself to be in His final revelation to us. When the glory of Jehovah is spoken about, it refers to the revelation of God's person, nature, and presence to mankind, sometimes with visible phenomena.[1]

When my grandfather used the word GLORY, he was making a statement about the honor, majesty, appearance, reputation, and recognition of God's presence. His declaration of "GLORY" was to embrace all that is excellent in the divine nature of God Himself. The result was the revelation of God's presence with us in that small congregation, revealing Christ in the hearts of the believers. The glory of God was not just present that day for the believers in that little storefront church. It also appeared as a sign to unbelievers to draw them to Himself.

When Phineas Bresee organized his first Church of the Nazarene in Los Angeles, California, he did so with simplicity, so that the poorest in the community would feel welcome. He called it the "Glory Barn" because, though meek and simple, the manifest presence of God was real in that place.

It is my desire that all of our churches be marked not by the name, but by the powerful presence of His divine glory!

1 Zodhiates, Spiros. *The Complete Word Study Old & New Testament: King James Version.* Ed. Warren Baker.

Let Us Rejoice | Carroll Bailey

"Rejoice always, pray continually, give thanks in all circumstances; for this is God's will for you in Christ Jesus." -I Thessalonians 5:17

As I was about to leave the house, I received a message asking for prayer. I said to my husband, "Do you ever feel overwhelmed by the number of people and situations that we need to pray for?" I was feeling the weight of people within our community who are suffering loss, cancer diagnoses, financial hardship, marital distress—not to mention the needs of those who do not know Jesus. I often feel like I could spend all day praying and it still wouldn't be enough time to pray over all the people, situations, and hurts of the world.

So how do we as followers of Jesus and ministers of the Gospel learn to shoulder the "burden" of praying continually? How do we not let this long list of needs get us down? We do this through praise—praising and rejoicing in what God is doing is just as much an act of worship as praying continually. We are called to praise and give thanks for what God has done, is doing, and will do in days to come. We must not forget this vital component in our spiritual walks. When we focus on praise, our Spirit will feel refreshed and the prayers that may at times feel like a burden will instead become a privilege to offer up.

Deeply Rooted | Janette Berge

"Therefore as you have received Christ Jesus the Lord, so walk in Him, having been firmly rooted and now being built up in Him and established in your faith, just as you were instructed, and overflowing with gratitude." –Colossians 2:6-7

The passage in Colossians encourages us to walk in Christ, being firmly rooted and built up in Him, and overflowing with gratitude. This reminds me of the importance of roots in plants. We often admire a plant's beauty, fragrance, and leaves, but we rarely appreciate its roots. However, without the roots, the plant would not exist.

A study at Rutgers University suggests that roots are the smartest part of a plant because they can sense their environment and grow towards the direction of water and nutrients. Moreover, the roots anchor the plant to prevent it from being blown away by the wind. Similarly, Paul urges us to be firmly rooted in Christ to avoid being swept away by the winds of life.

The significance of being firmly rooted in Christ is evident for those who have faced challenging times in their lives. When we intentionally grow our roots deep in Christ, we are better prepared for the dry periods of life. During those times, we may not have the strength to pick up the Bible or pray, but the Word we have stored up in our hearts will keep us nourished and encouraged.

Just as roots store water and nutrients, the love of Christ nourishes and stabilizes us as believers. Love is something that everyone seeks, and those who are rooted in the love of Christ have an endless supply of nourishment. However, damaged roots can cause symptoms of decline, such as lack of vigor and reduced growth. In the same way, if we neglect our roots in Christ, we may experience a decline in our faith.

See, we all fall into one of these categories—deeply rooted, newly planted and establishing roots, or damaged roots. So, let us strive to be like the smartest part of the plant—its roots—and seek to be firmly rooted in Christ. Let us grow deep in His love and be nourished by His truth so that we may bear fruit and witness to the love that grounds us.

The Flow State | Emily Heady

"I know a man in Christ who fourteen years ago was caught up to the third heaven. Whether it was in the body or out of the body I do not know—God knows."
–II Corinthians 12:2

I grew up in a fairly rigid church—KJV, biblical exposition and nothing else, hymns at a dirge-like tempo. I am deeply grateful for the rock-solid foundation in Scripture that church gave me, but one thing I had to learn outside of that church's walls was the sort of spiritual flow-state that I now, once in awhile at least, associate with whole-person worship.

My friends who are good runners (I am not a runner at all, much less a good one, so I have to take their word for it) tell me that somewhere around mile 16 in a marathon, they find this state: the place where they feel like they can run forever. Others achieve this while doing tasks whose motions they have internalized through much practice: artistic labors, building things, gardening. The Spanish mystic poet St. Teresa of Ávila described something like a spiritual flow state in her autobiography The Interior Castle, where she envisions her personal process of complete surrender to and union with Christ as something like the metamorphosis a caterpillar undergoes as it becomes a butterfly. As she describes it elsewhere, "a feeling of the presence of God would come upon me unexpectedly so I could in no way doubt that He was within me or I totally immersed in Him . . . The soul is suspended in such a way that it seems to be completely outside itself."[1]

I make no claims that I've experienced anything quite like this myself—or like Paul describes in the passage in II Corinthians above—but I do know that sometimes, after I've worked hard on a song and practiced a long time, when I have so deeply understood its logic and meaning that it has become automatic and intuitive for me, I feel something like what I imagine worship in Heaven must be like. There will be no need to think our way through it, to conjure an emotion with a well-placed minor chord, or to hesitate about whether to hold the fermata for an extra beat. We'll both be and do as God made us to do.

––––––––

1 Teresa of Ávila. *Life of St. Teresa of Jesus*. Ed. Benedict Zimmerman. Charlotte: Tan, 1997. 10.1

Together | Todd Thomas

"When the day of Pentecost came, they were all together in one place." –Acts 2:1

What follows this verse in Acts 2 is the incredible story of the outpouring of the Holy Spirit upon the disciples. This outpouring had such a profound and immediate effect upon the disciples that they began speaking the good news, and thousands of individuals became followers of Jesus.

As followers of Jesus, we love the idea of Pentecost. We even pray for a Pentecostal experience. We desire the Holy Spirit to fall and create a divine moment unlike anything we have experienced before.

Yet, it might be helpful to our hope if we gave attention to this phrase: They were all together in one place. Pentecost was a corporate event with individual significance.

About 120 believers had been together in prayer for ten days prior to this outpouring of the Holy Spirit.

Together.

John 17 records a prayer of Jesus in which He made urgent request that His followers would "be one." Unity would join them together in purpose, mission, service, and love. Unity creates a vessel that is able to receive the outpouring of the Holy Spirit.

I pray the Lord would help us to prayerfully and intentionally seek unity. May we humble ourselves by releasing our personal agendas driven by our personal preferences. May we recognize the need for reconciliation where there has been offense and division. May we once again embrace the high calling of serving one another. May we gather together with hearts of anticipation.

I believe that as we "come together," our Day of Pentecost will come.

SABBATH

A RHYTHM OF REST

⁹There remains, then, a Sabbath-rest for the people of God; ¹⁰for anyone who enters God's rest also rests from their works, just as God did from his. ¹¹Let us, therefore, make every effort to enter that rest, so that no one will perish by following their example of disobedience.

Hebrews 4:9-11

Post Pentecost Prayer - Part One | Kevin Griffin

"But the Spirit intercedes along with groans that cannot be expressed in words."
–Romans 8:26

So, what kind of devotional are you supposed to share for the day after Pentecost? I was thinking and praying about several ideas and asking the Lord what He wants, and it feels I'm still in process. Pentecost is celebrated, yet we sit in various places wrestling with a world that seems so opposed to the Spirit which came to guide and unite. It's as if many quietly whisper or loudly growl, "Where are you Lord, and what are you doing about all this?" If that's not you, bless you, but I confess as I type it has definitely been me. (For the record: I am not growling, but I have asked at various decibel levels what the days ahead hold and what my place is in them.)

Some of the earliest writers in church history, back as far as the fourth century, wrote much on the subject of prayer. A few of these writers (Ponticas/Cassie to be specific) stated that most people pray in levels that correspond to the lips, the mind, and the heart. They proposed that most of us utter prayers initially from our lips; these are familiar phrases that we learned as children. These are things we repeat, and they have a starting point and end like "In Jesus Name." Don't underestimate these prayers—we can mean them even though they're familiar.

The prayers from the lips then move at some point to prayers of the mind, a more cognitive prayer life that seems to have no start or ending. They are concepts, thoughts about God that are in front of and out in the open for God to hear. They move from thoughts about who He is and morph into conversation to Him and with Him. The intellectual concepts we have about Him inform what we say and how we pray. I seem to have more and more of these types of prayers, not because I am intellectual (I am not) but because I just have this daily on-going dialogue with God. But I want my prayer life to evolve not just because my language has moved past my formative years. I want it to grow because I trust Him more than I did before. I want to pray with my heart.

Post Pentecost Prayer - Part Two | Kevin Griffin

"But the Spirit intercedes along with groans that cannot be expressed in words."
–Romans 8:26

How do we engage our minds fully in prayer? It's hard, especially now. Recently I have spent more than my share of days wondering about the future: politics, a pandemic, and family issues all play a part. I have had tense moments of forcing myself to be still so I could recognize God. I want to recognize Him, but I also want to realize Him. I want to sense and know His presence in ways I never even dreamed could happen. To do this, I must quiet my mind.

Among the many things that I surely missed during the pandemic was corporate worship, hearing the Word and prayer with others. Being together in one place, calling out to the Lord and watching, waiting, hearing, seeing Him move, I'm craving it. (I'm craving Him!) The prayer Jesus taught His disciples to pray in Matthew 6 was an individual yet corporate prayer. "Our Father..." leads us into a way to pray both individually and in unison.

I would also encourage you to pray from where you are, not where you think you should be. Be honest, brutally honest with your heavenly Father. Say what you're thinking. If you are in pain, then pray from that pain and cast it on Him. He's a big God; He can handle it. I also want to pray today, with the Spirit's help, to listen to what He my Father have to say. I think only the Spirit at work in me can do that; He can help me hear from heaven. The Scripture says the Spirit will search our hearts. So please, Holy Spirit, search me.

My prayer today is that the Spirit would unite our thoughts and our hearts: Lord, I pray today that you would move in my own heart and mind and give me more of a burning desire to seek you with all my heart, to serve you while serving people. Take my words and my thoughts and receive them from my heart. When I'm struggling to conjure up the words, Holy Spirit, intercede and hit the mark. Holy Spirit, you are welcome here. I know where you are, Jesus, so now lead me as you live in me. Amen.

Post Pentecost Prayer - Part Three | Kevin Griffin

"But the Spirit intercedes along with groans that cannot be expressed in words."
–Romans 8:26

We have spent some time considering the ways that we can pray in a post-Pentecost way with our lips and with our minds—our words and our thoughts.

There is the third prayer, though, that I want to enter fully. This one—the one I think I am trying to articulate—is from the heart, from my soul. This prayer sometimes rises in those times when I can't seem to muster the words, when I am fumbling to even know what to say to Him, and when familiar phrases just don't cut it. It rises when I can't articulate a problem or request. I think the prayer I'm discussing is somewhere between "HELP!" and mere groaning.

I'm so glad the Spirit can help me here! Romans 8:26 states, "But the Sprit intercedes along with our groans that cannot be expressed in words." The Greek word for "intercedes" here has two meanings: It's a petition, or someone making a request on our behalf. It also translates "tygxano," which means "to strike, or hit the bull's eye." It's the antonym of "hamartia," which means to miss the mark. If hamartia sums up our traditional definition or view of sin, then tygxano—the groanings the Spirit utters on our behalf—look something like righteousness, or something pleasing to God that hits right where He wants us to aim.

I want to encourage you today to pray, to let your requests be made known, to pray out of your lips, with your mind, and from your heart and soul. Maybe you are like me—you look around and seemingly don't know what to pray. Maybe you're fearful, frustrated, and even angered by what you see in our world. But Paul reminds us in Romans that because of Pentecost we have an intercessor who will hit the mark when we can't even seem to formulate a sentence.

The Power of Questions | Mike Lyle

"On one occasion an expert in the law stood up to test Jesus. 'Teacher,' he asked, 'what must I do to inherit eternal life?' 'What is written in the Law?' he replied. 'How do you read it?' He answered, 'Love the Lord your God with all your heart and with all your soul and with all your strength and with all your mind'; and, 'Love your neighbor as yourself.' 'You have answered correctly,' Jesus replied. 'Do this and you will live.' But he wanted to justify himself, so he asked Jesus. . ." –Luke 10:25-29

There may be days I tell my kids to take out the trash as I leave for the day. When I return and see the trash piled up in the can, I might exclaim, "Why didn't you take out the trash?" They might respond, "I had a question about which trash you meant. I didn't know if you meant the trash in the kitchen or the trash in the bathroom . . . until I got clarity on that point, I didn't take out either one."

I'm sure this sounds somewhat familiar to parents—kids using questions to avoid obeying. This is the posture of the man in our text today. The expert in the law uses questions to test Jesus and to justify himself. I think we can use questions in the same way. We deconstruct our way into spiritual paralysis.

Just because we have this tendency, however, does not mean that questions are out of bounds. After all, Jesus does not scold this man for bringing his questions. In fact, He asks a question of his own—"What is written...how do you read it?" While questions can be used to prevent obedience, they can also be used to foster intimacy. My wife has asked me difficult questions before. These kinds of questions have needed to be asked and, indeed, have led to deeper connection between us.

I'm sure you have questions for God. Perhaps you were told that these questions are out of bounds or not welcome in the church. However, some questions need to be asked to pave the way for deeper intimacy. Ask your questions. As you ask, remember that we all have a tendency to use questions to keep us from obedience. So, while you're asking, go ahead and do what you know.

Let in the Glory | Marlon King

"Lift up your heads, you gates, And be lifted up, you ancient doors, that the King of glory may come in!" –Psalm 24:7

Sister Jones was a true warrior, and her favorite weapon was prayer. She was filled with the glory of God's Holy Spirit, and she left some glory residue everywhere she went. My father was her "sometimes pastor" for a couple of years when I was three years old. The church had split, and my dad was called to pastor the splinters—the carnal, prideful, and hurting people who in those days could only do one thing: fight.

Sister Jones went with the group who started the new congregation, but she had vested prayer interests in those who were left behind and would often return for a visit. On this particular Sunday morning, my dad and I were dropped off at the church early while Mom took the car to pick up some congregants who needed a ride. I was relegated to our pew, and Dad began to walk the aisles and pray. Before long, he was crying and begging God in earnest for a breakthrough because he was so tired of the fighting. I didn't know it then, but I later learned he was questioning God's call on his life. Soon, a few of those carnal, hurting leaders strode into the church and took up their positions in their pews. Dad prayed in lower, whispered tones but he looked defeated and completely broken. No one was talking now. The air was thick with evil, and I was getting scared.

By divine appointment that morning, Sister Jones was sent to our aid. She opened the door and took one step into that sanctuary and softly declared, "GLORY." She didn't stop there at the threshold or even at her old seat. She deliberately marched around that building praying and lifting her little handkerchief shouting, "GLORY, GLORY, GLORY!" The evil departed, and the carnal leaders looked a little embarrassed. My dad, still exhausted and weeping, stood to his feet and praised the God of deliverance. He preached a sermon that Sunday, but the Holy Spirit delivered the message through Sister Jones.

Years later, I heard from her pastor that at her funeral, they unrolled her prayer scroll and it encircled the sanctuary 1.5 times. Is it any wonder she carried the glory?

Sanctified by His Glory | Marlon King

"And there I will meet with the children of Israel, and the tabernacle shall be sanctified by My glory." -Exodus 29:45

I love the concept of the Mercy Seat as the place of propitiation or appeasement. God told Moses how to take common elements that were available to any man and with them, to build this dwelling place for the Glory of God. The craftsmen did their job and made this beautiful, gold-clad, wooden Ark of the Covenant; on the lid they placed the two shining golden cherubim, each with six wings extended very specifically to provide a place for the GLORY to dwell. When the Glory descended, it sanctified those common elements and made everything holy. It was supposed to be the unique place to encounter God's presence for about 1446 years until Jesus came, but His children disobeyed, so Ezekiel had the vision of His GLORY departing in 586 BC. Israel had not kept themselves, or the sanctified seat of God's GLORY, holy.

When Jesus came, He became the propitiation for our sin. As He arose from the dead, I can envision the angels on each end of the place where He lay in the tomb and the GLORY resting on Him just as the GLORY rested over the Mercy Seat between the two cherubim. The imagery is amazing—just like the Mercy Seat that God told Moses to build.

In the Old Testament, the GLORY rested on the Mercy Seat. In the early New Testament era, Jesus became the Mercy Seat on which God's GLORY dwelt. So where does His GLORY dwell today? His Holy Spirit dwells in us. We have become the seat of God's GLORY—not exactly a mirror image of the Mercy Seat as Jesus was, but a seat nonetheless.

So, as the Mercy Seat in the Tabernacle and the Temple began with common elements, so do we. I am a jar of clay that has been sanctified by His GLORY which came to live in me. That GLORY gives me power to do great things for the kingdom. But it is not my power, it is God's. May your life be sanctified by the GLORY sent by the Father.

"But we have this treasure in jars of clay to show that this all-surpassing power is from God and not from us" (II Corinthians 4:7).

SABBATH

A RHYTHM
OF REST

28 Then they cried out to the Lord in their trouble,

and he brought them out of their distress.

29 He stilled the storm to a whisper;

the waves of the sea[a] were hushed.

30 They were glad when it grew calm,

and he guided them to their desired haven.

Psalm 107:28-30

Patriot, Participant, or Piddler? | Gary Smith

"For me to live is Christ." –Philippians 1:21

My family is filled with people who served in the military or law enforcement. My great great grandfather served in the Revolutionary War in 1775-1783 and was wounded. My grandfather was killed in the line of duty as a Deputy Sheriff at age 36 (I never knew him), leaving a wife and ten children (one being my mother) to fend for themselves. There were three uncles who became Army, Navy, and Air Force soldiers. My dad was Army (nine years) and was at Pearl Harbor when it was bombed. The cost was high.

As I have reflected over the years on the lives of those individuals and countless others, I can say with confidence that they were all-in for the cause for which they were willing to give their lives. They were patriots!

But there are those who are not quite so committed to sacrifice. They will wave the flag and sing a national anthem with gusto but fall short of total commitment. I would call this group participants. They love the cause but shy away from being committed.

Then there are those who pay lip-service to the cause and recognize the good in it but do not see the value of participation. These I call "piddlers." Piddlers are self-centered, lack insight, and miss the purpose of living, having little understanding of the cost of preserving our freedoms. They will not realize the value of sacrifice and the rewards of it until it is too late.

As I reflect upon this idea, I can see spiritual similarities. There are those who are "spiritual patriots"—who embrace the mantra "Not I but Christ...and for me to live is Christ." They will pay the price to be overcomers! They will fight to win!

Then there are those who are "spiritual participants"—who love to be in the excitement of the moment and activity but are hesitant to go deeper in their relationships with Christ. Their lives do not consistently give testimony that Jesus is Lord.

Lastly, the "spiritual piddlers" rarely see the benefit of making Christ Lord but love to periodically be around people who demonstrate the love of Christ. They have "the form of godliness, but deny its power" (2 Timothy 3:5).

Grandma and the Admiral | Deb Huff

"All Scripture is God-breathed and is useful for teaching, rebuking, correcting and training in righteousness, so that the servant of God may be thoroughly equipped for every good work." -II Timothy 3:16-17

Grandma Eliza was a simple farm woman. My grandfather was paralyzed for the last five years of his life, and she had to work the 300-acre farm with the help of their sons. Every day before daybreak, she woke up, made her bed, dressed for the day, cooked food for the family, and read her Bible—all before she headed to the fields or barn to join her sons and do whatever needed to be done.

This was her routine every day—wake up, make the bed, dress, cook, and read the Bible all before going to work. It wasn't an easy life but she cherished it. Grandma was known in her community for helping those in need, for cooking Sunday dinner for the traveling pastor, and for teaching a Sunday school class of middle school children for more than 40 years.

I thought of her the other day when I heard the story about Navy Admiral William McCraven who addressed a graduating class at University of Texas at Austin and told students if they wanted to change the world, they should start by making their beds.

His speech went viral with 10 million views. The promotional site for his book reads, "Building on the core tenets laid out in his speech, McRaven now recounts tales from his own life and from those of people he encountered during his military service who dealt with hardship and made tough decisions with determination, compassion, honor, and courage."

Grandma Eliza never heard McCraven's speech, nor did she read his book. However, she began every day by making her bed and reading the Bible. That book is full of heroes who battled evil or who led a nation out of bondage. It has accounts of women who followed God's direction to save a nation or serve a meal to a traveling prophet.

Grandma Eliza would get a kick out of the Admiral telling college graduates to make their beds. Good advice. But she would also say that if graduates really wanted to change the world, they should read the Bible.

Authority and Authorship | Emily Heady

"Then Jesus came to them and said, 'All authority in heaven and on earth has been given to me. Therefore go and make disciples of all nations, baptizing them in the name of the Father and of the Son and of the Holy Spirit, and teaching them to obey everything I have commanded you. And surely I am with you always, to the very end of the age.'" –Matthew 28:19-20

When we hear the word "authority," we probably envision something having to do with power or brute force—a judge perhaps, or some kind of punishment. If we look closely at the word, though, we see that its root is "author." This fits: Jesus is the one whose voice can change things, or even create something from nothing. He's the first storyteller, the Word by whom all things were made.

Genesis is the setting of a scene. "Let there be light" is not just the turning on of a switch; instead, it's the creation of the very concept of light, of vision—and we know that it is good. It's a visual feast, an experience, and a moral judgment. And God does all this merely by speaking; His voice is that powerful.

As humans, we have some limited times where we can change things with our words alone. In philosophy, we call these speech-acts. Ministers, for instance, have the authority to pronounce a couple husband and wife. Parents can name their children. Presidents can declare prisoners pardoned. However, each of these speaks only with the authority the state confers. None of us can fundamentally change the nature of the world by speaking.

Interestingly, then, when Jesus chooses to announce His full authority after His resurrection, He uses His voice to give a commandment to His disciples—go forth and multiply. In some sense, it's the same commandment Adam and Eve got in the garden: Go make more of yourselves and fill up the earth. The story He's telling has never really changed. He's making and changing worlds, and He's doing it through us. And it is GOOD.

Dear God, please help us to recognize your authority and listen to your voice as you seek to bring us into your story.

Philip's Invitation | JJ Wyzinski

"The next day Jesus decided to go to Galilee. He found Philip and said to him, 'Follow me.' Now Philip was from Bethsaida, the city of Andrew and Peter. Philip found Nathanael and said to him, 'We have found him about whom Moses in the law and also the prophets wrote, Jesus son of Joseph from Nazareth.'" –John 1:43-45

A few months back, God called our church to begin taking more intentional steps to invite people for Easter. This wasn't simply a call to invite people, but to enter into a season of urgency that many churches have lost. We heard responses like, "I'm going to fill two whole rows by Easter!" and "I've been working on this person for a while so I think I can get them to come."

Business cards were printed, videos were recorded, and hearts were moved. As a member of the church, I was excited. It was life-giving to see God's people respond to the Great Commission. It wasn't new, but it was made new in us.

We saw the floodgates open as the building filled with invitees. It's amazing what an invitation can do. We saw people we've built relationships with walk into the doors of our church. But with each invitation, it became more obvious how little we'd done. We began to realize that our invitation wasn't the first they heard. God's was.

"I saw you under the fig tree before Phillip called you." I can't help but think that Jesus' words here are as much to Phillip as they are to Nathaniel. They are a beautiful reminder that we're not calling, just extending an invitation that God has already spoken. God's Spirit is calling people to Easter. To resurrection. All we need to do is follow. Our business cards, videos, and formal invitations aren't the reason people come. We don't fill rows. We don't work on the hearts of people. God does. God saw them well before we called them. Our invitation is just an echo. Our "Come and see" follows the God who said "Follow me," not just to Phillip, but to Nathaniel as well.

Prayer: Thank you, God, for seeing us. Help us be sensitive to your calling and to help others follow you. Amen.

Good News Logistics | Stephen Willis

"How, then, can they call on the one they have not believed in? And how can they believe in the one of whom they have not heard? And how can they hear without someone preaching to them? And how can anyone preach unless they are sent? As it is written: 'How beautiful are the feet of those who bring good news!'" –Romans 10:14-15

Seldom will you ever see me without socks. I just don't like looking at feet. However, even though I don't like looking at feet, I still appreciate them. Regardless of how they look, they are essential. This is why Paul calls feet beautiful: They are critical in promoting the gospel of Jesus Christ. This reality was on full display for me a number of years ago when I spent four days teaching the Old Testament to 27 rice farmers in Cambodia. These farmers showed up to learn the Word of God so that they could return home to share the good news. Here's the thing, though. They had no plans to just share it with their village. When their crops didn't need care, they would walk or ride bikes to the neighboring villages in order to proclaim the name of Jesus. They knew that their feet were a part of God's logistical plan for evangelism. These rice farmers lived as sent people, and it was deeply challenging to me personally because their intentions were laser-focused and came with great sacrifice (something most of us have lost in the western world!).

Paul asks, "How can anyone preach unless they are sent?" Our feet become beautiful when they are carriers of good news. In effect, the gospel moves on foot or it doesn't move. Have you ever connected this truth with the decision that Jesus made to wash the feet of His disciples in John 13:1-5? It was on this evening before sharing His "broken body" and "poured out blood" with His disciples that He washed their feet. In an upper room thousands of years ago, Jesus washed twelve sets of feet. One set of feet ran to betray Him but the other eleven, after being restored and empowered by the Holy Spirit, became the logistics team that would radically change the world.

Prayer: Lord Jesus, make my feet beautiful by connecting them with the good news of the gospel.

A Taco Truck Mentality | Reenie Peppers

"Therefore see that you walk carefully, not as the unwise, but as wise, making the very most of your time, because the days are evil. Therefore do not be foolish and thoughtless but understand and firmly grasp what the will of the Lord is." –Ephesians 5:15-16

Recently I saw on Facebook an advertisement for an event toted as a "Taco Truck" Festival. The idea of a taco truck makes me chuckle. Tacos used to be uncomplicated—ground beef, cheese, lettuce, tomato, and taco sauce. I would never think of going out for tacos as they were simple to make and much better when made at home. Today's tacos, though, have come a long way. You can have your tacos with pork, chicken, shrimp, or fish. You can garnish them with salsa, pico de gallo, guacamole, or slaw. And now you can have your tacos come to you on a truck.

As I think about tacos (I really need to get a hobby), it occurs to me that taco trucks reflect a mentality that permeates our society. We want life to be easy and uncomplicated; we want to have choices without excessive decision making; we want life and opportunities to come to us. I call this a "taco truck mentality."

A taco truck mentality is an entitled mentality. We want what we want without any complications such as hard work or difficulty. We want palatable choices but not the responsibility of sensible decision-making. We want opportunities without requirements or restrictions.

This is opposite of the mindset advocated by the apostle Paul in his letter to the Ephesians: "Therefore see that you walk carefully, not as the unwise, but as wise, making the very most of your time, because the days are evil. Therefore do not be foolish and thoughtless but understand and firmly grasp what the will of the Lord is." Real life is walking with a purpose and making the most of our time. Walking with purpose requires work and actively dealing with life's complications. Real life requires discernment in the choices we make, especially in the difficult choices. This life recognizes and takes advantage of opportunities; it does not wait for opportunities to be handed out on a silver platter.

The idea of taco trucks still makes me chuckle. Living with a taco truck mentality is not a laughing matter.

SABBATH

A RHYTHM
OF REST

Therefore, since the promise of entering his rest still stands, let us be careful that none of you be found to have fallen short of it.

Hebrews 4:1

My Witnesses | Kerry Willis

"But you will receive power when the Holy Spirit comes upon you. And you will be my witnesses, telling people about me everywhere—in Jerusalem, throughout Judea, in Samaria, and to the ends of the earth." –Acts 1:8

It was mid-July of 2017, a Sunday afternoon, and I had just preached passionately from the words of Jesus recorded in Acts 1:8, especially these three words—"Be my witnesses."

We were on our way to meet our extended family and to vacation together in our native North Carolina. In our journeying, we passed a young lady alongside the road with a flat tire as storm clouds were fiercely rolling in. She looked completely overwhelmed as she stood by her vehicle.

I quickly pulled the vehicle off and backed up to her front bumper. My wife, Kim, and I got out together. Twelve to fifteen minutes later, I had the tire changed and almost simultaneously the storm began, but Jackie called a timeout and started hugging us. With teary eyes she asked us, "Do you all go to church?" Yes, we said. Then she continued: "Thanks so much for helping me and please pray for my family. We had a cousin killed in a car wreck recently and our family is beyond devastated by it."

We pulled Jackie close in a holy highway huddle as a light rain began to fall. We assured her that God loved her and we loved her. Then, we prayed. As we said our goodbyes, we assured Jackie we would keep praying and told her that we believed God would help her and her family. (Jackie and her family remained in our intercessions for quite a while.)

As we pulled away towards our destination, the rain started falling really hard; however, my heart grew really soft. We had not said a word about God or church, yet the Lord somehow tenderly witnessed to her through us. It was so humbling and fulfilling.

When Jesus said, "Be my witnesses," surely He intended on being present with and within us always.

Abba Father, help us to remember that Christ in us truly is our hope and also the hope for everyone else we encounter. Amen. (Colossians 1:27)

Prayer for Christian Unity | John Henry Newman

"Neither pray I for these alone, but for them also which shall believe on me through their word; That they all may be one; as though, Father, art in me, and I in thee, that they also may be one in us: that the world may believe that thou hast sent me." –John 17:20-21

O Lord Jesus Christ, when you were about to suffer, you prayed for your disciples to the end of time, that they might all be one, as you are in the Father, and the Father in you.

Look down in pity on the many divisions among those who profess your faith and heal the wounds which the pride of man and the craft of Satan have inflicted on your people.

Break down the walls of separation which divide one party and denomination of Christians from another.

Look with compassion on the souls who have been born in one or another of these various communions and bring them all into that one communion which you set up in the beginning. Amen.

Debate | Cavan Carlton

"For it is God's will that you silence the ignorance of foolish people by doing good." –1 Peter 2:15

Growing up, competitive debate was an enormous part of my childhood. For a ten-year stretch from 1982-1992, at least one of the three Carlton brothers was eating, sleeping, and living high school cross-examination debate in northeast Oklahoma. Countless hours were spent researching and preparing for the next debate tournament, or even attending month-long summer debate camps in Texas, Michigan, New Hampshire, and Vermont. As the youngest child, my two older brothers loved to practice their debate skills on me, crushing me with their logic and reason until I had to yield.

Entering adulthood with polished argumentation skills served me well both academically and professionally; I relished good verbal sparring and was really skilled at winning.

Yet the Bible says that it is God's will that we silence the ignorance of foolish people by doing good. When I surrendered my heart and my life to Jesus at age 35, this was one of the radical truths I learned that seriously challenged me. I was used to silencing others' foolishness through verbal combat and debate! But God provided a different method: by doing good.

In the world today, there is much ignorance and much foolishness. As the culture has drifted away from Christ and the authority of Scripture, the void is being filled with the false wisdom of the world. This expanding and encroaching darkness is seen and felt, and as Christians it is our God-given duty to push back against the darkness with the marvelous light of Christ. But how are we to push back? How are we to silence the ignorance of foolish people? Not through debate and verbal warfare, but by doing good.

Let our actions, empowered by the Holy Spirit of Christ, speak louder than our words. Let us be the hands and feet of Jesus, shining His love and light into the darkness. Worldly logic and reason crumble before the power of God's love.

Love is... | Clay Bryan

"Love is patient, love is kind. It does not envy, it does not boast, it is not proud. It does not dishonor others, it is not self-seeking, it is not easily angered, it keeps no record of wrongs. Love does not delight in evil but rejoices with the truth. It always protects, always trusts, always hopes, always perseveres." –I Corinthians 13:4-7

Love. It's a word we hear often, and now has even become a controversy. The world says that "love is love," but we can rest assured that Scripture tells us exactly what love is.

First, love is patient. It goes beyond tolerance and extends grace, even in the face of difficulty. It teaches us to slow down and empathize with others, recognizing that everyone has their own struggles. Love is patient even when others don't agree.

Love is kind. It is expressed through gentle words, compassion, and a genuine concern for the well-being of others. It seeks to build up rather than tear down, to bring joy rather than sorrow. Love is kind even when others are not.

Love is selfless. It has no hidden agenda but is driven by a desire to see others flourish. Love compels us to serve and be okay with serving.

Love is not easily angered and keeps no record of wrongs. It lets go of past hurts, refusing to hold grudges or seek revenge. Love forgives.

Love protects, trusts, hopes, and perseveres. It provides a safe harbor, a place where others can find refuge. In a world filled with people searching for something real, love shows up time and time again.

As we reflect on these words, let us remember that love is not just a concept to read about. It is a call to action, a way of life. It is what we are called to share with all people, just as our Father loved all of His creation when He sent His Son to die for us all.

Let us pray for opportunities to share love with all walks of people. Let us have these words shape us and make us a people of true love: a people who don't need to explain what love is but who let our actions speak for us. Let the love of God be spread to all people and start an unstoppable movement that draws more and more people closer to Christ.

One Voice | Kerry Willis

"Then if my people who are called by my name will humble themselves and pray and seek my face and turn from their wicked ways, I will hear from heaven and will forgive their sins and restore their land." –II Corinthians 7:14 (NLT)

I recently wrote down these words during a quiet season of seeking God that I had set aside: "Lord, our world is in a seemingly wintry season spiritually. We sense that we need a God-appointed awakening."

Lord, I don't know what else I can do but to call people to prayer. Lord, let us resort to prayer, expecting a real revival to be the result.

My heart was drawn to 2 Corinthians 7:14 NLT: "Then if my people who are called by my name will humble themselves and pray and seek my face and turn from their wicked ways, I will hear from heaven and will forgive their sins and restore their land."

Shortly after saturating in this sacred Scripture verse, I took a prayer walk in the brisk morning winter breezes of the woods behind our cottage. As I walked, my prayers suddenly broke into wonder, love, and praise as I cried out to the Lord:

"Come Holy Spirit, we need Thee.
Come sweet Spirit, we pray.
Come in Your strength and Your Power.
Come in Your own gentle way."

My prayer continued:
Lord, if you are looking these days for one servant to stand in the gap so you can appoint an awakening in your world, here I am! Lord, I do not belong to myself; I belong exclusively to you! Have thine own way with your clay today! I know I only have one voice, but today I am using that one voice to call your people, Lord, to fervent prayer for such a time as this. Let the summer breezes of your Holy Spirit blow across the wintry season of your Church until this world of yours is once again lost only in your life and your love and your light!

In the name of Jesus!
Amen and Amen and Amen!

MY LIFE IS BUT AN INSTANT | ST THÉRÈSE OF LISIEUX

"So teach us to number our days that we may gain a heart of wisdom." –Psalm 90:12

My life is but an instant, a passing hour.
My life is but a day that escapes and flies away.
O my God! You know that to love you on earth
I only have today.
Lord, what does it matter if the future is gloomy?
To pray for tomorrow, oh no, I cannot!
Keep my heart pure, cover me with your shadow
Just for today.
O divine Pilot! whose hand guides me.
I'm soon to see you on the eternal shore.
Guide my little boat over the stormy waves in peace
Just for today.
Amen.

SABBATH

A RHYTHM
OF REST

7 Therefore Jesus said again, "Very truly I tell you, I am the gate for the sheep. 8 All who have come before me are thieves and robbers, but the sheep have not listened to them. 9 I am the gate; whoever enters through me will be saved.[a] They will come in and go out, and find pasture. 10 The thief comes only to steal and kill and destroy; I have come that they may have life, and have it to the full."

John 10:7-10

Take the Shot | John Swales and Andrew Horseman

"Then I heard the voice of the Lord saying, 'Whom shall I send? And who will go for us?' And I said, 'Here am I. Send me!'" –Isaiah 6:8

My name is Andrew. I grew up in the country and spent my entire life hunting. Out of all the months to hunt, April is my favorite. Hunting a gobbler (male turkey) is an adrenaline rush because of how difficult it is. You bring the gobbler to you by using a "call" to imitate a hen (female turkey). The call lures the gobbler, and the hunt begins.

My name is John. I grew up in the suburbs and wanted to give turkey hunting a shot (no pun intended). I purchased all the necessary camouflage gear I needed. Hitting the woods at first light, Andrew and I heard a gobble from the tree. I set us on course to get as close as we could without spooking him. I began calling the gobbler in.

We heard him gobble a few times and then he stopped. After a few minutes we heard him gobble again, but now he was much closer. Andrew leaned over to me and said, "He's coming...get your gun up." Andrew whispered, "Look to your left." Andrew saw the gobbler, but I didn't. The last thing Andrew whispered to me before going completely silent was, "Take the shot." All I could see was his head, but I remembered what Andrew said, so I fired. I harvested my first spring gobbler that morning because I "took the shot."

John and I talked about how many times we did not "take the shot" and completely missed a God-given opportunity. As a young boy, I was always taught that you will miss 100% of the shots you don't take. It could be a chance to share your faith with someone. Perhaps God has put someone in your life to invite to church. It could be an opportunity to serve the community. It could even be as simple as helping a stranger in need. God gives us shots every day, but do we take them?

What are some shots God has given you that you didn't take?
What are some ways you can build confidence in yourself to "take the shot?"
Will you commit today by taking the first shot God presents to you?

Are You Reaching Out to Those in Need? | Linda Shepherd

"For I was hungered, and ye gave me no meat, I was thirsty, and ye gave me no drink, I was a stranger, and ye took me not in, naked, and ye clothed me not: sick, and in prison, and ye visited me not." –Matthew 25:43

Let me ask you some questions: Have you ever seen a homeless person begging for food and you just passed them by? Perhaps you decided not to give them money because they might use it to buy beer or drugs. Has God ever whispered to you to buy them a sandwich or some food? Have you stopped to ask God what you could do for them? If you didn't have it to give, did you stop and pray for them? Has God put someone in your path that is spiritually thirsty? Did you introduce them to God or, if it was a Christian who was poor in spirit, did you encourage them? What about a stranger, or someone who was in need of clothes? Did you go check your closet and see what didn't fit anymore?

What about those in prison, whether behind bars or imprisoned by their own depression? Have you reached out to them and given them hope, or did you just assume it was a waste of time to even bother reaching out to them? What about those loved ones, friends, or strangers lying in convalescent homes? Have you thought about visiting them? Have you thought of maybe going with someone in your church that has an outreach ministry for the elderly?

One day we might be there, God forbid. We never know. Many people want ministry and keep waiting for it, but ministry is always around us, in front of us. There are always needs. If we are sensitive to the Holy Spirit, He will show us what to do. We will be surprised at how much God will entrust us to do for Him if we only seek, knock, and ask.

Prayer: Father, I am making myself available for you to use me today. May I not be blinded or choose to ignore the needs of others when it is in my power to help.

Eyes to See | Carla Pollard

"When He saw the multitudes, He was moved with compassion for them." –Matthew 9:36

I was watching a program from Istanbul when the host captured my attention with the resident artisans' beautiful creations as he said, "You can discover artistic craftsmanship all around you, if you look with a crafter's eye." Then he showed how the manhole covers had a touch of artistry in their design; you just needed the eyes to see it.

I experienced an eyes-to-see season when I was pregnant. Suddenly, I began to see pregnant women everywhere. I never noticed them before. They were not in my line of sight. I am certain they were around, but I did not see them. Sometimes we only see what is foremost in our minds and heart. While thinking about this I realized that the eyes of Jesus were unique. Like the crafter's keen eye for detail or my eyes for other pregnant women, our Savior saw what was foremost in His mind and on His heart: people.

The Bible tells us He saw the people and was moved with compassion. He had the eyes of a caring shepherd; He saw their deepest needs and was moved. Seeing a need and having sympathy were not enough for Jesus. He took action to meet those needs. When a thirsty, outcast woman headed for a well in Samaria, Jesus went out of His way to meet her there and He gave her living water for her soul. When the demoniac bound with chains cried day and night because of his torment, Jesus sailed the sea to find and deliver him.

Like Jesus, we can have eyes to see the needs of those around us. Jesus desires us to help the hurting souls in this world. He wants to place people in our line of vision so that we can be moved to action through His compassion working in us. We can make a difference in the lives of others. We just need to see with the eyes of Jesus and take action to meet those needs.

Prayer: Abba Father, help me to see through your eyes of love and compassion. Grant me the ability to empathize with those who hurt and to encourage those who are down and out so that they can move forward in their spiritual journeys.

Amen.

Lead by Example | Bruce Gardner

"Then Hezekiah and all the people rejoiced that God had prepared the people, since the events took place so suddenly." –II Chronicles 29:36

What does it mean to lead by example in today's society? Well, I believe it means the same thing it has always meant: to do the things yourself that you want those who are following you to do.

In II Chronicles 29, we find the story of Hezekiah. Here is a snapshot of the story. The kings of Judah had drifted badly when Hezekiah inherited an unholy mess from his father, King Ahaz. But Hezekiah repaired the Temple, restored legitimate worship, removed the idols, repented for the people, and required a change in the land. Once the population saw his example of worship, they followed suit. These events took place quickly, not only because their sovereign God had replaced Ahaz with the king's godly son, but because Hezekiah modeled the life he expected of others.

Hezekiah led the people by example.

There are many examples of the opposite style of leadership than what Hezekiah displayed. We've seen it in today's world as well. As John Maxwell, reminds us, "far too often, leaders drift. Once they get some experience under their belt and a track record of accomplishments, they often abandon the lifestyle that helped them reach the top. They abandon the very rules that they once established or endorsed. Sadly, leaders like these forget the number one management principle in the world: People do what people see. If they want to succeed, leaders must incarnate the life they desire in their followers." [1]

God sent His Son Jesus to be that example for us. He lived a holy life as one of us to give us an example to live by. His teachings give us clues on how to apply these principles to our daily lives. His call to us is to lead others to His way of life. His Holy Spirit teaches us daily on the things we must do to become more like Jesus in our lives. Then we can lead others to live the same way.

Let the Spirit lead you so you can lead others to lead others to Jesus!

---

1 Maxwell, John. *Maxwell Leadership Bible*. 3rd Ed. Nashville: Thomas Nelson, 2019. 526.

Keep God's Word Continually Before You | Reenie Peppers

"So commit yourselves wholeheartedly to these words of mine. Tie them to your hands and wear them on your forehead as reminders. Teach them to your children. Talk about them when you are at home and when you are on the road, when you are going to bed and when you are getting up. Write them on the doorposts of your house and on your gates, so that as long as the sky remains above the earth, you and your children may flourish in the land the Lord swore to give your ancestors." –Deuteronomy 11:18-21

I recently went to see the movie Jesus Revolution. This movie covers the Jesus Movement of the late 1960s and early 70s. Thousands, perhaps tens of thousands, of young people came to know Jesus during the movement. The movie raised the question, "What was the lasting impact of the Jesus Movement?" The movement did affect the Christian music industry and Christian media. However, we are barely one generation removed, and much of the original energy of the movement has dissipated.

Those who were influenced by the movement are now in the midst of raising families, and instead of continuing missionary efforts, those converted during the movement chose to stay put. Of course, we can live for Christ in whatever our context, but when life gets in the way, the revolution cannot be effectively passed on and passed down to the next generation.

In Scripture, we are promised that we and our children will flourish if we teach and keep the words of God continually in front of us. As we settle into the roles God has given us, may we work hard to keep alive and to pass on our passion for Jesus to the next generation. If everyone who came to know Jesus in the 1960s and 1970s had done so, surely our society would be in a much better place than it is today.

Prayer: Dear God, help me to keep your words continually before me and my household. Let me be passionate about passing on my legacy of faith to the next generation. In Jesus' name, Amen.

To Men on Father's Day | Brian Charette

"The righteous who walks in his integrity—blessed are his children after him!"
–Proverbs 20:7

In a piece entitled "Why Men Hate the Church," CBN's Spiritual Life blog posted:

"Cliff is a man's man. On the job he's known as a go-getter and a very hard worker. He's a good provider who loves his wife and kids. He's well respected by his neighbors. Cliff drives a humongous four-wheel-drive pickup. He loves the outdoors and takes every opportunity for a little hunting and fishing. He enjoys a cold beer and a dirty joke. He does not go to church. Ask him why he doesn't go to church, and he'll offer up words like boring, irrelevant, and hypocrite. But the real reason Cliff doesn't go to church is that he's already practicing another religion. That religion is masculinity."[1]

We all know some Cliffs and his friends, pinballing through a world that grows more and more confused about what it means to be a man of God.

And maybe we're tempted to give up on them. However, there is no ignoring the strong evidence that reaching men and empowering them to lead is central to a thriving church family in the twenty-first century. You may have heard the statistics. If a child is the first person in a family to commit to Christ, there is a 3.5% probability everyone else in the family will as well. If it's the mother who is first, that figure grows to a 17% probability. But if the father is first, then the figure skyrockets to 93% of the family or household following his lead.

But don't we already know this without the statistics? Don't we already have a sense that God wants men to lead and God's enemy doesn't? That, as critical as women are and as faithful as many have been, we want and desperately need our men to engage, to truly lead their families and their churches?

Would you consider praying just such a prayer in celebration of Father's Day?

———————

1 "Why Men Hate the Church." CBN, 2015, https://www2.cbn.com/article/not-selected/why-men-hate-church. Accessed 30 May 2023.

SABBATH

A RHYTHM
OF REST

The horse is made ready for the day of battle,

but victory rests with the Lord.

Proverbs 21:31

Give Hope Brad Robertson

"But in your hearts honor Christ the Lord as holy, always being prepared to make a defense to anyone who asks you for a reason for the hope that is in you; yet do it with gentleness and respect, having a good conscience, so that, when you are slandered, those who revile your good behavior in Christ may be put to shame. For it is better to suffer for doing good, if that should be God's will, than for doing evil." –I Peter 3:15-17

Set Jesus apart in your heart, giving Him an utterly unique place above all else, for He is our living hope, the only hope that we have. When his disciples were led to despair, Peter declared, "Lord, to whom shall we go? You have the words of eternal life." There is none other; only Jesus who gives hope and life. Our hopeless generation desperately needs Him!

We are called as His followers to share that hope with others, but how so? First, this appeal to give the "reason for the hope that is in you" is not meant to be a belligerent Bible beating that attempts to ram our beliefs down another's throat. This produces the opposite effect of inspiring hope. Instead, disciples are to share hope with others in "gentleness and respect." This means meekness, not arrogance: "Blessed are the meek, for they shall inherit the Earth" (Matthew 5:5). Perhaps if we refused to talk down to those outside the faith, they would be more inclined to listen. As William Barclay puts it, "Men can be wooed into the Christian faith when they cannot be bullied into it." Do we argue our faith to be right or do we share it to instill hope?

Last but not least, having a good conscience is our best appeal to hope! Your best witness is a pure heart: "In the same way, let your light shine before others, so that they may see your good works and give glory to your Father who is in heaven" (Matthew 5:16). Hope is the down payment of holiness (wholeness) of heart. Who you are and how you share the hope you have been given matters as much as what you say. We have been given a living, loving, personal Savior and been entrusted with leaving a legacy of hope to those caught in despair.

Reels or Nets | Stephen Willis

"And he said to them, 'Follow me, and I will make you fishers of men.' Immediately they left their nets and followed him." –Matthew 4:19-20

Many people love to fish. Not me. As the son of a net fisherman who has experienced catching thousands of fish at a time, I have never really gotten excited about catching one fish with a reel.

Sadly, over the years I think that the Church has thought that we are called to reach people with hooks and shiny objects. I don't think that is what Jesus had in mind—after all, Jesus called net fishermen to be his first disciples. Our text tells us that Jesus called these men to leave their profession of fishing for fish in order for them to fish for men. The men accepted the call of Jesus, and Matthew tells us that "immediately they left their nets." Could it be that Matthew included this line because he wanted us to see that the men called would actually become the net that Jesus would use to reach the lost world? (More on that in a moment.)

As a kid, I would watch my dad, sitting on an old stool in the backyard, mend nets. I would play ball around the nets as dad worked, and when I got tired I would simply watch him. Have you ever thought about what a net is? I learned early that a net is nothing more than a collection of organized knots that work together to accomplish its purpose. J.D. Walt proclaims, [1]"The knots are friendships in the tradition of the friends of Jesus. Yes, the knots are banded and bonded relationships; people learning to love one another with the very love of God."

Do you see it? Jesus transformed their lives and their relationships and united them to become the net that would be cast into the waters of the world to reach the lost. We know that relationships matter. Could it be that they matter more than we even realize? You see, the effectiveness of a net is found in the condition of the knots. Seek the Lord today. Allow Him to examine the relationships in your life. Are there knots that need to be mended? Will you do your part?

---

1 Walt, J.D. "From Shepherding To Fishing." Wake-Up Call, 26 July 2023. Seedbed.com.

Pushing Up Dandelions | Camelot Shuff

"'For I know the plans I have for you,' declares the Lord, 'plans to prosper you and not to harm you, plans to give you a hope and a future.'" –Jeremiah 29:11

Have you ever considered the dandelion? Are they weeds or grass? Are they flowers? Are they food?

I honestly do not know what dandelions are for, but I know that thinking of them helps me to appreciate the mind and work of God.

The good we find in dandelions, for instance, may depend on their use. Are you warming up to a hot cup of dandelion tea? Useful! Or are you glancing out at your lawn as it begs to not go another day without a mow? A nuisance! God the Father is the great gardener, and as He prunes, plants, grows, and sows seed, He alone knows the right way to grow a glorious garden. He knows the purpose of the dandelions.

As we seek to do our Father's will and pursue God's will in our lives, we may be tempted to look for the dandelions or other things that arise and then ask God, is this your will or is this not your will? Desired or not? This way or that way? What is this thing I'm facing—food or weed?

If we find ourselves asking these questions over and over, we reveal our need to understand and know NOW. It shows that in our minds, we do not trust someone's leading unless we already understand first. However, our best times of learning come when we have the wonder and hope of a child, who does not always understand but rather reveals to us two more important questions:

First, can I hear Him? Or—to put this differently—am I constantly in a place where I hear His voice?

And second, can I trust Him?

Once we can say yes to both of these wholeheartedly, we are, in that moment, living in the will of God as we obey Him. Everything else is just details.

A Kick in the Pants | Reenie Peppers

"The Lord will work out his plans for my life—for your faithful love, O Lord, endures forever." –Psalm 138:8a

We all had dreams and aspirations as we grew up. Some were lofty, some not so much. I had two ongoing aspirations as I navigated my teen and pre-teen years. I wanted to write, specifically scripts for Star Trek (the original series) and to be a New York City Rockette. Now, my family watched Star Trek religiously, so that desire to write scripts was logical. I also loved to dance (and still do). I knew I wasn't graceful enough for ballet so I turned my ambition towards becoming a Rockette.

I found out later the requirements for a Rockette are as follows: You must be at least 18 years old, between 5'6" and 5'10 ½", and skilled in jazz and tap dancing. What a kick in the pants! On a tall day, I barely reach 5'5". My inability to make myself grow any taller had derailed my dream of becoming a Rockette.

Now don't get me wrong, I've gone on to do some pretty awesome and out-there things. I was a color guard in the Pro Bowl. I was interviewed on National Public Radio. I even tried out to be a St. Louis Rams cheerleader. However, the most fulfilling aspirations of my life came after I entered into a relationship with Jesus. My current aspirations revolve around living a life according to God's plan. I know that "the Lord will work out his plans for my life—for your faithful love, O Lord, endures forever" (Psalm 138:8a).

So, while I may not be writing scripts for Star Trek, I am currently writing a devotional memoir. I never qualified to be a Rockette; however, I have participated in and lead sacred dance teams over the years. I have done many unusual things and many quiet, miraculous, led-by-God things. And as long as my ambition is to let "the Lord work out His plans for my life," I realize my ambitions and life will be amazing.

"Spiritual Lethargy Leads to Spiritual Garbage" | Deirdra Jones

"Do not love this world nor the things it offers you, for when you love the world, you do not have the love of the Father in you. For the world offers only a craving for physical pleasure, a craving for everything we see, and pride in our achievements and possessions. These are not from the Father, but are from this world. And this world is fading away, along with everything that people crave. But anyone who does what pleases God will live forever." –I John 2:15-17

One of my biggest ministry cheerleaders and mentors shared his books with me. It takes me a while to get through them mostly because there is so much to marinate and chew on. It's taken me four days to get past the first five pages of this one.

A.W. Tozer wrote these thoughts years ago, but I am watching it unfold in real time. Factions of the Church have become diseased and it is collapsing on itself. My heart breaks over the obvious collateral damage that will ensue...for generations.

How did we get here? We not only stopped looking at the world and every aspect of our lives and the things that touch it through the lens of Jesus, but we also took our eyes off Him completely. We have traded the truth for feelings. And in many ways the Church has become so intertwined with the world that one cannot tell the difference between them. This is not how it was or is supposed to be. We were and are called to change the culture, not the other way around. To negotiate or compromise leads to spiritual lethargy, which leads to spiritual garbage.

My prayer over these past few days and into the coming days is that the Church and the people of God would wake up and become "plagued with holy desire" and "hearts hungry for something only God could provide" (14).[1]
God, I pray for a spirit that is desperately hungry for you. Forgive me for the times I've tried filling the spaces in me meant for you with something counterfeit. Plague me with holy desire for you and the things of you. May it be contagious and spread like spiritual wildfire among your people and as a result, to those you desire to be your people.

---

1 Tozer, A.W. , and James L. Snyder. *Dangers of a Shallow Faith: Awakening from Spiritual Lethargy*. Blooming-ton, MN: Bethany House, 2012.

The Grateful Tour |Gary Smith

"'For I know the plans I have for you,' declares the Lord, 'plans to prosper you and not to harm you, plans to give you hope and a future.'" –Jeremiah 29:11

Making plans for special trips with family is always an exciting part of summer activities. Plans stir the imagination, anticipation builds excitement, and when those plans come to fruition, the journey speaks to the soul and spirit.
This summer, we had anticipated a trip that would take us places we have not been before: the Black Hills of South Dakota, Mount Rushmore, and the Badlands. We planned to spend a few days in that region and curve back to Oskaloosa, Iowa, where we had pastored. We would cap the nearly two weeks off at the "Sweet Corn Serenade," a wonderful time to celebrate the abundance of corn and soy bean harvests. Plans were set and tickets bought. We were ready for the adventure!

This is where God's "interruptions in the affairs of men" took a strange turn. A friend of ours in Miami where we had previously ministered passed away, and the family asked if we would conduct the service—which was during the middle of our anticipated vacation. For a minister, the schedule is almost always in question, so I said "yes" and week one was taken from the vacation. During that time, I decided to take the lemons and make lemonade. We visited folks we knew there and expressed our appreciation for their service to the Lord and to our ministry. What an incredible experience! Expressing gratefulness to folks we hadn't seen in 49 years was a huge blessing in disguise.

Could it be that the Lord was revealing His plan while trumping ours? This brought an astounding revelation that changed our whole vacation. We canceled the South Dakota tour and decided to make our whole vacation time a "tour of gratefulness." We listed 15 people in Iowa who had impacted our lives and that of our children through ministry there. Most were elderly now. As we visited these dear folk, an overwhelming sense of God's presence and confirmation gripped our hearts. God's plan was a blessed and wonderful diversion from our regular vacation. It will forever be our greatest vacation, confirming to our hearts what brings the greatest happiness and joy: expressing gratitude to those of the household of faith.

SABBATH

A RHYTHM
OF REST

The Lord replied, "My Presence will go

with you, and I will give you rest."

Exodus 33:14

Nativity of John the Baptist | Emily Heady

"Then I said, 'I have labored in vain, I have spent my strength for nothing and in vain; yet surely my just reward is with the LORD, and my work with my God.'" –Isaiah 49:4

On or about June 24 each year, our brothers and sisters in liturgical traditions celebrate a feast dedicated to the nativity of John the Baptist. From his miraculous birth, John's path was laid out for him. He was to be the voice crying in the wilderness, making straight the path for Jesus. And this is just what he did, though he did it in a way that—to say the least—likely seemed counterintuitive to those around him.

John was no priest, arrayed in costly garments and occupying a role front and center at the Temple; John was neither wealthy nor privileged, attracting the masses with his glamor; John was no inspirational sweet-talker promising peace and prosperity. Instead, he was a rough-looking guy who ate locusts and preached a message of repentance. And he drew a massive crowd.

Why was this? Perhaps it is because deep down, John was speaking to the deepest desires of those around him—a desire for a way through the tangle of confusion that resulted from trying (and failing) to keep the 613 commandments the religious leaders of John's time had extracted from Scripture, a desire for a simple and straight path to God.

Yet John's true message offended some as well, most notably the wife of Herod the King, who didn't care for the fact that John had called out their adulterous relationship. That act of truth-telling got John killed—beheaded as an act of vengeance from a guilty person who did not want to face her sin. Waiting in that prison cell, did John feel he had labored in vain? Did he feel he had spent his strength for nothing? I don't think so. John, more than anyone before him, saw this world clearly. He could help make a straight path for Jesus because he knew how truly close God is to those who love Him, how fulfilling our work can be when we do it for the one who always sees its worth.

Jesus, as we go through this world, help us to stay on the straight path and not to waste our labors on things that don't matter.

Holy Spirit, Lord of Light | Traditional

"But the Comforter, who is the Holy Ghost whom the Father will send in My name, He shall teach you all things and bring all things to your remembrance, whatsoever I have said unto you." –John 14:26

Church history gives us a prayer discipline called the novena–or a cycle of nine prayers on a topic. The next few days here give us the bones of a novena for the fresh infilling of the Holy Spirit, something we all need!

DAY ONE: Holy Spirit! Lord of Light! From Your clear celestial height, Your pure beaming radiance give!

Almighty and eternal God, Who hast vouchsafed to regenerate us by water and the Holy Spirit, and hast given us forgiveness all sins, vouchsafe to send forth from heaven upon us your sevenfold Spirit, the Spirit of Wisdom and Understanding, the Spirit of Counsel and Fortitude, the Spirit of Knowledge and Piety, and fill us with the Spirit of Holy Fear. Amen.

Prayer for the Seven Gifts of the Holy Spirit

O Lord Jesus Christ, Who, before ascending into heaven, did promise to send the Holy Spirit to finish Your work in the souls of Your Apostles and Disciples, deign to grant the same Holy Spirit to me that He may perfect in my soul, the work of Your grace and Your love. Grant me the Spirit of Wisdom that I may despise the perishable things of this world and aspire only after the things that are eternal, the Spirit of Understanding to enlighten my mind with the light of Your divine truth, the Spirit of Counsel that I may ever choose the surest way of pleasing God and gaining heaven, the Spirit of Fortitude that I may bear my cross with You and that I may overcome with courage all the obstacles that oppose my salvation, the Spirit of Knowledge that I may know God and know myself and grow perfect in the science of the Saints, the Spirit of Piety that I may find the service of God sweet and amiable, and the Spirit of Fear that I may be filled with a loving reverence towards God and may dread in any way to displease Him. Mark me, dear Lord, with the sign of Your true disciples and animate me in all things with Your Spirit. Amen.

On My Knees | Traditional

"And do not grieve the Holy Spirit of God, by whom you were sealed for the day of redemption." –Ephesians 4:30

DAY TWO: Act of Consecration to the Holy Spirit
On my knees before the great multitude of heavenly witnesses, I offer myself, soul and body to You, Eternal Spirit of God. I adore the brightness of Your purity, the unerring keenness of Your justice, and the might of Your love. You are the Strength and Light of my soul. In You I live and move and am. I desire never to grieve You by unfaithfulness to grace and I pray with all my heart to be kept from the smallest sin against You. Mercifully guard my every thought and grant that I may always watch for Your light, and listen to Your voice, and follow Your gracious inspirations. I cling to You and give myself to You and ask You, by Your compassion to watch over me in my weakness. Holding the pierced Feet of Jesus and looking at His Five Wounds, and trusting in His Precious Blood and adoring His opened Side and stricken Heart, I implore You, Adorable Spirit, Helper of my infirmity, to keep me in Your grace that I may never sin against You. Give me grace, O Holy Spirit, Spirit of the Father and the Son to say to You always and everywhere, 'Speak Lord for Your servant heareth.' Amen.

DAY THREE: Come. Father of the poor. Come, treasures which endure; Come, Light of all that live!

Come, O blessed Spirit of Holy Fear, penetrate my inmost heart, that I may set you, my Lord and God, before my face forever, help me to shun all things that can offend You, and make me worthy to appear before the pure eyes of Your Divine Majesty in Heaven, where You live and reign in the unity of the ever Blessed Trinity, God world without end. Amen.

DAY FOUR: Thou, of all consolers best, Visiting the troubled breast, Dost refreshing peace bestow.

Come, O Blessed Spirit of Piety, possess my heart. Enkindle therein such a love for God, that I may find satisfaction only in His service, and for His sake lovingly submit to all legitimate authority. Amen.

Thou in Toil Art Comfort Sweet | Traditional

"When you pass through the waters, I will be with you; and when you pass through the rivers, they will not sweep over you. When you walk through the fire, you will not be burned; the flames will not set you ablaze." –Isaiah 43:2

D A Y   F I V E :   Thou in toil art comfort sweet, Pleasant coolness in the heat, solace in the midst of woe.

Come, O Blessed Spirit of Fortitude, uphold my soul in time of trouble and adversity, sustain my efforts after holiness, strengthen my weakness, give me courage against all the assaults of my enemies, that I may never be overcome and separated from Thee, my God and greatest Good. Amen.

D A Y   S I X :   Light immortal! Light Divine! Visit Thou these hearts of Thine, And our inmost being fill!

Come, O Blessed Spirit of Knowledge, and grant that I may perceive the will of the Father; show me the nothingness of earthly things, that I may realize their vanity and use them only for Thy glory and my own salvation, looking ever beyond them to Thee, and Thy eternal rewards. Amen.

D A Y   S E V E N :   If Thou take Thy grace away, nothing pure in man will stay, All his good is turn'd to ill.

Come, O Spirit of Understanding, and enlighten our minds, that we may know and believe all the mysteries of salvation; and may merit at last to see the eternal light in Thy Light; and in the light of glory to have a clear vision of Thee and the Father and the Son. Amen.

Heal Our Wounds | Traditional

"Heal me, LORD, and I will be healed; save me and I will be saved, for you are the one I praise." –Jeremiah 17:14

D A Y E I G H T : Heal our wounds--our strength renews; On our dryness pour Thy dew, Wash the stains of guilt away.

Come, O Spirit of Counsel, help and guide me in all my ways, that I may always do Thy holy will. Incline my heart to that which is good; turn it away from all that is evil, and direct me by the straight path of Thy commandments to that goal of eternal life for which I long. Amen.

D A Y N I N E : Bend the stubborn heart and will, melt the frozen warm the chill. Guide the steps that go astray!

Come, O Spirit of Wisdom, and reveal to my soul the mysteries of heavenly things, their exceeding greatness, power and beauty. Teach me to love them above and beyond all the passing joys and satisfactions of earth. Help me to attain them and possess them for ever. Amen.

Thou, on those who evermore Thee confess and Thee Adore, in Thy sevenfold gift, Descend; Give Them Comfort when they die; Give them Life with Thee on high; Give them joys which never end. Amen.

Come, O Divine Spirit, fill my heart with Thy heavenly fruits, Thy charity, joy, peace, patience, benignity, goodness, faith, mildness, and temperance, that I may never weary in the service of God, but by continued faithful submission to Thy inspiration may merit to be united eternally with Thee in the love of the Father and the Son. Amen.

Holiness Equals Possession | Kerry Willis

"Abide in me and I in you." –John 15:4

Since Pentecost, Jesus isn't primarily looking for followers. Because He wants holiness to happen, He's now looking for sanctuaries. Yes, holiness is all about who owns us and who indwells us. In other words, holiness equals possession. Jesus calls us beyond merely imitating Him to increased intimacy with Him. Yes, it's ownership of us and oneness with us that He wants...and what He wants is what we need.

Let us not live beneath the inheritance line He has lovingly afforded us. In John 15:4, His invitation is clear: "Live in Me and I will live in you!" That's more than follower-talk. That's possession-language.

Holiness is indeed what I long for, Jesus, an ever-increasing intimacy with you. I want you to totally own me. I want to be one with you. I want to be exclusively yours. It is all joy for me to say, "Yes, Lord, I'll be your holy place. Make your home and set up your throne in me! Amen!"

Presence matters most!

SABBATH

A RHYTHM OF REST

Jesus answered, "Everyone who drinks this water will be thirsty again, but whoever drinks the water I give them will never thirst. Indeed, the water I give them will become in them a spring of water welling up to eternal life."

John 4:13-14

Forgiveness | Todd Thomas

"For if you forgive men when they sin against you, our heavenly Father will also forgive you. But if you do not forgive men their sins, your Father will not forgive your sins." –Matthew 6:14-15

I see Matthew as he remembers the occasion of this moment. I see him pause, deep in thought, recalling the wording Jesus used. The word he remembers Jesus using when speaking of forgiveness is a strong and powerful one. It had been used for centuries to describe the act of sending away, hurling away, releasing, letting go, leaving behind, abandoning, dismissing, or setting aside. It was a word used to describe a decisive, intentional, and final act.
This act is completely contrary to our nature.

We often say we forgive but cannot forget: "Fool me once, shame on you; fool me twice, shame on me." We just won't forget. We keep the memories fresh by telling the story of our injury over and over and over. We seldom give grace the opportunity to fade not only the scars, but also the story.

In this postscript to prayer, Jesus gives us a hard reality: Forgiveness must be active to be received. We cannot hold unforgiveness, however we define it, and expect the forgiving grace of the heavenly Father to remain currently active in our own lives. We cannot live with an unforgiving spirit toward others and live in the necessary flow of the Father's forgiveness.

We must forgive others. We must let go of past hurts. We must abandon the story. We must dismiss the record. We must take decisive, intentional action with a sense of finality. If we refuse to take such action something powerful happens: The wrong done to us become the wrong that is now in us.

I believe a great, sweeping flood of the presence and power of God will be known among us the moment we allow the convicting and cleansing grace of Christ to wash away our spirits of unforgiveness.

Forgiveness - Part Two | Todd Thomas

"This is how my heavenly Father will treat each of you unless you forgive your brother from your heart." –Matthew 18:35

In this portion of Scripture (Matthew 18:21-35), we find the story often known as the Parable of the Unmerciful Servant. In this parable, Jesus tells of a man with an impossible debt. If the average wage of that day were applied to the debt in its entirety, it would take several lifetimes to satisfy the debt. Yet the king, in an act of great mercy, forgave the debt. This servant then went out and demanded payment of a small debt from a fellow servant. As a result, the king's leniency was reversed and full payment of the impossible debt of the first servant was demanded. Jesus ends the story with these words: "This is how my heavenly Father will treat each of you unless you forgive your brother from your heart."

It has often been said that forgiving another person is an act of setting yourself free. While I understand the sentiment, I am still troubled by the thought. I am troubled because forgiveness of this sort is motivated by self-interest.

When the king of our text forgave the impossible debt, he gained nothing. Actually, by forgiving the debt, the king absorbed the financial loss while the servant was set free.

This is an apt description of the forgiveness God gives to us. We owed a great debt, an impossible debt. No amount of penance, no amount of good works, could settle that debt. Apart from God absorbing the debt and paying the price, we would never be free.

In this story are challenging principles of forgiveness:
1. In forgiving another, we are not finding freedom for ourselves; we are giving freedom to the offending person.
2. In forgiving another, the debt owed does not simply vanish. We embrace the debt, take on the burden, and release the offender. Our heart, our actions, our words, all declare: "You no longer owe me anything." We no longer hold them to account, not even for an apology.
3. Once we are forgiven, we are under divine obligation to offer the same as we have received: absorbing, releasing grace.

Forgiveness, rather than an act motivated by self-interest, is an act of deep sacrificial humility. Help us, Jesus.

Forgiveness Withheld | Chad Moler

"Bear with each other and forgive one another if any of you has a grievance against someone. Forgive as the Lord forgave you." -Colossians 3:13

Have you ever known someone to carry a grudge? Not the sort of grudge that gets carried from a small misunderstanding over lunch and that is quickly forgotten about by the time dinner rolls around. I mean the sort of grudge that gets remembered for a week, a month, or decades.

Whenever the offender's name is brought up or is thought about, there is a rehashing of all their wrong doings. A little stroll down hurtful memory lane conjures up all the "feels," and not in a good way. All the things the offender did are hung out on the line to air out—again and again and again.

Lewis Smedes said, "To forgive is to set a prisoner free and discover that the prisoner was you."[1]

In the moment of seeing that person or hearing their name, it feels right and just to grind them down—but what that really does is continue to keep us bound up. When we continue to harp on how we were wronged or what injustices were done to us, we can never experience true healing, the healing that can only ever come from God.

As Paul told the Christians in Colossae, "Forgive one another, if you have a grievance." The offended person is the one who needs to take the initiative, make the first move, and offers forgiveness or attempts to reconcile.

Paul reminds us that we are to do this as the Lord has forgiven us. The one who knew no sin, who was wrongly accused, forgave those who hung Him on the cross, those who heckled Him and deserted Him.

Heavenly Father, teach us how not to withhold forgiveness from anyone. Help us to recognize our role and responsibility in reconciliation, and to act first in humility. Amen.

---

1 Smedes, Lewis B. *Forgive and Forget: Healing the Hurts We Don't Deserve*. New York: Harper & Row, 1984.

Resolved to Forgive | Ashley Gomez

"...[T]hough we live in the world, we do not wage war as the world does...[W]e take captive every thought to make it obedient to Christ." –II Corinthians 10:3, 5b

I'll never forget the day I finally saw my self. I was retelling, for probably the hundredth time, how I'd been personally wronged, and worse, by people who claimed to be Christians. As I told my story to a listening friend, I watched as the lack of comprehension and a non-committal expression came over her face. And in that moment, it hit me: how I had become so captivated by my hurt I literally made myself a slave to it, as it consumed my thoughts and speech. The friend to whom I was telling the story wasn't even a believer, and here I was, maligning other believers! How ugly in spirit I had become, bent on bringing about my misguided version of justice to those who had caused me pain!

In Romans 12:18-19, sandwiched between words of living sacrifice and being humbly submitted, Paul further urges us to "as far as it depends on you, live at peace with everyone. Do not take revenge, my dear friends . . ." The truth is, we, as children of Adam, are broken. And though we have knowledge of good and evil, the ability to judge aright belongs to God alone. We do not see that clearly. But as children of God, redeemed from that brokenness, we are responsible to daily live out God's peace, which always yields restoration.

I resolved to pray every single time even the slightest thought of my situation came to mind—to "take captive every thought." Christian communicator Allison Allen shares it this way: "[Y]ou cannot carry . . . unforgiveness into a new season."[1] And just so, God propelled me into a new season after healing me of my hurt and anger. What joy to forgive and to fully trust that God knows what He is doing!

---

1 Allison Allen, cohost. "We Will See God Blurry Until We Get Better at Saying "I'm Sorry." Lisa Harper's Back Porch Theology, Season 1, Episode 4, January 2022.

Who is My Younger Brother? | Lynne Goodwin

"But to Jonah this seemed very wrong, and he became angry...'Now, Lord, take away my life, for it is better for me to die than to live.'" –Jonah 4:1,3

I was working on an illustration for the parable often called the Prodigal Son. But, instead of the bad behavior of the younger son, this picture would focus on the father. He would watch the horizon for his lost son; he would joyfully embrace his returning son, and he would urge the older brother to share in that joy as he celebrates the lost son that was found.

I worked out my composition and started sketching but soon faltered. I knew how I would show the longing of the father as he searched the horizon for the son who had taken his inheritance and run away. I had the desperate embrace of the father and his younger son as they were reunited in repentance. But I couldn't figure out the body language in the last scene, as the father begs his older son to come into the party for the younger brother.

I was struggling with the older brother; I couldn't figure out how to make his posture communicate his reason for refusing to join the celebration. "The older brother feels like he deserves a party for his obedience, how does that look?" I wondered aloud.

"He's Jonah, sulking on the hill, so angry he could die," my husband suggested thoughtfully. He had an answer for the posture of both the older brother's body and heart.

Our pastor often challenges us to find ourselves in the Scriptures as we read. The older brother is easy to identify with if you grew up in the church. His obedience, in contrast to the younger brother's rebellion, seems overlooked. However, the anger of Jonah because God chose to spare Nineveh made me see unforgiveness behind the older brother's refusal to join the party.

In both stories, the one who had been wronged was willing to forgive. But the self-righteous hearts of Jonah and the older brother would not let go of their anger to make room to celebrate the repentance of others.

My husband's suggestion made me consider how I can learn to share in the Father's joy for everyone's repentance.

Be Still | Chad Moler

"Be still in the presence of the Lord, and wait patiently for him to act..." –Psalm 37:7

I'm going to be honest and say that sometimes I have a difficult time slowing down. There are times when I am extremely busy and still try to find room in my schedule to fit more in, as if somehow I can create more hours in the day. If I am not careful, I will sacrifice my own personal time in order to get more done. Thankfully, God has placed people in my life to help guard me against that.

C. S. Lewis said, [1]"I am sure that God keeps no one waiting unless he sees that it is good for him to wait"(9).

Being still and sitting before the throne of grace is a practice that I am continuing to learn. There are times when I still feel the urge to get up and do something (anything!), and yet I feel like I need to stay. That it is not time to act, or at least not for me. That things are happening behind the scenes that I cannot see.

It very well could be that it is necessary for me to sit and wait because my actions would not help whatever situation I feel needs my attention. My actions may be a hindrance to the work God is doing, so I must wait patiently for Him to act, fully accepting that there may be more for me to learn in this time of waiting. In the waiting, not only will my faith be strengthened as I see God do more than I ever could, but my faith will also be strengthened by being in His presence.

Father, help me to see that being in your presence, waiting for you, is how I will grow in my faith. Continue to teach me to be patient as you act in your timing, not mine. Amen.

---

1 Lewis, C.S. *Mere Christianity*. London: HarperCollins UK.

SABBATH

A RHYTHM
OF REST

Be still before the Lord and wait patiently for him;

do not fret when people succeed in their ways, when

they carry out their wicked schemes.

Psalm 37:7

Ordinary Time | Emily Heady

"Then the apostles gathered to Jesus and told Him all the things, both what they had done and what they had taught. And He said to them, 'Come aside by yourselves to a deserted place and rest awhile.' For there were many coming and going, and they did not even have time to eat. So they departed to a deserted place in a boat by themselves." –Mark 6:30-32

July falls between liturgical seasons—after Easter and before Advent. It happens during what our liturgical brothers and sisters call "ordinary time." It's a prosaic term, but there's beauty in it, for so much of our Christian lives unfold in everyday routines. We are sanctified less through the dramatic moments that make for great storytelling than through the moment-by-moment work of the Spirit in us.

When I picture the scene above, I can imagine the apostles' childlike joy as they report back to their teacher what has happened—the miracles, the people who came to believe, the words they said. Each must have been jostling to speak, overcome with the need to share what he had seen and done. Their enthusiasm must have been like my children's, returning from summer camp or field day at school.

For His part, Jesus must have loved their enthusiasm and joy, and His response shows that He loved them too. If Jesus were a corporate manager, in charge of His salvation mission like a foreman overseeing a construction project, He might have said, "Good job, team. Now let's bring this same level of 'can do' to the job site tomorrow. If we can keep being this productive, we'll see it in our profit margin!" Instead, He responds as I did when my own children's enthusiasm peaked. Knowing that they were so excited they would soon crash, and knowing they'd eaten only Little Debbies and Kool-Aid, I sought not to push them farther but to bring them back to ordinary time. To rest, to reflect, to enjoy.

It is in the moments of rest and reflection that we can most clearly see the Spirit working—what He has done out there in the world and how He is also changing the landscape of our inner lives to look more like Eden.

Jesus, as we work hard, let us also remember to make room for ordinary rest so we might see you more clearly.

The Story: Part One – The Prologue | Mike Lyle

"In the beginning, God created the heavens and the earth...By the seventh day God had finished the work he had been doing; so on the seventh day he rested from all his work. Then God blessed the seventh day and made it holy, because on it he rested from all the work of creating that he had done." –Genesis 1:1, 2:2-3

A prologue is an introduction. When there is a prologue to a story, the author is inviting the reader into the world being created. I'm always tempted to skip the prologue and get right to the story parts of the narrative. However, when I do that, I find myself disoriented and uncertain about the setting. A good prologue helps the reader understand when and where they are in the story. Here are some famous ones: "It was the best of times, it was the worst of times..."; "Two households, both alike in dignity, In fair Verona, where we lay our scene...," or "A long time ago in a galaxy far, far away..."

To that list, perhaps we can add "In the beginning, God created the heavens and the earth." The prologue of our story can be found in the book of Genesis. It answers questions about the world we are in. Is it a world marked by scarcity, competition, and survival of the fittest, or is it one of abundance, completion, and rest? Without a doubt, the first two chapters of Genesis depict a world exploding with life and potential. Then, we are told that the maker of this world rested.

Why would God rest? Was God tired? I don't think so. I think we are being invited into a world marked by "enough." God knew when to stop creating because His creation was very good. We are told this world is good and that God has provided all we need to live and thrive in this world.

I wonder what kind of world you are living in. Is it the world we see in the prologue (the one God made) or are you living in the counterfeit world of scarcity, survival, and competition (the one we made)? One of those worlds invites us into rest and the other into destruction. Won't you hear God's invitation to enjoy His rest? You can trust Him. In HIS world, there is enough.

The Story: Part Two - The Introduction | Mike Lyle

"Then the man and his wife heard the sound of the Lord God as he was walking in the garden in the cool of the day, and they hid from the Lord God among the trees of the garden. But the Lord God called to the man, 'Where are you?'"—Genesis 3:8-9

If the prologue of a story orients the reader to the setting, the introduction introduces the characters and sets the trajectory for the plot. A good introduction can "hook" a reader by presenting a compelling character or story within the world created by the prologue.

In our introduction, we see a God who is a creator. We aren't given a reason for the making; we are just given a picture of a God who speaks and worlds are formed. This God enjoys creating. He keeps announcing that what He is making is good. Then, we see image bearers. These people are going to reflect the Maker in creation and rule and reign within it. However, there is another character—a snake—who is in rebellion against God. This snake lies to the humans, wanting them to believe that God is holding out on them. The snake tells them that they can decide between good and evil themselves; they don't need God to tell them. So, these humans reach and grasp to define good and evil for themselves.

At this point, God comes walking in the garden. I don't think this was the first time God came to walk with them. There are different ways to ask the question God asks in our text. There is a Hebrew phrase that means, "I can't find you." This is not the one used. In Genesis 3, we see another Hebrew phrase that means "You're not where I left you, where are you?" It isn't that God couldn't find Adam and Eve. God was expecting them to walk with Him, to learn from Him about how His creation works, to be discipled by Him within the world He made. However, Adam and Eve were not where they should be—walking with Him. The rest of the story is about how God will fix that broken relationship.

Maybe at this point, you could hear that question personally—"Where are you?" Are you walking with God in His story or are you writing your own?

The Story: Part Three - The Rising Action | Mike Lyle

"'You yourselves have seen what I did to Egypt, and how I carried you on eagles' wings and brought you to myself. Now if you obey me fully and keep my covenant, then out of all nations you will be my treasured possession. Although the whole earth is mine, you will be for me a kingdom of priests and a holy nation.' These are the words you are to speak to the Israelites." –Exodus 19:4-6

In any story, there's a point where the narrative takes off, where the plot's focus is revealed and the characters must make some decisions. This is called the rising action. In our story, the good creation is now filled with destruction, death, and corruption. God comes to Abram and invites him into partnership. Note: God is still committed to ruling His creation with human partners. God tells Abram that He will bless the whole world through him and his family.

This family, however, has trouble trusting God and eventually finds themselves in slavery. They cry out, and God comes to their rescue. He brings them to a mountain where He reminds them of the promise and blessing. On this mountain top, God tells them that He's trying to rescue the whole world through them. He will show this family what He is like so they, in turn, can show the rest of the world. This is what it means to be a kingdom of priests and a holy nation. This will require them to be different from the other nations and to represent the character of the Maker to a lost world.

This family will struggle to be faithful to God's mission. They will demonstrate both radical obedience to God and utter failure. Sometimes the failure will come from a lack of understanding or a lapse in judgment, and sometimes from opposing God and forsaking the mission. Throughout this part of the story, we see God's unending patience for people who are trying but failing to live up to the mission. We also see, however, that God judges those who completely ignore the mission and oppose Him.

Maybe you need to be reminded of God's patience today as you wrestle with being a holy priest. Maybe you need to remember that God opposes those who oppose Him. It's His mission. Are you with Him or against Him?

The Story: Part Four - The Climax | Mike Lyle

"Just as Moses lifted up the snake in the wilderness, so the Son of Man must be lifted up, that everyone who believes may have eternal life in him. For God so loved the world that he gave his one and only Son, that whoever believes in him shall not perish but have eternal life. For God did not send his Son into the world to condemn the world, but to save the world through him." –John 3:14-17

The climax of a story is when the conflict of the plot is resolved. In our plot, we see that God is looking for partners who will help Him restore His broken creation. The conflict that arises again and again is the fact that these potential partners are also broken. Sin is not only something "out there" that is destroying God's good creation; it is also working inside God's potential partners like a poison.

In our text today, we are reminded of when poisonous snakes were biting the Israelites in the desert. How could they be a kingdom of priests when they were dying from poison? Moses asks God for help and is instructed to make a bronze snake and put it on a pole. When the people are bitten, they are to look at the snake for healing.

Maybe we should recall the story in Genesis when a snake tempted Eve and recollect the curse against the snake and the prophecy about how a son of Eve would crush the snake's head even as the snake bit and poisoned him. Israel is invited to look upon a defeated snake in hope for a cure from its poison. When Jesus is lifted up on the cross, we are invited to see a defeated snake and hope for a cure from his poison.

The cross of Christ is the climax of the long story of God's rescue plan for His good creation. Jesus draws the poison into Himself, thereby setting us free to partner with Him in the restoration of all things corrupted by the snake's poison.

Has the conflict of your story been resolved? Do you believe that the snake has been defeated by the cross and, as a result, sin no longer has a hold on you? If so, it's time to join Jesus in the work of saving the world.

The Story: Part Five - The Falling Action | Mike Lyle

"On the evening of that first day of the week, when the disciples were together, with the doors locked for fear of the Jewish leaders, Jesus came and stood among them and said, 'Peace be with you!' After he said this, he showed them his hands and side. The disciples were overjoyed when they saw the Lord. Again Jesus said, 'Peace be with you! As the Father has sent me, I am sending you.' And with that he breathed on them and said, 'Receive the Holy Spirit.'" –John 20:19-22

A story's falling action takes place after the climax as the story moves toward resolution. Our story would be incomplete without the resurrection. Paul even said that our faith is useless if Jesus didn't rise from the dead (1 Corinthians 15:14). If God's plan was to restore a broken creation, the resurrection is the beginning of that restoration.

God has a goal for His creation—a new heaven and a new earth. In this new creation, there will be no death or sickness or any of the poison that corrupted the old creation. Jesus is the first born of this new life and, in His resurrection, we see what it looks like. We aren't simply invited to look upon a new creation, however. We are invited to participate in it.

Jesus offers us the Holy Spirit as a deposit of the new creation and as a means to live within it. We can now partner with Jesus to move the story forward toward its glorious end. N.T. Wright explains this idea: "What you do in the present—by painting, preaching, singing, sewing, praying, teaching, building hospitals, digging wells, campaigning for justice, writing poems, caring for the needy, loving your neighbor as yourself—will last into God's future. These activities are not simply ways of making the present life a little less beastly, a little more bearable, until the day when we leave it behind altogether. They are part of what we may call building for God's kingdom."[1]

Are you moving the story toward its resolution? Perhaps you have a role to play in ushering in God's new creation. May His kingdom come and His will be done on Earth as in heaven.

---

1 Wright, N.T. *Surprised by Hope: Rethinking Heaven, the Resurrection, and the Mission of the Church.* San Francisco: HarperOne, 2008.

SABBATH

A RHYTHM OF REST

"This is to be a lasting ordinance for you: On the tenth day of the seventh month you must deny yourselves[c] and not do any work—whether native-born or a foreigner residing among you—because on this day atonement will be made for you, to cleanse you. Then, before the Lord, you will be clean from all your sins. It is a day of sabbath rest, and you must deny yourselves; it is a lasting ordinance.It is a day of sabbath rest, and you must deny yourselves; it is a lasting ordinance."

Leviticus 16:29-31

God's Grandeur | Emily Heady

"See, I am doing a new thing! Now it springs up; do you not perceive it? I am making a way in the wilderness and streams in the wasteland." –Isaiah 43:19

Gerard Manley Hopkins' poem "God's Grandeur" is a sonnet—eight lines explaining a problem, then six more answering it. Here, in Hopkins' mind, is the situation that needs remedying: The world is full of God's glory, yet people don't notice it.

The first four lines describe the glory we're missing. God's grandeur is everywhere, Hopkins says: It reveals itself in flashes, like light on a piece of tinfoil. It shows in high-pressure situations, as oil emerges from an olive when it is pressed hard enough. Why don't we notice it?

The next four lines offer at least one reason for this: We are just too busy. We go back and forth, hither and yon, working and doing and messing and mucking things up. We insulate ourselves with labor, with busyness. We encase ourselves in the everyday, as shoes encase our feet.

Still, God speaks to us daily in nature, and the last six lines help us see how. Beneath the surface, life springs forth: Blades of grass push through dirt; springs bubble from the deep. Every morning, after the darkest dark of night, the sun rises. Hopkins doesn't see this as a machine doing its business; no, nature with its ever-renewing cycle of life is a reminder of how the Spirit moves in each of us:

The world is charged with the grandeur of God.
It will flame out, like shining from shook foil;
It gathers to a greatness, like the ooze of oil
Crushed. Why do men then now not reck his rod?
Generations have trod, have trod, have trod;
And all is seared with trade; bleared, smeared with toil;
And wears man's smudge and shares man's smell: the soil
Is bare now, nor can foot feel, being shod.
And for all this, nature is never spent;
There lives the dearest freshness deep down things;
And though the last lights off the black West went
Oh, morning, at the brown brink eastward, springs —
Because the Holy Ghost over the bent
World broods with warm breast and with ah! bright wings.

Starving for Love | Chad Moler

"Jacob loved Joseph more than any of his other children . . ." –Genesis 37:3

If you have a family or if you have ever seen a movie or sitcom, there is a good chance that you have witnessed a sibling rivalry. Maybe you have heard a child say their parents have a favorite child, or have heard the parents admit that for themselves.

This was the situation in Jacob's family, where he blatantly declared his great love for Joseph in front of his other children. Not only did he make this known verbally, but he lavished Joseph with gifts, like the famous colorful coat, all of which drew his older brothers' ire.

This great love that Jacob had for Joseph caused his brothers to hate him, to the extent that the brothers didn't have one positive thing to say about Joseph. Even though the crux of this story is about the favoritism Jacob showed to Joseph, the story really is about a lack of familial love. The brothers desperately tried to win their father's love, or at least to get a fair share of it from Joseph. After years of trying, the only way they could level the playing field was to strip Joseph of the displays of affection from their father, destroying his coat and writing him off. Joseph, in turn, was desperate for his brothers' love—to fit in, to be accepted, to be a part of the group.

The challenge this story poses is to view people through the lens of love—to recognize that the person who we think doesn't like us may be crying out for love, or that the person who is harsh may be desperately reaching out for connection. Maybe people aren't mean or nasty but just suffering from a starvation of love.

Through Jesus, we have an opportunity to do exactly that: to connect. We can look past the faults of others and satisfy that hunger for love that so many feel. Why not lavish on others the same love that has been lavished upon us by our heavenly Father? As Bishop Victor Rivera says, "Christ's love always helps us see beyond other's faults."[1]

Father, help me to see others the way that you do. To look beyond faults and love people with the love of Christ. Amen!

---

1 Rivera, Victor Manual. *In Search of True Freedom: Seven Keys to Discover the Best Way to Live.* Maitland, FL: Xulon P, an imprint of Salem Media Group, 2010.

Train a Child | Doug Fry

"Train a child in the way he should go, and when he is old, he will not turn from it."
–Proverbs 22:6

My parents were raised in godly homes, and I believe it was 1951 when they made that final commitment for Jesus Christ. I really do not remember a time when they were not Christians. Our family became members of the Roanoke, Virginia First Church of the Nazarene.

Five years after becoming Christians and members of the Nazarene church, my parents joined three other families to start a new Nazarene church in the northwest part of our city. Looking back now, I realize those were some of the most exciting years of our lives. You see, when my parents made that commitment to follow Jesus, they were all about doing His work. My dad became Sunday School Superintendent and my mother became a Sunday school teacher and taught small children for over 40 years.

In just a few years we had a brand new church building and were very involved in our community. During times of revival, VBS, and Easter, adults and children would canvas our church neighborhood and hand out flyers and invitations to come and worship with us. These were exciting days as our church grew in all areas every year. Church attendance was paramount in our home. We were there every time the doors were open and the lights were on.

During one of our revival services, I felt convicted and knelt at an altar of prayer. I asked Jesus to come into my heart and to please forgive me of my sins. When I got up from praying, I knew Jesus had done something special in my heart. During my high school years, peer pressure would get the best of me, but eighteen years later the bottom fell out of my life. During the time that I was away from the Lord, there was not a day that I wasn't reminded of the lessons learned in my childhood home. My parents had given me the best training possible. They believed Proverbs 22:6.

Today, there are so many activities that compete with the Church for our children. While Proverbs 22:6 is not a guarantee, it's a strong reminder to give our children the best training for life possible.

Child-Like Faith | Darcy McAlinn

"And he said: 'Truly I tell you, unless you change and become like little children, you will never enter the kingdom of heaven.'" –Matthew 18:3

What does it look like to "become like little children"? I had the privilege of speaking at a camp one summer. I had spent months planning out what stories I thought the kids would relate to. Most of the kids that went to this camp had been coming for years and had a strong foundation in the main stories of the Bible, but this particular year we had a child who was new to the Church. We were talking about how Jesus spent His life and started His ministry when this little boy raised his hand and started jumping up and down. Of course, I was in full swing of the lesson and didn't want to get sidetracked, but when he nearly fell out of his seat, I called on him. With the most excited voice he said, "Wait! Jesus was a real person?!" His amazement was so contagious that the kids then basically took over and told this little boy all about Jesus.

This is a moment that I will never forget. It is such a great reminder of how exciting and amazing the gospel really is. It's easy as we get older to become somewhat numb to the gospels. I've been guilty of that myself, but then I think about that little boy and how he could hardly contain his excitement.

When I think about this verse from Matthew, I think of kids spending all morning in class having to sit still and work on assignments, but then recess comes along and they all line up and as soon as the door to the playground opens those kids run full speed ahead, laughing and full of joy. That's how I want to enter the kingdom of heaven.

Dear Lord, thank you for the stories that allow us to see and connect with you. Thank you for the moments that encourage me, the moments that renew my heart for you, and the moments that make me long for relationship with you. Please give me faith like a child's, to be in awe of you and so excited to know you that I can hardly sit still. I love you so much. Amen.

The Children | Kerry Willis

"...future generations will be told about the Lord." –Psalm 22:30b

The Word of God is so very powerful and wonderful. Recently, in Mark's record of the gospel, the words written in chapter 10 (the whole chapter) have been really riveting to me personally—heart, mind, soul, and strength.

Here's one portion of the passage:
"One day some parents brought their children to Jesus so He could touch and bless them. But the disciples scolded the parents for bothering Him. When Jesus saw what was happening, He was angry with His disciples. He said to them, "Let the children come to Me. Don't stop them! For the Kingdom of God belongs to those who are like these children. I tell you the truth, anyone who doesn't receive the Kingdom of God like a child will never enter it." Then He took the children in His arms and placed His hands on their heads and blessed them" (Mark 10:13-16 NLT)

How must the disciples have felt when they realized they were not allowing those that Jesus wanted to come to Him to actually come to Him? The little children, that is.

In the culture of that day, children were not often highly valued. Generally speaking, they were to be invisible and silent. Yet, Jesus did not succumb to the culture of His day. He went against the culture and let everyone know that children were highly valuable to Him. Why? Truly, "Jesus loves the little children, ALL the children of the world!"

This thought is on my mind today. In the culture I live in now, do I highly value those that the world does not highly value? Is there anyone I think Jesus does not want coming to Him? If so, Lord forgive. Lord forbid.

My prayer is this: Lord, let the little children realize your loving presence for them through me. And not just the little children, but ALL the children of the world, especially the ones who are seemingly invisible and have sadly lost their voice. Reach through me to save those created in your image. All of them are precious in your sight. Make them to also be precious in mine. Amen.

Launch Out | Bobbie Jo King

"When he had stopped speaking, He said to Simon, 'Launch out into the deep and let down your nets for a catch.'" –Luke 5:4

Have you ever heard the Lord whisper your name? I believe children are especially sensitive to His voice. The first time I remember to have "heard" Him speak was at the tender age of 8. In the middle of the night, I was weeping over the fact that Papa had died. I did not get to say "goodbye" or "I love you" one last time. My heavenly Father gently spoke words of comfort that allowed me to say "goodbye." Years later in 2020, I heard Him whisper again, "Bobbie, are you ready to stop talking and to launch out into deep new territory I have for you? Are you ready to let down your nets for a catch of lost souls?" Yes, Lord! "Are you ready to experience MY power?" Yes, Lord! "Will you do as I say? Will you trust me, and not fear?" Yes, Lord! "Will you walk with me and learn from me?" Yes, Lord! I will.

At this point, Marlon and I had been married eight years so I knew that God was also speaking to him. That conversation began the journey of planting a church in Norfolk, Virginia. It has been an uphill climb but worth it all. His plans are not like ours, and we have spent many hours praying and planting seed in expectation of a great harvest. Launching out into the deep is never as easy as it sounds, but the harvest is sure to come as we walk in step with the Master Fisherman and the Spirit who goes before us, softening the hearts of men, women, and children to be ready to receive the good news of Jesus.

I have learned that fishing requires patience, whether you want to fill your nets with fish or people. We must trust God, the one who calls us, to do the work as we partner with Him. We must listen, obey, believe, and cast our nets out knowing that "we can do all things through Christ who strengthens us" (Phil. 4:13). We can do anything God commands or asks us to do.

Do you hear Him whispering, "Are you ready to launch out into the deep and let down your nets for a catch?"

SABBATH

A RHYTHM OF REST

¹ *Shout for joy to the Lord, all the earth.*

² *Worship the Lord with gladness;*

come before him with joyful songs.

³ *Know that the Lord is God.*

It is he who made us, and we are his[a];

we are his people, the sheep of his pasture.

Psalm 100

Christ in Us | Cavan Carlton

"I have given them the glory that you gave me, that they may be one as we are one—I in them and you in me—so that they may be brought to complete unity. Then the world will know that you sent me and have loved them even as you have loved me." –John 17:22-23

Many important life lessons arrive in tandem with our first wrinkles and gray hair.

When I was 35 years old, I learned a very important life lesson. I learned that there is an enormous difference between being a believer in Jesus and a true disciple of Jesus. You can't become a disciple without first being a believer, but you can become a believer and never advance to becoming a disciple. The distinction between the two never really occurred to me early in life, and for decades I stayed stuck, believing in Jesus but not following Him, not obeying Him, not loving Him, and not being His true disciple. I wanted to be like Him; I just wasn't.

It is possible to learn about Christ and to have a strong desire to emulate Him. He's the greatest person ever to walk the face of the earth—who wouldn't want to be like Him? But all of the learning about Him and the striving to be like Him can be done without the infilling presence of His Holy Spirit permeating our being. However, it will be false and impure. It will be sourced in our personal desire and effort, not in Jesus Himself.

To be genuine, to be real, to be a true disciple of Jesus and truly powerful for Jesus, our Christlikeness must be sourced in the infilling presence of the Holy Spirit in us. The Holy Spirit of Christ has to permeate our entire being and literally change us from the inside out.

Only when I truly repented of my sins and fully surrendered my heart and life to Jesus did I receive the full blessing of His Holy Spirit. That changed everything.

We can only truly be like Jesus if Jesus is truly inside us.

A Second Coat | Janette Berge

"And I am sure of this, that he who began a good work in you will bring it to completion at the day of Jesus Christ." –Philippians 1:6

Have you ever tackled a task that seemed overwhelming, like painting a room? Maybe you love the idea of a fresh coat of paint, but the actual process is something you dread. I know I feel that way about painting, but as a homeowner it's something I end up doing quite often.

Recently, I decided to paint the guest bathroom because the previous owners had painted it a color that I affectionately called "urine yellow." I wanted to change things up. So, I gathered my painting materials, turned on some worship music, and got to work. But after finishing the task, I noticed spots where the original color was still visible. Ugh! A second coat was needed.

As I started on the second coat, I was getting more and more frustrated. That's when I heard the Lord speak to me and say, "Aren't you glad I am never tired or annoyed of repainting you?" It was a powerful moment that reminded me of Philippians 1:6, which reminds us that He will bring His work in us to the finish line. When we accept Christ as our Savior, we receive the first coat of crimson red that transforms our lives. But God doesn't stop there. He continues to work in us, shining His light in the areas where our old self still shows through.

When we invite God into our lives, we open ourselves to the transformation He can bring about from the inside out. It's not always easy to let Him into every area, but when we do, we begin to see areas that need a little more work. Maybe it's a habit or a hurt we need to work on. Whatever it is, God's light can prompt us to let Him apply another coat of paint.

Even though tragedies come in many forms, we can still see God at work in our lives, perfecting His masterpiece. He is constantly working to make us more like His Son. Instead of shying away from those times when God "repaints" us, let's embrace them and trust that He will bring us to completion.

Spirit Walk |Gary O'Shell

"Whether you turn to the right or to the left, your ears will hear a voice behind you, saying, 'This is the way; walk in it.'" –Isaiah 30:21

I'm told it's a wonderful spiritual experience to visit Israel. Many who have made the trek have especially noted "walking where Jesus walked." But there is a question that comes to my mind. Do we wish more to walk where Jesus walked, or where He is walking today?

We can make idols out of most anything, including our spiritual past and heritage. Nostalgia over what God has done can dominate our hearts and minds to the degree we cannot see where He is and what He's doing right now. We know where He has walked, but we miss where He's currently walking.

I realize that pastors and leaders can inject their flesh, pride, and carnal desires into an agenda for moving people in the direction they want them to go. The Word gives us a clear safe-guard for this. It is an intimate walk of fellowship with God. I love the Scripture from Isaiah 30. This is a portrait of what the believer's walk with Him looks like. At any point in the journey, His voice will speak if we walk in intimacy with Him. Our yielded heart and spirit can know that wherever we are walking, His voice will continually speak direction. If we are facing the wrong way, His voice will speak behind us to reveal the right one. We will walk where He is walking today and in our close fellowship with Him, we can trust that we will continue to walk where He is leading tomorrow.

I go back to those Holy Land trips. Some have said that when we take them, we stand on holy ground. Yet I remember someone else saying that wherever we stand with Him, that place becomes holy ground. Do we walk there now? In our marriages, parenting, workplaces, neighborhoods, churches, and ministries, do we walk with Him on holy ground? Jesus is walking His holy ground right now. In all of these aspects of our lives, do we walk with Him on His holy ground? Or is it just our ground we walk?

Far-Flung Forgiveness | Emily Heady

"As far as the east is from the west, so far hath He removed our transgressions from us." –Psalm 103:12

I know a couple that has a strong, twenty-year marriage. Yet both spouses will separately narrate how that marriage—which God has blessed and redeemed—started with an affair. Both regret that bad start daily, and on really bad days, they forget that when God forgives, He does it completely.

How far is the east from the west? There is no number high enough to measure that distance. If you're going north around the globe, eventually you'll cross the North Pole and go south—and vice-versa when you get to Antarctica. Yet if you're going east, you're always going east. There is no end to how far east you can go. What is the Psalmist's point? That when God forgives, there's no way that we can chase those sins down again: They're just that far gone.

What would it mean if we could grasp how wide and how deep is the gulf God has placed between us and our past sins? For my friend, it would likely mean that she wouldn't be so tempted to call herself names like "sinner" or "adulterer." It might mean she saw herself first as a beloved daughter of God, one for whom He intends only good.

It might mean other things as well:

That when we see a neighbor with whom we exchanged harsh words, we will approach in a spirit of reconciliation, knowing that God has already forgiven the part we played in that tense exchange.

That when we enter into prayer, we will do it knowing that we are fully and completely accepted—that God isn't going to bring our past up to us again.

That (gulp) we can extend that same grace to others—to the friend who spread a rumor about us, to the coworker who wrongfully blamed us for a failed project, to the church leader who abused our trust, or to the child who cheated us. God has forgiven us so much, and He has cast our sins so far away that they will never be remembered again. Knowing this, we can release others as well.

God, thank you for forgiveness. May we live in it every day.

Innocent of Charges | Stephen Willis

"Be kind and compassionate to one another, forgiving each other, just as in Christ God forgave you." –Ephesians 4:32

Sadly, conflict inside the family and within the relationships that matter most to us is more common than we want to admit. Much of my time as a local pastor is spent helping to reunite people who are supposed to be living together under the bond of peace. It never ceases to amaze me how differently each person involved in the conflict often sees the details. The temptation for people found in such a stalemate is to proclaim, "I am in the right and I have done nothing wrong."

It is in times like this that I challenge people to consider the details of their relationship with Jesus and the foundation of the gospel message itself. As people who have been adopted as children of God and welcomed into His household, we must see relationships through the lens of the gospel message. What does this mean? It means that we failed the test, while Jesus came along and aced it. We were locked in our personal prisons of sin and Jesus released us. We had a debt load that was impossible to carry but He came and canceled it. There was only one who lived who was innocent of the charges, and we are not it. Yes, we need forgiveness, and we also are in need to forgive.

Have you been hurt by someone? I think we all have. Is God calling us to remain in situations that are dangerous or hurtful to us? Probably not. However, He has called us to make forgiveness a priority in our lives, even when it is hard. Why? Because our willingness to forgive is likely more about us than it is about the person we are forgiving. Nelson Mandela proclaimed, "Not forgiving someone is like drinking poison and expecting the other person to die." With this truth in mind, let us call upon His Spirit to free us from unforgiveness. I know that we can do it with His help, and I know that as a result, our lives can testify to the miracle message of the gospel.

Prayer: Lord Jesus, help me through your Spirit to be a person who is actively working to forgive and to be forgiven. May my life exemplify the gospel.

Do You Really Love Me? | Jonny Bailey

"If you [really] love Me, you will keep and obey My commandments." –John 14:15

Why would Jesus make this proclamation? Here's some context:
Often in Scripture, God invites us to imagine our relationship with Him as a marriage (Revelation 19:7-9; Isaiah 54:5). In a healthy marriage, there are things that you do and don't do after you have taken the vows. Our relationship to Christ is meant to be even stronger than an earthly marriage. Yet we generally do not give it such reverence.

Try to recall times and places in your life where you have not let God enter. Jesus does not want to just be Savior, but Lord in your life. If we want to really love God, we must follow His ways, His character, and His commands. Just like in a marriage, living in relationship with God is not a one-time decision, but a willful decision to work out our vows daily.

Do you love the Lord with all your heart, soul, strength, and mind (Luke 10:27)? Ask God to search you (Psalm 139:23-24) and find the places where you can better obey this command. For example, do you love your neighbor as Christ loves you? Jesus positions Himself with forgiveness and restoration towards us, and in relating properly to others around us, we affirm our vows to Christ. Do we seek restoration with the people with whom we find ourselves in conflict (Matt. 5:44)?

Take time now and ask the Holy Spirit to make known the areas where you can be in more complete obedience to Him. Ask Jesus to forgive you, and ask Him to fill you with the power to live a life that displays your love for Him in the way He asks.

SABBATH

A RHYTHM
OF REST

Whoever dwells in the shelter of the Most High

will rest in the shadow of the Almighty.

Psalm 91:1

Hope In the Midst of Failure | Carla Pollard

"Then began he to curse and to swear, saying, 'I know not the man.' And immediately the cock crew. And Peter remembered the word of Jesus, which said unto him, Before the cock crow, thou shalt deny me thrice. And he went out, and wept bitterly."
–Matthew 26:74-75

Peter hid as Jesus was laid in the tomb. Peter disowned knowing Jesus. He even cursed in denial as he warmed himself by the fire on the night Jesus was taken to be tried. Peter, the one with the fight-or-die attitude and the bold proclamations of an undying allegiance denied his association with the Lord. I'm certain Peter felt the profound weight of his failure and it broke him. But Peter had hope even in the midst of his failure.

Hope is still the answer for overcoming our faults and failures. We all experience times of failure, but the one thing that helps us wake up in the morning with renewed joy and strength is when we place our hope in Jesus, a living hope found in the grace of God through His Son.

This living hope is a testimony to the power of Christ to forgive our sins and transform our lives. It is through Jesus we find forgiveness and restoration. It is through Jesus we have new life and can experience victory over our failures. Our hope is bigger than any failures or problems we may face, even death. We can face our failures, say I'm sorry, and ask for forgiveness because our hope is not a "hope so" hope. Our hope is a "know so" hope—a biblical hope which is grounded in the anticipation and assurance of a future reality.

Are you losing hope over your failures and thinking things can never change? Trust Jesus. Our past failures can't be undone, but our future can be bright. Our failures are swallowed up in hope restored through our trust and faith in Christ today.

Abba Father, impart to us your grace and mercy so that we may experience this living hope which leads us to forgiveness, freedom, and transformation. Help us to know hope in a way that always brings us to Jesus when we fail and helps us to cling to your promises no matter what our circumstances may look like. Amen.

Coordinates | John Lawson

"The Lord himself goes before you and will be with you; he will never leave you nor forsake you. Do not be afraid; do not be discouraged." –Deuteronomy 31:10

If I'm in a small town or rural area, I enjoy wandering by foot or on my bike for the sole purpose of discovering something new and unfamiliar...getting lost, even if just for a few disconcerting moments. After all, if I can spot a familiar peak (or valley) or river or a sign for another town that I've only heard of, I can typically get back on track within minutes...if I'm ready to, that is.

Recently, I visited Nashville. I was blessed to have my wife with me, who has a better sense of direction than I. Yet we were out of our element; we are small town folks at heart. Within our first 36 hours, we had little sense of direction. We couldn't see the river. We couldn't see any mountains. Even if there was a landmark we should've been looking for, it would have been as unfamiliar as everything else we were experiencing. We were discovering, but we weren't "on mission," and for some reason, even Google kept changing its mind about where we were. We did not do all we had hoped to do—but hopefully next year's visit will be much different.

In your life, what is your intended destination? What map are you using (and do you know how to read it?)? Are you able to identify some landmarks, obstacles, and turns you were previously aware of? Which obstacles and turns, for better or worse, did you not see coming? Remember: Where you will be, where you want to be, and where God wants you to be aren't always clear indicators of where you are at the moment. It's ok. You can, in fact, still get there from here.

God is good and He knows every turn. And if He has called us, then He has gone before us and He has seen and can see what we're clueless about it. What we MUST remain sure of is who He is and that He loves us. Whether in the small town or in the deepest, darkest alleyway of the biggest city, you are seen and known and loved.

He is With You | January Marshall

"Even when I walk through the darkest valley, I will not be afraid, for you are close beside me. Your rod and your staff protect and comfort me. You prepare a feast for me in the presence of my enemies. You honor me by anointing my head with oil. My cup overflows with blessing." –Psalm 23:4-5

Psalm 23 comes to mind often due to its comforting prose and language. It is used at funerals and repeated in times of trial, struggle, and even opposition. If anyone had enemies and trials, David was certainly no stranger. Yet he knew God would take care of him as long as he remained faithful.

Psalm 23 does not mean we will not have struggles. It does not mean that people will not still disappoint or hurt us. What it does mean is this: Even through all that, God is preparing you for greatness, to fulfill your purpose and bless you. He does this in the midst of people who have hurt you, broken your spirit, and convinced you that you aren't worthy. Just sit and watch. It means that even in the darkest valley, He is there. Even when life doesn't make sense, He is there. Even when we stumble and make mistakes, He is still there. Even when we start to doubt Him or lose faith, He is still there, calming us, protecting us, and defending us all the days of our lives.

Prayer: Lord, You have promised to bless me even in times of pain, even in front of my enemies. When life becomes hard, Lord, and I begin to struggle, or when people hurt or disappoint me again, help me to continue to seek you. Help me to remain faithful and to hold onto the promise that you will never leave and will always have my back. In Jesus' name, Amen.

Crossing the Bar | Emily Heady

"We have this hope as an anchor for the soul, firm and secure." –Hebrews 6:19

My grandmother died when I was in graduate school. It was summer, and I got a call while I was working my summer job at an event photographer's. We photographed a lot of graduations, and we had a busy summer wedding season. I helped as I could with the photos—but more often, my role was to support the people whose loved ones were making transitions across the stage or at the front of the church.

Graduation is a crossing—the walk across the stage signals both an end and an entry into a new phase in life. So is marriage: a moment when two become one, making a new thing altogether.

At my grandmother's funeral, the minister read Alfred, Lord Tennyson's poem "Crossing the Bar." I have spent much of my life studying Victorian literature, so this is one of my favorites. I didn't know until that day that this was one of my grandmother's favorites, too. Tennyson speaks of death—crossing the bar— as a journey into deep waters, where a divinely appointed tide will carry him home. Once he has arrived, he says, he hopes to see his Pilot face to face.

Even though he sails by faith and not sight, the crossing he makes is ordained: God steers his ship. So also does He steer us all from one life phase to another, from one home to another. May we look with joyful anticipation to the day when we too will meet our Pilot.

Crossing the Bar
Sunset and evening star, And one clear call for me!
And may there be no moaning of the bar, When I put out to sea,
But such a tide as moving seems asleep, Too full for sound and foam,
When that which drew from out the boundless deep Turns again home.
Twilight and evening bell, And after that the dark!
And may there be no sadness of farewell, When I embark
For tho' from out our bourne of Time and Place The flood may bear me far,
I hope to see my Pilot face to face When I have crost the bar.
(Alfred, Lord Tennyson, 1889)

Pilot and God, please steer us safely through these deep waters until we meet you face to face. Amen.

Heaven Promised | Kerry Willis

"We are confident, yes, well pleased rather to be absent from the body and to be present with the Lord." –II Corinthians 5:8

My dad and I did lots of talking on the phone over the years. Especially when I became a pastor and moved away from our little, coastal, island home, I was ever thankful for a way of staying in regular touch with my dad's voice.

On Tuesday, August 19, 2014, in the late afternoon, I was looking towards the end of the second day of my sabbatical season when Dad and I had the blessing of catching up with one another on the phone. Dad had just come through a seven-month season of trusting God with cancer and chemotherapy. All of the most recent, post-cancer reports were the best we could expect — "all-clear." Yet, over the more recent few days, seemingly out of nowhere another "something" showed up to challenge Dad's health again. His left elbow and arm were really causing him pain and making his after chemo days even more full of fatigue than they already were.

As I listened to my dad share, his tenderness was inspirational to my eternal soul, as always. After about a half-hour of conversation, the topic turned to heaven. We discussed how we would all be together someday soon, in the nonstop, realized presence of Jesus, and enjoying a reunion with our loved ones who have gone on ahead of us.

Finally, Dad said he had made his mother—my Granny Margery—a promise on her death-bed. His promise was that he would see her one day again in our forever home. Instantly, these words just came out of my mouth as my tears began to flow: "Daddy, if you get to heaven before I do, please promise me you will come with Jesus to meet me when I make my arrival." He promised he would.

Prayer: Abba Father, my dad went to be in your forever presence on November 17, 2014. I hold onto these words of hope... "Heaven promised!" Amen.

Anticipation | Nan Jacobs

"The Lord will perfect that which concerns me; Your mercy, O Lord, endures forever..." –Psalm 138:8

Did you ever wake up in the middle of the night with your heart pounding and the acute awareness that something you eagerly anticipate—leaving on your dream vacation, getting married to your lifelong crush, or holding that first grandbaby—is really going to happen? My heart-pounding night actually took place when I woke up from a very real dream that will one day be my reality. Heaven, yes, HEAVEN! I woke up thinking, it is really going to happen to me!

The wonder of God's plan to create us and give us free will to choose what we want or what He knows to be best is awesome, but to know we will have to give an account for our choices can seem—at least at first—to be something else. I have made so many poor choices that I have often said, "I am the queen of bad choices, but I know the King who has redeemed each of them." In the dark times of regret, it is possible to see God's hand in the reshaping of our ways; though our actions have consequences, He can use each one as a jumping-off point to learn valuable life lessons. As today's verse reminds us, He will through His power perfect us and make us holy, working the sanctification process in us—making us ready for heaven.

I am grateful for God's mercy to me throughout my life and for what it promises about my future. My excitement motivates me to consider what obedience to His Spirit looks like in my daily life. I have learned that I cannot obey without surrendering my will to His—every single day. He is teaching me to live not in shame, that bad feeling that accompanies getting caught, but in repentance, which leads to obedience and the peace He promises. The choices we make daily contribute to the process of transformation, and when they align with the Holy Spirit it results in growth and Christlikeness—as well as joy, peace, and anticipation of what's to come. To a hurting world this can be very attractive! Not only do we anticipate heaven when we die, but we also show the world what it looks like here on Earth.

SABBATH

A RHYTHM
OF REST

[1] *Then I saw "a new heaven and a new earth,"[a]*

for the first heaven and the first earth had passed

away, and there was no longer any sea. [2] I saw the

Holy City, the new Jerusalem, coming down out of

heaven from God, prepared as a bride beautifully

dressed for her husband. [3] And I heard a loud voice

from the throne saying, "Look! God's dwelling place

is now among the people, and he will dwell with

them. They will be his people, and God himself will

be with them and be their God.

Revelation 21:1-3

Seeing Beyond the Veil | Emily Heady

"His head and hair were white like wool, as white as snow, and His eyes like a flame of fire; His feet were like fine brass, as if refined in a furnace, and His voice as the sound of many waters; He had in His right hand seven stars, out of His mouth went a sharp two-edged sword, and His countenance was like the sun shining in its strength. And when I saw Him, I fell at His feet as dead. But He laid His right hand on me, saying to me, 'Do not be afraid...'" –Revelation 1:14-17

The scene in the first chapter of Revelation is—without a doubt—terrifying. Interestingly, though, the writer John has seen it, or at least something like it, before. He was there, after all, when Jesus was transfigured before His disciples on the mountain. In that first scene, as in this last one, Jesus responds to His disciples' terror in the same way—by reassuring them.

During the first week of August, the Church celebrates the Feast of the Transfiguration. It is a time to reflect Jesus' full glory, which He graciously revealed to His chosen disciples on the mountain. Granted, the disciplines did know who Jesus was before that. Just a chapter before, Peter had said to Jesus, "You are the Christ, the Son of the Living God" (Matthew 16:16). Still, there is something different about knowing something because we have wrapped our heads around it and seeing it in the flesh. What a grace it is when Jesus lets us see directly into who He is!

Paul reminds us that "now, we see through a glass, darkly; but then face to face: now I know in part; but then shall I know even as also I am known" (I Corinthians 13:12). Jesus gave His disciples a glimpse of His glory, and it changed them forever. One day we will see Him as well. Until then, we can rest in knowing that He sees and knows us fully, and He loves us anyway. His message to us—don't be afraid—carries us through.

Jesus, thank you for knowing us fully and loving us still. As we see you more, may we love you more as well.

Know | Matthew Lesniak

"Behold, the days are coming, declares the LORD, when I will make a new covenant with the house of Israel and the house of Judah, not like the covenant that I made with their fathers on the day when I took them by the hand to bring them out of the land of Egypt, my covenant that they broke, though I was their husband, declares the LORD. For this is the covenant that I will make with the house of Israel after those days, declares the LORD: I will put my law within them, and I will write it on their hearts. And I will be their God, and they shall be my people. And no longer shall each one teach his neighbor and teach his brother, saying, 'Know the LORD,' for they shall all know me, from the least of them to the greatest, declares the LORD. For I will forgive their iniquity, and I will remember their sin no more. " –Jeremiah 31:31-34

Jesus is 100% human. He is also 100% God. Diving deeply into the mystery of the Incarnation is not the subject of this devotion, but the fact remains that we have a massive amount to learn about being human. This man, Jesus, walked on water, healed, appeared in rooms and to individuals instantly, and most of all truly forgave others. He was a person, a human, doing these things.
God's Word declares that we are being made more and more into the image of Jesus. Wow! Imagine being like that! We are going to grow, and we have so much more in store once we have arrived at our destination. Personally, I cannot wait to be truly human in Christ Jesus.

These lines in Jeremiah are such a comfort to me today because they promise the most important thing of all: that we will know God. I have always been a searcher. My interest and training in the sciences has fed a desire "to know." I look at nature and the world around me and ask, "How, why, when, what...?" God promise that we will know the best thing of all—Him: "For they shall all know me!" What questions could be left after that? Every question, riddle, event, inquiry, disappointment resolved. The meaning not simply revealed but understood. We will KNOW GOD!

Today, bask in the promise of Jeremiah 31.

Understanding the Identity of Jesus | Torrie Slaughter

"And the Word became flesh and dwelt among us, and we beheld His glory, the glory as of the only begotten of the Father, full of grace and truth." –John 1:14

As believers, we must clearly understand who Jesus Christ is and what He accomplished for us. John chapter 1 is a powerful and compelling opening to the gospel of John, where we are introduced to the person and work of Jesus Christ.

The opening verses of John 1 give us a clear understanding of Jesus' divine identity. John affirms that Jesus was with God from the beginning and that He is, in fact, God Himself. This assertion is critical to our faith because it confirms that Jesus is not just a good teacher or a prophet but is God Himself.

John continues to reveal Jesus' identity by stating that "the Word became flesh and dwelt among us" (John 1:14). Jesus is fully God and fully human. As human beings, we can relate to Jesus and understand His experiences. At the same time, as God, Jesus can redeem us from our sins and offer us eternal life.

John the Baptist also plays a vital role in affirming the identity of Jesus, saying, "Behold, the Lamb of God, who takes away the sin of the world" (John 1:29). This statement indicates that Jesus is the Savior of the world who came to take away the sins of humanity and reconcile us to God.

John chapter 1 is a beautiful and powerful passage that affirms Jesus' divine identity as the Son of God and our Savior. It tells us that Jesus is the Word with God and that He came to Earth as a human being to redeem us from sin and reconcile us to God. This truth should fill us with awe and wonder, and we should strive to live our lives in light of it.

Let us hold fast to this truth as we live for His glory. May we be reminded that Jesus is not just a good teacher or a prophet but is God Himself who came to save us from our sins. May we continually seek to know Him more and share His love with those around us.

The Same Power | Gary O'Shell

"The Spirit of God, who raised Jesus from the dead, lives in you. And just as God raised Christ Jesus from the dead, he will give life to your mortal bodies by this same Spirit living within you." –Romans 8:11

I heard a woman named Rebecca Morgan tell a powerful story recently. She was speaking of her recent participation in a 26-mile marathon run. She had trained and prepared for it, but it was a distance she had never run before. As she neared the 20-mile mark, she felt her strength waning and her body breaking down. She wanted to quit. Along that route was a young girl in a wheelchair. She held a sign that said, "The same power that raised Jesus from the dead lives in you." Rebecca was impacted by the power of that truth. She determined that she would trust in that power above and beyond how she felt or what her body sought to get her to do. By His strength, His resurrection power, she would finish the race.

What would happen in our lives if we could dare to believe that promise? What if we believed it speaks to our physical, emotional, and spiritual concerns, our circumstances and all the things in our lives that seem impossible? What would our lives look like if we could believe the truth that that infinite resurrection power is alive within all who believe and trust in Him? What wonders would we see? We would surely experience the truth of His promise that "we can do all things through Christ who strengthens us."

A young girl, physically confined to a wheelchair, lived above the confines of that wheelchair. Whatever we believe our limitations to be, real or imagined, in Christ we too can rise above them by the power of His risen life within us. We who are in Christ have been given that life. It remains for us to fully receive it. We then live in the power of a life that cannot be destroyed. The final enemy of all humans is death. For the people of God, that enemy has been fully conquered. The same power that raised Him from the dead lives in you. Can you believe that? Can you live that?

Absolute Promises | January Marshall

"'No!' Peter insisted. 'Even if I have to die with you, I will never deny you!' And all the other disciples vowed the same." –Matthew 26:35

"Always." "Never." Experts tell you not to use these words in a conflict—yet we use them. "You always do this." You never do that!" Think about the last time you heard one of them. Did you feel good? Was the statement even true? Now, think about the verse that opened this devotional—Peter's "never" statement. I am sure he wanted to believe he would never betray Jesus, but ultimately he did. He denied Him three times, and the other disciples? They ran away, too.

There are absolutes mentioned elsewhere in the Bible—promises of "always" and "never" made that are absolutely true and that are fulfilled by God Himself. He is the one who can actually fulfill the promise of each always and never that He speaks. In Deuteronomy 31:8, God promises to never leave or forsake us, and He has not. We have left Him a time or two. But He remains faithful to us. And in Matthew 28:18-20, as Jesus is giving the disciples the Great Commission to go out and make even more disciples, He is letting them know that even though He is leaving them, He is always with them, just as He is always with us. As we go throughout the world sharing the good news, He is always with us. We do not shine the light of His love alone. We do not suffer alone. His Spirit, His love, and His light always go before us, beside us, and behind us. This is an absolute we can count on. It is a never and an always that proves true each and every time.

Prayer: Lord, I have used absolutes in arguments to prove a point time and time again. I admit I have even used "never" and "always" to make promises to others, and unfortunately even let them down. For this I confess, and I ask forgiveness. Lord, You are the only one who can speak in these kinds of absolutes, as You are the only One who truly will keep the "always" and "never" promises You speak. May I be forever reminded of each and every one of the absolutes You speak. In Jesus name, Amen.

Praying Big Dreams | Carla Pollard

"Now unto him that is able to do exceeding abundantly above all that we ask or think, according to the power that worketh in us. Unto him be glory in the church by Christ Jesus throughout all ages, world without end. Amen." –Ephesians 3:20-21

What has God placed in your heart that you think is too big for you to accomplish? Do you have a dream deep inside? Are you afraid of your dream, thinking there is no way you could ever achieve it? Someone once said, "If your dream doesn't cause you to tremble, you're not dreaming big enough." When we have a God-inspired dream, He provides us with everything we need to accomplish it. He brings us what we need when we take those first bold steps in prayer and follow God's directions toward fulfilling that dream.

The apostle Paul reminds us of the amazing way God can answer our prayers. Paul has just prayed a big prayer for the church in Ephesus. God has given him great desires for that local church, and he is asking God for big things to happen in their hearts and lives. In Ephesians 3, Paul concludes this prayer with an exhortation of God's ability to respond above and beyond whatever we pray. These words which we have preserved in our Bibles show us how much God desires for us as we seek Him and believe in His ability to answer our prayers in big ways. When we embrace His ultimate purpose for our big dream and pray for His direction, God moves. The ultimate purpose, Paul writes, is for the glory of God.

Abba Father, I ask you to help free me from the fear of bold prayers and big dreams. Encourage my heart with your presence and grant me the vision you desire to pass through my life. Amen.

SABBATH

A RHYTHM
OF REST

3 And I heard a loud voice from the throne saying, "Look! God's dwelling place is now among the people, and he will dwell with them. They will be his people, and God himself will be with them and be their God. 4 'He will wipe every tear from their eyes. There will be no more death'[b] or mourning or crying or pain, for the old order of things has passed away."

Revelation 21:3-4

Living Sacrifice | Matthew S.E. Waggoner

"God helping you: Take your everyday, ordinary life—your sleeping, eating, going-to-work, and walking-around life—and place it before God as an offering." –Romans 12:1

Have you ever watched a movie and put yourself in the shoes of the starring actor or actress? What about listening to your favorite song while dreaming that you were the lead guitarist with a top hat shredding to your guitar solo? I suspect every person who has heard the beat drop from Phil Collins' "In the Air Tonight" has, at some point in their car, beat out that drum solo on every surface in the car.

My entire childhood, I remember dreaming of being famous in every movie or every music video I watched on MTV. I wanted to be extraordinary so badly that I would put a headband on like Rambo or turn my pants backwards like Kris Kross singing "Mac Daddy." The problem? I'm just ordinary.

I have no special musical abilities, nor do I have any special acting skills. But that is just what God wants—us, however we are! You and I do not need to be extraordinary people to be living sacrifices, but we must be willing to surrender to God in our ordinary lives. In the process, we get to witness God moving on the front lines in our day-to-day interactions. We get to give Him our ordinary sleeping, eating, going to work, and walking around lives as a sacrifice.

But what does it mean to be a living sacrifice? It means laying down our lives for the sake of others and for the glory of God. God uses ordinary lives just as much as He uses extraordinary lives. Think about this for a moment: Just as God can use an extraordinary life (like the life of a famous person) to reach more people, you and I who live ordinary lives have the privilege of living for God every day and seeing the Spirit impact people right in our local communities. Ordinary people just like you and I are being baptized and made alive in Christ! Ordinary people are serving as ushers and kindergarten teachers. God loves and uses the ordinary!

Abba Father, help me today to see that you work in the ordinary life. Amen.

The Good Guy | Stephen Willis

"Here is a trustworthy saying that deserves full acceptance: Christ Jesus came into the world to save sinners—of whom I am the worst." –I Timothy 1:15

As a kid, I spent countless hours playing basketball outside. Often, the only company I had was the ball, the hoop, and my imagination. I can't tell you how many game-winning shots I made to win the championship. However, I can tell you that I was undefeated in every single game. How is that? Well, even if I missed the shot at the buzzer, I would always pretend that I was fouled. If I happened to miss the foul shots, I would pretend that there was a lane violation on the other team so that I could shoot again. You see, in my mind I was the good guy, and in my personal fantasy world the good guy always wins.

When I was a kid, this perspective regarding myself was absolutely fine. It made me happy, and it didn't hurt anyone that I went undefeated in my make-believe games. However, if we carry this perspective over into our adult spiritual lives, it can be extremely dangerous. Brace yourself for this truth: You aren't the good guy in the story. No matter how hard you try to be good we are informed by Isaiah that "all our righteous acts are like filthy rags" (Isaiah 64:6).

In the world today, many people have the false assumption that their goodness will guarantee them eternal life. They come to this conclusion by comparing their lives to others'. This is the big mistake. As we understand the gospel, we realize that the standard isn't other people. The standard is Jesus Christ Himself. Paul proclaims, "Christ Jesus came into the world to save sinners—of whom I am the worst." What do we surmise from this one text? There is only room for one good guy in the story, and we aren't it. That position is reserved for Jesus Christ alone.

Prayer: Lord Jesus, you are the "good guy" in our story. Thank you for coming to Earth and saving us from our sin. As a result of your sacrifice may we offer our lives as living sacrifices. Help us, LORD, to release our old identities as sinners and embrace our new positions as your sons and daughters.

Have We | Gary O'Shell

"Mary Magdalene found the disciples and told them, 'I have seen the Lord!' Then she gave them his message." –John 20:18

"We talk about the resurrection, but have we seen the Lord?" –Vance Havner

After Mary Magdalene's wondrous encounter with the risen Christ, she reported to His disciples, "I have seen the Lord!" We can only imagine the emotional, mental, and spiritual state of the disciples; they were depressed, discouraged, and fearful. They also had surely been talking about His words about His death not being final, and His promise that they would see Him again. They didn't understand all that was involved in that, or what His resurrection would look like, or if it was even possible. Now, Mary was with them and proclaiming that she had indeed seen Him.

With this announcement, a whole new level of conversation must have arisen: excitement, hope, joy...as well as doubt and even unbelief at the report of His resurrection. However, all that they were talking about was just that—talk. None of them had seen and experienced Him, their risen Lord. Only Mary had. That's where we get to Havner's question, and it's a timely one. In His Church, do we just talk about His resurrection, about our risen Lord, or have we actually seen and experienced Him?

Only those who truly have can understand how to answer that question. To believe upon Him is to have the eyes of a living faith. To believe upon Him opens the door to experience Him and, in a very spiritual way, to see Him. We know He's real. We know He's risen. We know that He's alive. With our eyes of faith, we see the one who is invisible, and we hear His whispers into our hearts and spirits. If you've only heard the report and have talked about what you've heard but never stepped out in faith with a heart yearning to experience Him, then your experience of the risen Lord remains little more than talk. He wants to be seen and experienced. He wants us, you and me, to see and experience Him. Have you? Do you want to not merely speak of Him, but see and experience Him? You can and will when your talk turns into faith. Are you ready to really see and experience the risen Christ?

The Great High Priest | Brian Marker

"Therefore, since we have a great high priest who has ascended into heaven, Jesus the Son of God, let us hold firmly to the faith we profess. For we do not have a high priest who is unable to empathize with our weaknesses, but we have one who has been tempted in every way, just as we are—yet he did not sin. Let us then approach God's throne of grace with confidence, so that we may receive mercy and find grace to help us in our time of need." –Hebrews 4:14-16

Are you someone who deals with impostor syndrome? You know...that feeling of self-doubt that makes you question if you are good enough or spiritual enough to be in a leadership role? Sadly, this feeling has become more and more prevalent in recent times. For whatever reason, we put this pressure on ourselves never to make a mistake or fall short. We try so hard to be perfect or an expert in our field that we miss what God has for us right now. We end up listening to lies from the enemy instead of the truth. The truth is, we aren't going to be perfect. But we are going to continue to mature as we grow closer to God every day!

I wish I could say I wasn't one of those people, but I often put this pressure on myself as a newly-licensed pastor. Do I know everything I need to know? If people knew that I was tempted or I fell short, what would they think of me? Would I lose all credibility? I have so much more to learn... Am I ready? Do I have what it takes?

Good news, friends...our Lord and Savior is the Great High Priest! Read Hebrews 4:14-16 again and let it sink in. He has been there too!

Jesus empathizes with our weakness! He was tempted just like we are! Instead of having a spirit of uncertainty and doubt, I challenge you (and myself) to approach God's throne with confidence. Receive that mercy and grace when you are feeling that doubt well up inside you. When we firmly hold to the faith that we profess, we get to live in the freedom and authority of someone who only has to worry about the opinion of one individual: Jesus.

Not Enough | Jenn McCamant

"Brothers and sisters, think of what you were when you were called. Not many of you were wise by human standards; not many were influential; not many were of noble birth. But God chose the foolish things of the world to shame the wise; God chose the weak things of the world to shame the strong." –I Corinthians 1:26-27

I am a runner. I've always been athletic, but in my adult years, longer distance running has become a passion of mine. It is part of my quiet time. I love to run outside on a local rail trail—just me and the Lord. However, there are days that the weather doesn't cooperate and I find myself on our family's treadmill. Don't get me wrong, I am grateful for an indoor place to run, but it doesn't compare to running outdoors. Time and miles drag as I run in place staring at the cold, gray cement walls in my dark basement and get nowhere.

For much of my life I've found myself on a similar treadmill. I'll call it the "Not Enough Treadmill." I've always found myself driven to succeed, to try and be the best, though I'd find myself falling short time and time again. No matter how hard I'd try, as I looked at the people around me and considered the world's standards, I'd find myself not enough: not influential enough, not trendy enough, not beautiful enough, not smart enough, not talented enough… the list of "not enoughs" went on and on.

For many years those "not enoughs" paralyzed me, especially as I found myself in places of leadership. I would avoid situations, fail to try new things, and skirt certain social interactions because I felt inferior or unqualified, or because I feared I wouldn't measure up to others' expectations.

Ironically, I was allowing the very thing God was looking for to hinder me. God was calling me to embrace my "not enough." In God's kingdom, weakness is strength and foolishness is wisdom. It's in the areas that I am weak and foolish, the very areas where I am not enough, that God's power and wisdom can work. I truly am not enough—but Christ in me is enough.

Prayer: Lord, it seems strange to delight in my weaknesses like Paul. However, I thank you because your power is made perfect in my weakness.

No Response | Chad Moler

"My grace is all you need. My power works best in weakness." –II Corinthians 12:9

When I was younger, I would wonder if my prayers would make it to God's ears. I mostly believed that they would, but there were times I wondered if they would make it beyond my ceiling. That worry was further bolstered by feeling like my prayers were often not answered. One thing would lead to another, and I would start to question whether I prayed the right way, prayed hard enough, prayed loud enough. All the usual doubts started to creep in.

As an adult, praying can be complicated. Some may feel hesitant and view their prayers as bothersome to God, like He has better things to do. Others may pray out of obligation, and at the same time doubt that it will do any good because they have never witnessed a response.

C.S. Lewis struggled with this same feeling. But he viewed it this way:"I know now, Lord, why you utter no answer. You are yourself the answer. Before your face questions die away. What other answer would suffice?"[1]
How often do we pray in this way, not praying solely about an issue, but with the acknowledgment that God Himself is the answer? When Paul prayed for God to take away the thorn in his side that plagued him, God said, "My grace is all you need." In other words, He reminded Paul that He was enough. Do we really believe this?

I think sometimes we miss that. We become so hyper-focused on taking our problems to God, laying them at His feet and expecting that He will fix everything, that we miss the significance of Paul's statement. God is enough.

Whatever you are bringing to the feet of Jesus, do so with the understanding that He Himself is the answer to our problems, and that His power works best in our weakest moments.

Father, help us to remember that you want to hear from your children and that your grace is sufficient for every one of the concerns that we carry. Amen!

———

1 Lewis, C.S. *Till We Have Faces: A Myth Retold.* 1956. New York: HarperOne, 2017.

SABBATH

A RHYTHM
OF REST

Yes, my soul, find rest in God; my hope comes from him.

Psalm 62:5

You and Your Gift | Deirdra Jones

"This is why I remind you to fan into flames the spiritual gift God gave you..."
–II Timothy 1:6

At the time of Timothy's ordination, he received special gifts of the Spirit to enable him to serve the Church. Perhaps Timothy felt like he was missing something to accomplish what God had called him to do, so Paul encouraged Timothy to hang on to the gifts that God had already given him. Paul reminded Timothy that he simply needed the courage and follow-through to use them.

Have you ever found yourself envying the gifts that others have? Perhaps it's not even what would be considered a "gift." Somehow, and maybe not even in a way you can put your finger on, there is just something about them....if you could just have the gift like that then maybe you would be better at [fill in the blank].

The truth is, God has given you exactly what you need be who He needs you to be and to do the task He has given you. Your responsibility is to walk in obedience and steward your gifts well, right now. You don't need to be anyone else or have what they have. He is building your faith and your testimony with who you are, your gifts, and your call. He wants to do something different in and through you—something different from what He has done or is doing in and through someone else.

God has gifted you specifically for right here, right now. He is building your story to reach people in a way that someone else's story cannot.

Warning: That twinge of envy...don't entertain it for a second. Our thoughts become attitudes that can become actions.

Father, help me to embrace who you made me to be, the gifts you have given me, and the capacity that you have given me to use them. If and when more is required to accomplish your call, I believe and trust that you will provide exactly what or who I need on time, every time. Amen.

"Y'all Come on, Go with Us" | Lynne Goodwin

"As each has received a gift, use it to serve one another, as good stewards of God's varied grace." –I Peter 4:10

My mother used to say to me, "You are just like your granny, and I pray for you every day." This was not meant as a good thing. There was much about Granny that was unpredictable, but she loved Jesus.

My granny may have been the only woman in her farming community that owned a car. She used it to give people rides to the store, the doctor, church.

I have been thinking about her generosity and how she looked at everything she had as a gift for someone else. She came from a poor place where there was never quite enough of the necessary things. I think that made her love a bit desperately. I think she wanted to save everyone she met.

As a child, I would ride along with her as she took people to church or on errands. When they got back home, there was always the chatting that happens in driveways; she never hurried off. The last thing she would say as they opened the car door was, "Y'all come on, go with us."

This was met with, "Thanks, but I've got to get dinner started," or "Maybe, another time." I don't remember anyone accepting her offer. Maybe they just saw it as a reflex. But I think it was a little gift, to let people know that they were welcome in her life, not just her car.

As an adult, I have had more opportunities than my granny did. I have more to give, but I wonder if I give as well. I give money; she offered herself. As a woman with few resources, she used what she had to love people in practical ways: a ride, a visit, a meal...I saw it all the time, so I didn't understand that it was special.

But now I understand. She was offering the ministry of presence. She would probably have called it "company." Her willingness to be with people was Jesus shining out of her, loving whoever she was with right then.

I miss my granny. There was more that I could have learned from her, but I am pleased to consider that I could still grow up to be like her.

His Name | Stephen Willis

"Then they said, 'Come, let us build ourselves a city, with a tower that reaches to the heavens, so that we may make a name for ourselves.'" –Genesis 11:4

The fall of man is recorded in Genesis three. As you move into chapter four and the chapters that follow, you'll see just how sizable of a fall it was, and that the heart of man apart from God is a pathetic thing.

In Genesis 11, we see humanity build its first city which would include the first ever tower construction project. The ingenuity of our predecessors is impressive: They continued to improve on their ability to design and execute a building project on a larger scale. However, the impressiveness of their activity is significantly impacted when you consider their motive. Why did they build the tower? Did they do it so that they could get closer to the stars? Was it to be able to see enemy armies? Was it to maximize the land that they were given? No, none of these had anything to do with their motive. The Holy Scripture is clear that their motive was "to make a name for themselves." That's it?

The first ever recorded city was built by those who wanted to "make a name for themselves." Some things never change. A great majority of those who are moving into urban areas still have the same motivation. Many years ago, Frank Sinatra sang about it. In his hit song "New York, New York" he proclaimed,

"I want to wake up in a city that doesn't sleep
And find I'm king of the hill
Top of the heap."

However, we also must know that this temptation isn't just for those in the urban jungle. The temptation is alive and well for rural folk as well. I don't live in a major city, but If I spend any time at all entertaining my own desires instead of the Spirit, I find myself also longing to be "king of the hill, top of the heap."

As God's people, let us rediscover that meaning is found in promoting the name of Jesus. When our activities have this motive, we discover the joy that leads us and others to eternal priorities and life.

Pray with me: Lord Jesus, help me to decrease that you may increase.

Glorify Him Alone | Lisa Willis

"For since the creation of the world God's invisible qualities—his eternal power and divine nature—have been clearly seen, being understood from what has been made, so that people are without excuse. For although they knew God, they neither glorified him as God nor gave thanks to him, but their thinking became futile and their foolish hearts were darkened. Although they claimed to be wise, they became fools and exchanged the glory of the immortal God for images made to look like a mortal human being and birds and animals and reptiles. Therefore God gave them over in the sinful desires of their hearts to sexual impurity for the degrading of their bodies with one another. They exchanged the truth about God for a lie, and worshiped and served created things rather than the Creator—who is forever praised. Amen." –Romans 1:20-25

To know God and to glorify God are separate things. We can know God and still live to glorify ourselves and our own desires instead of the one who deserves it.

As we read Romans 1:20-32, we understand that God's character and reality are revealed to us "without excuse." Many—including us—who know God have chosen not to glorify Him or give thanks to Him, and so have become futile thinkers with darkened hearts. We have exchanged the glory of the immortal God for idols (entertainment, comfort, food, money, status). Because of this, God has given us over to our sinful desires because we have exchanged the truth of God for a lie and worshiped created things instead of the Creator. What is the lie? The lie is that any of these idols in our lives will satisfy us the way that our Father will.

So, what is the solution?

Clearly, if we are glorifying God and giving thanks to Him through worship, prayer, time in the Word, and thanksgiving, then we will not easily turn to these sinful desires and idols because we will recognize the truth that is in Christ.

Why don't we start a list of things that we are thankful for and reread it and add to it each day? I believe that we will become more attuned to Him about what we should listen to, watch, say, and read. Our hearts will therefore be guarded against anything that does not glorify Him.

Unbearable Hunger | Chad Moler

"Esau said to Jacob, 'I'm starved! Give me some of that red stew!'" –Genesis 25:30

Have you ever been so hungry that you have thought your stomach was going to eat itself? I mean, have you felt the type of hunger that not even a famous candy bar would satisfy? Usually, it happens on those days when you forget to eat breakfast and start to get a headache by lunch—but you are too busy and work through lunch and get home just in time to eat dinner, starved beyond belief.

In the passage from Genesis, Esau famously came home from a long day of hunting to the smell of freshly made lentil stew. It smelled so good that he sold his birthright to his younger brother Jacob, giving up what was culturally and rightfully his for a bowl of soup. Esau settled. Even though the promise before him was immense and would give him unimaginable and lasting security, he settled for temporary security, a good feeling that would come right then.

St. Augustine famously said, "You have made us for Yourself and our hearts are restless until they find their rest in Thee."[1]

We all have inside of us an unbearable hunger inside that causes us to search for more, to want to do more. Spiritually, we do the activities we think we are supposed to do, like going to church, reading our Bibles, and singing songs, all in hopes that it will get us through to the next Sunday. Sometimes it does, but often it does not last. How many times in the middle of the week are we satisfying our small hunger pangs with a figurative mess of pottage? We feel them constantly, and we settle for the little things that really do not satisfy.

Yet our creator desires to walk daily with us in close intimacy; it is in that activity that we will find satisfactions for our hearts' deepest longings. And satisfying that deepest longing of our soul, all the smaller hunger pangs will seem so much less important as we rest content in God.

Father, allow me to understand that my deepest longing is to be in sweet communion with you. You are the one who will satisfy all my hungers. Amen.

---

1 St. Augustine. *Confessions*. New York: Penguin, 1979.

The Outsiders | Caleb Atkins

"He grew up before him like a tender shoot, and like a root out of dry ground.
He had no beauty or majesty to attract us to him, nothing in his appearance that we
should desire him." -Isaiah 53:2

I used to daydream about being a rock star—for Jesus, of course. I just knew that my favorite band would somehow fall on hard times and miraculously need a new bass player. As I waited for the phone to ring, I would rehearse my moves. I knew I would change the world (for Christ) through fame and bright lights. I could just hear the crowd chanting my name... I mean Jesus' name.

The call never came.

The dream remained. But the paradigm began to shift.

As I continued to learn about Jesus I started to become familiar with the ordinary life of the most extraordinary man history has ever known.

Questions like "Can anything good come out of Nazareth?" started to resonate with me in a new way. The Jesus I was learning to love looked a lot more grassroots than glamorous. Here was one who had no beauty or majesty or obvious outward attraction, yet He was the most compelling figure I could ever imagine.

To follow Jesus meant to embody the ordinary.

The bio of Jesus' band—if I were to write it—would say first that they are a crew of misfits.

How about mother Mary? She was just a young, innocent teenager, pregnant out of wedlock. Then there's blue-collared, work-hardened Peter. What about the widow who empties her pockets of the last two pennies she owns? Or how about the smelly shepherds who must have tracked all kinds of sheep dung into the stable as they rushed to meet the Messiah? What a group of rag-tag, rough-and-tumble, kingdom-minded ordinaries! His beloved. The outsiders.

I'm still waiting for that call. But for now, I'm learning to look a little more ordinary, like Jesus.

SABBATH

A RHYTHM
OF REST

Ascribe to the Lord the glory due his name; bring an offering and come before him. Worship the Lord in the splendor of his holiness.

1 Chronicles 16:29

Walk with God - Part One | Mike Lyle

"Now there is in Jerusalem near the Sheep Gate a pool, which in Aramaic is called Bethesda and which is surrounded by five covered colonnades. Here a great number of disabled people used to lie—the blind, the lame, the paralyzed. One who was there had been an invalid for thirty-eight years. When Jesus saw him lying there and learned that he had been in this condition for a long time, he asked him, 'Do you want to get well?' 'Sir,' the invalid replied, 'I have no one to help me into the pool when the water is stirred. While I am trying to get in, someone else goes down ahead of me.' Then Jesus said to him, 'Get up! Pick up your mat and walk.' At once the man was cured; he picked up his mat and walked." –John 5:2-10

Because we are told specifically where this story takes place, we can assume that this setting holds some significance. What could John be saying by telling us Jesus healed a paralyzed man outside the sheep gate where lambs were brought in for the sacrifice?

This is one of the only miracles where nobody asks Jesus for help. Jesus simply spots this man and goes to him to provide the healing he needed. Jesus, as the sacrificial Lamb of God, enters creation without being asked. And He does it at the sheep gate—making a small sacrifice that prefigures His bigger one later. God loves the world so much that He sends His only Son to lay down His life for it. When we are paralyzed and hopeless, when we cannot walk with God and we're leaning on all the wrong things to help us get through life, God breaks in and provides a way to walk. Through His loving sacrifice, God enables us to walk with Him before we even ask for it; while we were still sinners, Christ died for us.

We may have areas of our lives that seem lame. These areas usually take on an aura of shame; however, this story reminds us that these sorts of blemishes call out to God and invite Him to approach. Don't be afraid of your areas of apparent paralysis, because it is through these areas that God enters and invites you to walk. In your weakness, God is made strong.

Where do you feel inept with God? Where are you struggling? Don't hide from those things anymore. Enter that struggle and hear God's invitation to walk.

Walk with God - Part Two | Mike Lyle

"Now there is in Jerusalem near the Sheep Gate a pool, which in Aramaic is called Bethesda and which is surrounded by five covered colonnades. Here a great number of disabled people used to lie—the blind, the lame, the paralyzed. One who was there had been an invalid for thirty-eight years. When Jesus saw him lying there and learned that he had been in this condition for a long time, he asked him, 'Do you want to get well?'" –John 5:2-6

We should notice that this man isn't lying in front of the Temple (the place of religion) and Jesus is seemingly ignoring the expectations of Sabbath-keeping (the time of religion). This miracle is happening in a different time and place.

Could it be that what the paralyzed man is looking for isn't found in the religious system? Perhaps the answer for a paralyzed life is not found in religion, but in relationship. Religion might be able to tell us how we ought to walk, but in relationship, we are empowered.

We are told that the man sits outside a pool that is surrounded by five colonnades or porches. With John's writing style, we can be fairly confident that these porches represent something. Perhaps they represent the five books of Moses, which make up the Jewish books of law[1] (Bernard 225-35). These books are supposed to provide a way to walk with God, yet all around this "law" (or all around these five porches), we see paralyzed and broken people. Jesus doesn't wait to be invited; He enters the human paralysis and provides a way to walk. Jesus died so that we might walk.

Remember God loves you enough to go looking for you. Where have you been resting in something other than God's love as you walk with Him? Your Father is able to move you into movement. Take some time to allow your heart to commune with His. Ask to feel the love of the Father. Securely place your heart in the relationship of your loving Father.

---

1 Bernard. J.H. *A Critical and Exegetical Commentary on the Gospel According to St. John.* New York: Scribner's, 1929.

Walk with God - Part Three | Mike Lyle

"When Jesus saw him lying there and learned that he had been in this condition for a long time, he asked him, 'Do you want to get well?' 'Sir' the invalid replied, 'I have no one to help me into the pool when the water is stirred. While I am trying to get in, someone else goes down ahead of me.' Then Jesus said to him, 'Get up! Pick up your mat and walk.' At once the man was cured; he picked up his mat and walked." –John 5:6-9

Jesus asks this man what we might consider to be a strange question. Don't all sick people want to get well? Why would Jesus even have to ask? It's like asking, "Do you want a million dollars?" Who in their right mind would answer, "No, thank you"? However, the man's answer provides some insight to his heart and, I think, to ours.

This story is presented as a hopeless situation. The man has been paralyzed for a long time.

According to Haenchen, he likely "knows only one possibility [for healing],... the healing powers of the pool, and that possibility has eluded him repeatedly for many years"[1] (239-60). There is no solution to his problem—a fact the man is more than willing to let Jesus know about. I think this is why Jesus asked the question. He sees the hopelessness of the paralyzed man and is inviting him to hope again.

Perhaps you have encountered some seemingly hopeless situations, thrown your arms up, and approached life as a paralyzed person. But remember: Walking isn't very different from falling. To walk, you must fall from one foot only to be caught with the other. Moving forward requires letting go. In light of this, walking starts to look like surrender. This man is invited to surrender all other sources of potential healing and embrace the one source of true healing. Through this text, God might be pointing out areas in which you are paralyzed, hopeless, or standing still. Hear His invitation to walk—which kind of sounds like an invitation to surrender. This is why it's phrased as a question. Do you want to get well? It might cost you everything. But, then again, you just might start walking.

---

1 Haenchen, Ernst. *John: A Commentary on the Gospel of John*. Philadelphia: Fortress P, 1984.

Seeking God's Guidance: The Path to True Life | Torrie Slaughter

"There is a way that appears to be right, but in the end, it leads to death."
–Proverbs 14:12

When I was living life according to my own understanding and desires, I thought I had it all figured out, making decisions based on what seemed clear-cut and straightforward. Little did I know that I was about to learn a powerful lesson through the words of Proverbs 14:12.

One day, as I stumbled upon this verse, it struck me like a lightning bolt. It was a wake-up call, a nudge from God to seek His guidance in every aspect of my life. With newfound humility, I embarked on a journey of seeking God's wisdom. I started by setting aside intentional time for prayer and reflection, pouring out my heart to Him, and listening for His still, small voice. As I surrendered my desires and plans, I discovered the beauty of aligning myself with His will.

The Bible became my faithful companion, a wellspring of wisdom and truth. I immersed myself in its pages, meditating on the teachings and allowing them to shape my perspective. I sought guidance from trusted mentors and friends who walked closely with God, drawing from their experiences and insight.

As I opened my heart to God's leading, my life began to change in remarkable ways. Doors opened that I never could have imagined and opportunities unfolded before me. Sometimes, His guidance led me down unexpected paths, requiring sacrifices and choices that seemed daunting. Yet with every step, I witnessed His faithfulness and experienced His abundant blessings.

Through this journey, I discovered the beauty of active faith and a teachable spirit. I realized that seeking God's guidance was not a passive endeavor but required active participation. It meant embracing responsibility and intentionally aligning myself with His plan.

So, my friend, I encourage you to embark on your own journey of seeking God's guidance. Let go of the need to control every outcome and humbly surrender your desires to Him. Embrace the teachings of Proverbs 14:12 and trust that His plans for your life are far greater than anything you could imagine. You are not alone on this path; God is with you every step of the way.

Percentages for Christ | Stephen Willis

"Jesus said to him, 'No one who puts his hand to the plow and looks back is fit for the kingdom of God.'" -Luke 9:62

I recently saw that a high-profile baseball player was immediately benched by his coach after a key play. What did he do? He didn't give 100% running around third base. He got thrown out at the plate, and then he got taken from the game. In the press conference the coach essentially said, "No matter your name, there is a right way to play the game." (I like to rhyme.)

In a similar vein, E. Stanley Jones (missionary to India) presented a question that startled me and also stuck with me. He asked, [1]"Are we twenty-five, fifty, seventy-five, or one hundred percent Christians?" It is a penetrating question that I had never been asked.

In Luke 9, Jesus made it clear the sacrifice required for following Him. He warned the early disciples that He didn't even have a place to lay His head (Luke 9:58). Within the same text, He talked about the sacrifice of leaving family for the sake of the mission.

As I sit and write, I can't help but think about some of the things that I am tempted to hold onto and that decrease my percentage of Christian commitment. There is a war that wages within our flesh to play it safe and not surrender everything. In many ways, the longer we walk with God the more tempting this can become. Yet the call of God is to completely trust Him and in so doing completely surrender to His will.

Recently, I heard a worship leader pray this prayer: "Lord, take what you want and give what you give." I have adopted this prayer as my own. Each time that I feel a compulsion to put my trust in things that aren't the Father, it helps me submit and return to simply trusting Him. I haven't arrived, but it truly is my desire to round third base 100% committed to getting safely home.

Prayer: Lord, take what you want and give what you give. I need not test you. I simply should trust you.

----

1 Jones, E. Stanley. *Growing Spiritually: E. Stanley Jones*. Potomac, MD: The E. Stanley Jones Foundation, 2019.

Let God Do His Thing | January Marshall

"For just as rain and snow fall from heaven and do not return there without saturating the earth and making it germinate and sprout, and providing food to sow and food to eat, so my word that comes from my mouth will not return to me empty, but it will accomplish what I please and will prosper in what I send it to do." –Isaiah 55:10-11

In January, we anticipate snow in many parts of the world, but as it can also knock out power and cause other problems, we quickly find snow isn't always something we are equipped to handle. Some love it, some even hate it—and we may feel both at any given point in time. It's beautiful as it's falling but a pain to clean up and dangerous when it thaws and refreezes for days or weeks at a time. Then, when snow carries over into spring and damages our precious flower buds, we want it to melt right away so we can get back to business as usual.

Waiting is hard! We plant seeds for flowers and expect them to grow overnight—but growth takes time, as does the exodus of the long winter. And so does the process of change that comes when His word is sent. Spiritual growth is not an overnight process. It's not a light dusting of snow. Sprinkle the Word and all is good in a day? No, it takes time. But rest assured, if you sowed the seed and sent out His Word, God is continuing to work on the harvest. He's watering those plants, even in extreme conditions. Just give it time.

Prayer: Lord, I praise you for providing the "water" needed to continue to allow the harvest to grow, both in my life and the lives of those for whom I pray. Each time I make a request to you, do not leave me empty, but help me to remember your Word will not leave a void where it is sent. When it is shared, Lord, allow it to prosper and bring change in the lives willing and ready to hear it. Lord, I pray that those to whom I have shared your goodness, your mercy, and your Word may come to know you through my obedience in sharing your good news. Amen.

SABBATH

A RHYTHM
OF REST

Truly my soul finds rest in God;

my salvation comes from him.

Psalm 62:1

Willing One Thing - Part One | Emily Heady

"And Elijah came near to all the people and said, 'How long will you go limping between two different opinions? If the Lord is God, follow him; but if Baal, then follow him.'" –I Kings 18:21

As I write this, a chapel service that began over ten days ago at Asbury University is still in full swing. Why is this? Perhaps God chose to honor the sincere and single-minded confession, repentance, and seeking of Himself that He saw there.

The verse for today points out a fundamental human problem—if we seek God while we are also seeking other things, we end up limping. We have to choose. One of my favorite authors, Søren Kierkegaard, puts it this way: "If it be possible for a man to will the Good in truth, then he must be at one with himself in willing to renounce all double-mindedness"[1] (68). To choose one thing is not to choose another; to say "yes" to God is to say "no" to all the other competing things.

Granted, there are many good things worth wanting in the world. I want to sit in the sunshine with my dog on my lap. I want to retire before my health requires it so my husband and I can enjoy some time traveling. I want my children to flourish in their faith. I want God to be pleased with my labors, with the words I speak and the things I ponder. One thing I wanted in particular was to be able to travel to Asbury to participate in person in this outpouring of the Spirit.

Life didn't permit me to drive the seven hours to Wilmore, Kentucky. Yet as I prayed through my disappointment—a disappointment lessened, I have to admit, by the dog on my lap and a 65-degree February day—I was reminded of the fact that if we seek God, He will shape our desires so, as we go on our way, we will run towards Him.

Jesus, please help us to will one thing—for your kingdom to come. Amen.

---

1 Kierkegaard, Søren. *Purity of Heart Is To Will One Thing: Spiritual Preparation for the Office of Confession.* 1938. Trans. Douglas V. Steere. New York: Harper & Row, 1948.

Willing One Thing - Part Two | Emily Heady

"I am crucified with Christ; nevertheless I live; yet not I, but Christ lives in me. And the life which I now live in the flesh I live by the faith of the Son of God, who loved me, and gave himself for me." –Galatians 2:20

When I was in graduate school, my pastor at the Bloomington Free Methodist Church was a good and godly man named Mel Nead. He was a straight-laced and good-humored fellow, inclined more toward quiet discipleship training than hard-driving theology. So one day, when Mel began describing an experience from his seminary years with an edge in his voice and a level of passion that I found uncomfortable to witness, I sat up and took notice. To this day, it's the one sermon of his that I can remember point for point. Mel asked us, I recall, if we really wanted God. It's a good question. He asked us if we wanted God more than we wanted to be who we thought we were. Another good one—and not one that I found it easy to answer honestly.

Mel was a seminary student at Asbury in 1970 when the campus was experiencing a strong outpouring of the Spirit. He told us about being in the chapel, so overwhelmed by the presence of the Lord that he lost all track of time. As Mel narrated it, the presence of God felt so strong to him, so heavy and thick, that he thought he couldn't bear it any longer—but he also prayed that even if it killed him, God would increase. He wanted more God, and nothing but God.

Of course—and Mel Nead's testimony of total sanctification suggests that he knew this—as God fills us, we shrink. Surrendering turf we might think of as our own so that God's kingdom will increase is one version of what it means to die to self. Indeed, the self is the primary territory in which God is interested. He wants us, and to surrender is to be crucified with Christ. With each surrender, we drive the nails into our own hands; we nail ourselves to our crosses. Still: Though we are dead, yet do we live.

Jesus, help us to take up our crosses and follow you—no turning back, no turning back. Amen.

How's Your Memory? - Part One | Deb Huff

"Keep my commands and you will live; guard my teachings as the apple of your eye. Bind them on your fingers; write them on the table of your heart." –Proverbs 7:2-3

A beautiful, fifteen-year-old girl had just sung with the youth choir at her church. It was a lovely night of praise and worship. On the way home with her parents and brother, their car was struck by someone under the influence. While her brother received minor injuries, both parents were rushed to the hospital in serious condition. The girl suffered a fractured skull and severe brain injury. Medics flew her to a larger hospital in a nearby town, giving the family little hope for her survival. For the next several weeks, friends joined the family in a prayer vigil over her in a critical care unit.

The girl was in a coma for more than a month, and when she finally regained consciousness, the honor roll student couldn't remember what two plus two was. Yet, she could recite God's word! Every Bible verse she had ever memorized in the children's program at her church stayed with her and gave her strength and courage to fight what seemed like an unwinnable battle.

God instructs us to memorize Scripture. Through Solomon's words to the youth of his day, God tells us to "Keep my commands and you will live; guard my teachings as the apple of your eye" (Proverbs 7:2). If we keep God's commands, He will bless us maybe not with monetary gain, but with family, health, and a spirit of joy. The apple of the eye refers to the pupil of the eye that lets in light for us to see. Without the pupil, we cannot see and would live in darkness, void of the blessings of God.

How does this story end? Stay tuned.

How's Your Memory? - Part Two | Deb Huff

"Keep my commands and you will live; guard my teachings as the apple of your eye. Bind them on your fingers; write them on the table of your heart." –Proverbs 7:2-3

To get the imagery of what it means to bind Scripture on our fingers and write them on our hearts, we have to look at the tradition of Old Testament life where Scripture was copied and placed into little boxes, phylacteries, that were worn by Jewish men during morning prayers. One box was placed on the forehead and tied around the head, while the other was placed on the left arm. To draw attention to the verses inside, a leather strap from the case circled down the arm seven times and was wrapped seven times around the middle finger. The leather strap around the fingers would be a visible reminder of verses inside the box. Just imagine wearing a box on your forehead and one on your arm with the strap connected to your middle finger. Would that help you remember the words inside the box?

The last part of that verse says to write God's commands "on the table of your heart." We are to internalize those verses—not just memorize them so we can say them, but make them a part of who we are and a guiding light for how we live.

Joshua 1:8 makes the admonition a bit stronger: "Keep this Book of the Law always on your lips; meditate on it day and night, so that you may be careful to do everything written in it. Then you will be prosperous and successful." If this were talking about a television show, it would be a command for binge watching. In essence, this is a command to binge on Scripture. Meditate on it day and night.

Jen Barrick, the young woman who came through the coma and had to rebuild her life, did so with the strength and courage she received from her relationship with the Lord and the Scripture He had written on her heart so long ago. The accident occurred in 2006 and since then, she spends her days sharing God's Word wherever and whenever possible, working with her family in a ministry called Hope Out Loud. When she speaks to audiences those old familiar scriptures uplift and encourage others in their walk with the Lord.

Rivals | Gary O'Shell

"Your kingdom come, your will be done, on earth as it is in heaven." –Matthew 6:10

"When you ask the Kingdom of God to come, you ask for rival kingdoms to go." –Chris Tiegreen

I've a question for you and for me today. How many times have we, in some way or another, prayed for Matthew 6:10 to be our reality? I know in one group that I participate in, it's the way we close each time together. We pray for His kingdom to come. If we're sincere in that prayer, what happens to all the other kingdoms that we've allowed to secure a foothold in our hearts?

Our great problem is that I don't think we're all that anxious for our other kingdoms to go. We've grown fond of them, even fallen in love with them. We welcome His kingdom, but we don't want it to be our only kingdom. We feel, even though we'd never expressly say so, that there is room for His kingdom and others in our lives. Many others. Jesus said that we couldn't serve even two masters, but we feel we can find a way to manage not just two, but many.

Somewhere in our consciousness, we know that the Father does not share power, though we deceive ourselves into thinking He'll tolerate rivals to His Lordship. He will not, but we're very good at deluding ourselves into thinking that He will. But our deception goes deeper than we know. Our enemy, Satan, will tolerate no rivals as well, and since all other kingdoms are ultimately his kingdoms, the only one he will seek to destroy is the Father's. Therefore, our only choice is to renounce every kingdom but His, and then trust Him, through His Spirit, to eradicate their presence in our hearts. The only place this can happen is at the cross. It's the place where all rivals go to die. Have you, we, taken them there...to be crucified and die? Or do they—will they—live on? In whose kingdom do you abide?

Walk It Like We Talk It | January Marshall

"So practice and obey whatever they tell you, but do not follow their example. For they don't practice what they teach." –Matthew 23:3

"Do as I say, not as I do." Ever heard this statement before? If you have, I can imagine it was spoken to you as a child by adults who desired that you listen to them but who also didn't exactly do what they were asking you to do. We can probably even remember some people who fell into this category—those who told us what not to do, but then did the exact opposite.

The same was true in Jesus' day. Though He states it much differently, Jesus speaks in Matthew 23:3 about the Pharisees and makes a similar point. Teachers of the law, these Pharisees knew their stuff, but they didn't practice what they taught. Instead, they desired that others simply do what they said, but not what they did.

As Christ-followers, we are to be the opposite and are called to do what the Word says. However, we must ensure we do not do this for show, to make ourselves look righteous, or for mere lip service. As those who call Jesus our Savior, we are called to not only do what the Word says, but also to live it out in our lives. We are to be living examples of Jesus for those who do not know Him, living in such a way that we are a worthy example of Him for others to follow.

Prayer: Lord, I pray that I will not only practice and obey what Your word says, but that I will also be humble in the ways that I live Your commands out in my life. May I be a worthy example of Your love, mercy, grace, and forgiveness, as well as of holy living, so that others can know You through my daily walk and interactions. Lord, if I become like the Pharisees, merely obeying for show or praise, please correct this in me and steer me in the right direction. In Jesus' name, Amen.

SABBATH

A RHYTHM
OF REST

"Do not forget the covenant I have made with you,

and do not worship other gods. Rather, worship the

Lord your God; it is he who will deliver you from the

hand of all your enemies."

2 Kings 17:38-39

The Vote | Stephen Willis

"'We can't attack those people; they are stronger than we are.' And they spread among the Israelites a bad report about the land they had explored. They said, 'The land we explored devours those living in it. All the people we saw there are of great size.'"
–Numbers 13:32-33

One of the saddest moments in the history of God's people is when His people decided that the will of God could be voted on. It is hard to believe that God Himself could lose a vote, but He did. It wasn't even close: 10-2. The people of God, overwhelmed by the size of the opposition, lost sight of the size of their God. The people forgot that God is a promise keeper. God often uses the faithfulness of His people to help deliver on His promises. However, in this instance (like many), although God was willing to fulfill His end of the bargain, His people fell short by doubting what He promised. The obstacles before them just seemed too big.

What was the result? An entire generation of people found themselves walking in a spiritual circle in the midst of the desert for forty years. I once heard Dr. Gustavo Crocker proclaim, [1]"Spiritual circles lead to downward spirals away from God." Think about it. When the people of God become entrenched in the old, fearful to advance because of the possibility of failure, and ignore the call of God to advance forward, they have no choice but to go in circles. These spiritual circles negatively affect their relationship with God and hinder their ability to move into the Promised Land. In many ways, the journey of faith is itself the real destination, as we walk in relationship with God with steps of faith that require and reveal His provision.

I for sure don't want to identify with the majority in Numbers 13! Rather, sign me up with Caleb and Joshua who proclaimed, "We should go up and take possession of the land, for we can certainly do it" (Numbers 13:30). How would things be different if we prayed prayers, dreamed dreams, and acted with faith that matched the size of the God we serve?

Pray with me: Lord Jesus, help us to never take a vote on the promises you have made. Help us to trust in your provision.

---

1 Virginia District Assembly, 2023.

Jesus Is the Smartest Person Who Ever Lived | Mike Lyle

"Therefore everyone who hears these words of mine and puts them into practice is like a wise man who built his house on the rock. The rain came down, the streams rose, and the winds blew and beat against that house; yet it did not fall, because it had its foundation on the rock...When Jesus had finished saying these things, the crowds were amazed at his teaching, because he taught as one who had authority, and not as their teachers of the law." –Matthew 7:24, 28-29

Recently, I was talking to a woman who had been wronged by someone and was very upset. She was so angry that she wanted to take this person to court and sue them for all they're worth. After making this comment she quickly added, "I know Jesus would not do that, but this is not Jesus, this is me...I'm doing this." At that moment, I realized there is a major disconnect between the way of Jesus and the way people often live their daily lives. This woman was essentially saying that what Jesus would or would not do had no relevance for her "real" life.

Dallas Willard sheds some light on this kind of mentality in The Divine Conspiracy. He explains how Jesus is actually the "smartest man who ever lived...[and] knows the truth about our lives and the universe"[1] (Willard 94). The problem is that most of us do not believe this to be true about Jesus. For most of my life, I lived like the woman above; for me, Jesus was "hardly conscious...looked on as a mere icon, a wraithlike semblance of a man, fit for the role of a sacrificial lamb or alienated social critic" (134). It isn't until we believe that Jesus knows and "conveys an understanding of human life that actually works" that we will listen to Him (136).

Do you see Jesus as the smartest person who ever lived or do you think of Him as far removed from your actual life? What would change if you believed He was better at your job than you are; or was better at parenting than you are; or better at being married than you? He knows how to live. This should give us some confidence in living life His way and hearing Him as a teacher who has authority.

---

1 Willard, Dallas. *The Divine Conspiracy*. New York: HarperSanFrancisco, 1998.

"Oh, to Vex Me" | Emily Heady

"I do not understand what I do. For what I want to do I do not do, but what I hate I do. And if I do what I do not want to do, I agree that the law is good. As it is, it is no longer I myself who do it, but it is sin living in me.... For I have the desire to do what is good, but I cannot carry it out. For I do not do the good I want to do, but the evil I do not want to do—this I keep on doing." –Romans 7:15-19

It is clear from John Donne's nineteenth and last Holy Sonnet that he has spent some time living with Paul—he, like Paul, offers a vivid description of the constant back-and-forth, the frustrating self-division that we feel as the two natures inside of us go to war.

He feels that he is wavering and inconstant—though with some good habits (lines 1-3). He cannot keep his promises; his contrite repentance is sometimes as much a slave to his carnal desires as his more base affections (lines 3-6). His godliness goes hot and cold, prayerful and wordless, everywhere and nowhere. Spirituality comes on him at times like a virus—it overtakes him, then is suddenly gone (lines 12-13).

Donne, however, knows that there is one emotion and practice that truly does draw him near to God: reverence, or holy fear. If he can only imagine a right relationship between his small self and God's infinity, he knows the rest will fall into place.

Oh, to vex me, contraries meet in one:
Inconstancy unnaturally hath begot
A constant habit; that when I would not
I change in vows, and in devotions.
As humorous is my contrition
As my profane Love, and as soon forgot:
As riddlingly distemper'd, cold and hot,
As praying, as mute; as infinite, as none.
I durst not view heaven yesterday; and to day
In prayers, and flattering speeches I court God:
Tomorrow I quake with true fear of his rod.
So my devout fits come and go away
Like a fantastic Ague: save that here
Those are my best days, when I shake with fear.

Jesus, please inspire us with holy fear. May our reverence for you help to shape and unify our will.

God's Governance | Stephen Willis

"Of the greatness of His government and peace there will be no end." –Isaiah 9:7

A significant amount of my undergraduate studies focused on government and economics. Before entering full-time pastoral ministry, I taught both subjects in high school. It doesn't take a college degree to know that both our history books and our current headlines are filled with examples of how governments have failed the very people they were called to govern. I don't think we should be shocked by these facts simply because we know that these governments are run by sinful and flawed people.

However, have you ever considered the governance of God? Unlike the temporary governments that have limits and failings, God governs perfectly. As a part of His perfect governance, God gives us the choice to allow Him to govern us. He won't advance into our hearts and lives with military aggression or force. He gives us the option because His rule over us has much more to do with love than control. As one who has welcomed the governance of God into my own life, I have discovered that the only role I play in my sanctification is my willingness to surrender my will and desires to Him. As I continue to grow, I desire that my ongoing answer to God is "yes" because I am discovering that I can trust God much more than I can trust my own desires. As a part of this journey, I am finding that the more I allow God to govern me, the more He is able to develop me.

Today I rejoice that God pursued me and saved me from my sin. I hope you are also rejoicing in this reality. However, are you also rejoicing in the governance of God upon your entire life? The truth is this: All of us are under the authority of someone or something. The only one we can truly trust is the one who governs perfectly.

Pray with me: Lord Jesus, it is the nature of my human heart to often white knuckle the things of this world. It is so easy for me to depend on my own desires and understanding. Today, I humbly surrender my heart and will to your rule and governance. Fill me afresh today with your Holy Spirit, that I may be set apart for your purpose.

Small Voices | Doug Fry

"Trust in the Lord and do good; dwell in the land and enjoy safe pasture. Delight yourself in the Lord and he will give you the desires of your heart. Commit your way to the Lord; trust in him and he will do this: He will make your righteousness shine like the dawn. Be still before the Lord and wait patiently for him." –Psalm 37:3-7

Sometimes God uses small children to speak to us.

It was a cool winter night when I came home from work really worn out. My position with the company that I worked for demanded long hours. These were very difficult times, and my marriage was in deep trouble.

The year before I had just recommitted my life to the Lord after many years of doing my own thing. Each night after dinner and some family time, I would read the Bible and pray with our children before putting them to bed.

This particular night I was tired and depressed and had decided that we were going to bed without Bible reading or prayer. My seven year-old son would have none of that. He picked up our Bible and brought it to me. He placed his hand on a particular page and kept demanding that I read it.

I grudgingly agreed to read the Bible and pray. As soon as I began to read what he suggested, I knew this was the Lord speaking to me; it was Psalm 37.

As I began to read this passage of Scripture, verses 3 through 7 spoke loud and clear. All of sudden, I was no longer depressed or tired. I felt His presence and decided not to worry but to trust in His promises. I prayed with our children and put them to bed. I remember going to bed feeling like He had personally touched me and assured me that everything would be all right.

After a couple of years, my rocky marriage did end. But through it all I had perfect peace knowing that my God would provide.

Born Again | Jennifer Burgett

"'How can someone be born when they are old?' Nicodemus asked. Jesus answered, 'Very truly I tell you, no one can enter the kingdom of God unless they are born of water and the Spirit.'" –John 3:4-5

I was taught that eating from the Tree of Knowledge is how man came to know right and wrong—but I'm not sure that's true. They understood that before ever eating this fruit. God told them not to eat the fruit, and they knew they were disobeying.

So, what actually happened here?

Let's start with two phrases Satan used at the fall of man: "Did God actually say..." and "...you will be like God..." Satan first causes Eve to doubt what God said. If she can't trust what God said, shouldn't she instead trust her desire to be like God? That's exactly what Eve and Adam do: They give into their own desires above the Word of God.

Now let's look at their first thought after sinning: "We're naked." This is probably not the first thought I would have if I had disobeyed the only rule God gave me, but it makes sense if the "knowledge" they gained was a shift in their worldview. Instead of putting their desires aside to prioritize how God called them to live, they instead viewed the world through the lens of their own desires first.

God has given man desires—healthy ones!—but they need limits. That's why the tree was there. It was not a temptation set up by God but rather a limit or a boundary. When Adam and Eve's desires took priority, God had to set up harder limits—pain in childbirth, hard work, death.

We are all born into a world that tells us to put ourselves first: Do what feels good! Follow your dreams! You deserve this! This is why we need to be born again. Salvation is about believing that God's way is better. We see this best through the testimony of Jesus, who, being fully human, was not bound by human desires and put the will and Word of God first.

Jesus died on the cross so we could spend eternity with God, but He lived on Earth to show us how to begin that eternal life here and now. Being born again is about starting a new path towards that life.

SABBATH

A RHYTHM OF REST

You rule over the surging sea;

when its waves mount up, you still them.

Psalm 89:9

In Our Temptation, God's Power is Within Us! | Kerry Willis

"There isn't any temptation that you have experienced which is unusual for humans. God, who faithfully keeps his promises, will not allow you to be tempted beyond your power to resist. But when you are tempted, he will also give you the ability to endure the temptation as your way of escape." –I Corinthians 10:13

Many of the Holy Scriptures are hard for us as believers to understand on our own. We surely need the mind of Christ to triumphantly trust in "what saith the Lord." Perhaps one of the seemingly most difficult Scriptures for believers to decipher is I Corinthians 10:13. Here it is once again from God's Word Translation of the Holy Bible:

"There isn't any temptation that you have experienced which is unusual for humans. God, who faithfully keeps his promises, will not allow you to be tempted beyond your power to resist. But when you are tempted, he will also give you the ability to endure the temptation as your way of escape."

As I have sought the mind of Christ in relation to this Scripture, I have come to believe that the way to understand this verse victoriously is to realize that God "will not allow us to be tempted beyond what His power can resist within us."

So, what am I saying exactly? I am saying that the answer to our confusion with I Corinthians 10:13 is found in another verse of Scripture—Colossians 1:27: Christ in you (us), the hope!

Let us never forget that in our temptation, God's power is within us!

Greater | Gary O'Shell

"And Elisha prayed, 'Open his eyes, LORD, so that he may see.' Then the LORD opened the servant's eyes, and he looked and saw the hills full of horses and chariots of fire all around Elisha." –II Kings 6:17

"May God help us to not let what's visible distract us from what's true." –Alicia Britt Chole

Elisha the prophet and his servant were surrounded at Dothan by the chariots of the Syrians. His servant panicked, but the cool, measured response of Elisha never ceases to inspire me: "Do not fear, for those who are with us are more than those who are with them." Then Elisha prayed that the eyes of his servant be opened, that he might see what Elisha saw. God answered, and the servant beheld the surrounding mountain filled with horses and chariots of fire. Then Elisha prayed that the Syrians would be struck with blindness, and they were, with Elisha now turning his captors into his captives. Elisha was living out the exhortation from Alicia Britt Chole: He would not let what was visible before his natural eyes distract from what he knew was true: that his God was greater than the sum of all that was against him or could be against him. Do you and I live in such a place? Do we walk with eyes of flesh or the eyes of the Spirit?

In our staff meeting this morning, we spoke of what it means to believe. It is vastly more than agreement with facts. It is being in possession of the truth through experience. Paul said that he knew whom it was he believed and he was persuaded that He would keep all that was his life "until that day." Paul lived always seeing the Father's chariots of fire, not the chariots of the devil and those he works through. Do we? Can we? Will we?

The enemy's chariots will surely show up for us in some way at some time. What will we believe? The eyes of flesh or the eyes of our heart? As we face that day, may He open our eyes to see His chariots of fire all about us. As He does, we will take captive the enemy that means to capture and enslave us. Greater is He that is with us than he that will ever be with them.

In the Penalty Box | Reenie Peppers

"God, in His grace, freely makes us right in His sight. He did this through Jesus Christ when He freed us from the penalty of sin." –Romans 3:24

Recently I've encountered situations that have made me contemplate the concept of penalty. The first was about a week ago. I was putting new seat cushions on my dining room chairs and had to cut off the tags. As I was cutting off the tags, I noticed the warning—"Under penalty of law this tag not to be removed except by the consumer." When I was a child, I believed those tags on mattresses and pillows read "Do not remove under penalty of death"—and of course, all our pillows and mattresses while I was growing up continued to sport their tags. I thought this was humorous until I mentioned it to my husband. He shared with me that in our early years of marriage I refused to let him remove these tags as I was firmly convinced it was illegal to do so. Seriously?

The second instance to raise the idea of penalty is the Stanley Cup finals. The St. Louis Blues and Boston Bruins are currently battling it out for the championship. My husband is from St. Louis, and my family is from Boston. It has made for an interesting dynamic in our house this past week. Of course, you can't have hockey without players being sent to the penalty box, where a player must sit for a period of time due to a rule violation.

I've often felt I was living my life in and out of the penalty box. I feared that eventually I would cause an offense severe enough to get me expelled from the good life. But in my second year of college, I accepted the truth that "God, in His grace, freely makes us right in His sight. He did this through Jesus Christ when He freed us from the penalty of sin" (Romans 3:24).

Jesus has already served my penalties. Do I still live with the fear of messing up enough to merit expulsion from a life of hope and blessing? Certainly not. I live under God's grace and have been freed from the penalty of sin.

Now if you will excuse me, I am going to go cut the tags off all my pillows and mattresses.

DAY BY DAY

Praise be to Thee, O Lord Jesus Christ,
For all the benefits which You have given us,
For all the pains and insults which You have borne for us.
O most merciful Redeemer, Friend and Brother,
May we see You more clearly, love You more dearly,
And follow You more nearly, Day by day.
Amen.

St. Richard of Chichester

Called Compassion | Stephen Willis

"When he saw the crowds he had compassion on them, because they were harassed and helpless, like sheep without a shepherd." –Matthew 9:36

When we made the decision as a church leadership to change the name of our local church to Compassion, I never really considered the full impact it would have. I knew the Spirit had birthed the desire in my heart, and I knew the name embodied who we were and who we were striving to be. What I didn't know was how it would challenge me to do better. The Spirit continues to remind me regularly that I am the lead pastor of a church called Compassion and that my life should reflect and not contradict such a powerful name. I get it wrong often, but I am learning that there is power in a name and significance in what we call ourselves.

I told one of my sons today that he is good at relationships. Why? Because Satan is trying to convince him that he isn't. He had started to believe it himself. I could tell that my words served as a salve for his soul. This simple affirmation reclaimed territory that had been stolen by the enemy.

I tipped the woman overseeing the complimentary breakfast at my hotel today. Why? Mostly because God is challenging the pastor at Compassion to be more generous but also because I could tell in the midst of her diligence that she felt unseen. My tip shocked her. I suspect it had to do more with me seeing her effort and being appreciative than with the small amount of cash that she received.

Simple words and acts of compassion are a big deal. They not only impact those we serve, but they also help us see the world as Jesus does.

I have been reminding myself that God sees me as a son and as a saint instead of as a sinner. As a part of this reminder, I believe that my past sin won't define my life but that the Holy Spirit's power will.

So let me ask: What words define your life? The answer to these questions will deeply impact the trajectory of your influence and life.

Prayer: Jesus, help me to see myself as you see me. Help me to overcome the lies of the enemy so that I can live with abundance and victory.

Love God, Love Others, Serve Both | Gary Smith

"Love the Lord your God with all your heart and with all your soul and with all your mind and with all your strength...and love your neighbor as yourself." –Mark 12:30-31

This Scripture says it all! For mankind to survive and for peace to be upon the earth, it is imperative that we embrace this Word and carry out its admonition. It is our local church's mission statement, and it embodies how we ought to live. The Savior poured this message into the hearts of His disciples even though it was hard to live it.

Being filled with the Holy Spirit would complete the call of this passage. In order to be holy (I Peter 1:16), we must live in the power of His Holy Spirit, and in so doing, we allow His cleansing stream to wash us clean from all committed sins and to lead us into a holy walk by putting death to our inborn carnality. It is receiving all of God and allowing Him to lay the groundwork to demonstrate the love of God to others, the greatest commandment.

As life speeds onward, I am growing more aware of how powerful this message is. You cannot love God, love others, or serve both without doing all three! "As Christ followers, we are defined by His power "living in us" to display His pure love (holiness) made possible by the infilling of the Holy Spirit (Eph. 5:18). We cannot truly love others unless the Holy Spirit has done His cleansing work in us to purify and cleanse from "all unrighteousness" (I John 1:7-9). In doing so, He begins to teach us things we could not understand without the Spirit's holy work in us. Then and only then can we experience and demonstrate this love to others (Luke 10:17).

As I have reflected on our mission statement for several years now, the Lord has added additional meaning and it has become a personal life motto for me. It is a phrase that I can view often and embrace fully with great hope and promise: the hope of hearing Him say, "...well done" (Matt. 5:23)!

It may be that this message will grow even more, but for now I am happy with...

"Love God...love others...serve both...live holy...finish well...to hear Him say 'well done.'"

SABBATH

A RHYTHM
OF REST

Return to your rest, my soul,

for the Lord has been good to you.

Psalm 116:7

Saving Lives - Part One | Kerry Willis

"For the Son of Man came to seek and to save the lost." –Luke 19:10

Into the foyer of the local church that I once pastored in Harrisonburg, Virginia, just to the left sat a glass case where an old book was opened to two pages that displayed a powerful story. Here's the first part:

"On a dangerous seacoast notorious for shipwrecks, there was a crude little lifesaving station. Actually, the station was merely a hut with only one boat... but the few devoted members kept a constant watch over the turbulent sea. With little thought for themselves, they would go out day and night tirelessly searching for those in danger as well as the lost. Many, many lives were saved by this brave band of men who faithfully worked as a team in and out of the lifesaving station. By and by, it became a famous place.

Some of those who had been saved as well as others along the seacoast wanted to become associated with this little station. They were willing to give their time and energy and money in support of its objectives. New boats were purchased. New crews were trained. The station that was once obscure and crude and virtually insignificant began to grow. Some of its members were unhappy that the hut was so unattractive and poorly equipped. They felt a more comfortable place should be provided. Emergency cots were replaced with lovely furniture. Rough, hand-made equipment was discarded and sophisticated, classy systems were installed. The hut, of course, had to be torn down to make room for all the additional equipment, furniture, systems, and appointments. By its completion, the life-saving station had become a popular gathering place, and its objectives had begun to shift. It was now used as sort of a clubhouse, an attractive building for public gatherings. Saving lives, feeding the hungry, strengthening the fearful, and calming the disturbed rarely occurred by now.

Fewer members were now interested in braving the sea on lifesaving missions, so they hired professional lifeboat crews to do this work. The original goal of the station wasn't altogether forgotten, however. The lifesaving motifs still prevailed in the club's decorations. In fact, there was a liturgical lifeboat preserved in the Room of Sweet Memories with soft, indirect lighting, which helped hide the layer of dust upon the once-used vessel."

Saving Lives - Part Two | Kerry Willis

"For the Son of Man came to seek and to save the lost." –Luke 19:10

Here's the conclusion of our story:

"About this time a large ship was wrecked off the coast and the boat crews brought in loads of cold, wet, half-drowned people. They were dirty, some terribly sick and lonely. Others were black and 'different' from the majority of the club members. The beautiful new club suddenly became messy and cluttered. A special committee saw to it that a shower house was immediately built outside and away from the club so victims of shipwreck could be cleaned up before coming inside.

At the next meeting there were strong words and angry feelings, which resulted in a division among the members. Most of the people wanted to stop the club's lifesaving activities and all involvements with shipwreck victims . . . ("it's too unpleasant, it's a hindrance to our social life, it's opening the door to folks who are not our kind"). As you'd expect, some still insisted upon saving lives, that this was their primary objective—that their only reason for existence was ministering to anyone needing help regardless of their club's beauty or size or decorations. They were voted down and told if they wanted to save the lives of various kinds of people who were shipwrecked in those waters, they could begin their own lifesaving station down the coast! They did.

As years passed, the new station experienced the same old changes. It evolved into another club...and yet another lifesaving station was begun. History continued to repeat itself...and if you visit that coast today you'll find a large number of exclusive, impressive clubs along the shoreline owned and operated by slick professionals who have lost all involvement with the saving of lives.

Shipwrecks still occur in those waters, but now most of the victims are not saved. Every day they drown at sea, and so few seem to care...so very few. Do you?"

Give away your life...to the true lifesaver and let Him rescue the perishing through you.

God Is Holy | Cavan Carlton

"You are to be holy to me because I, the LORD, am holy, and I have set you apart from the nations to be my own." –Leviticus 20:26 (NIV)

We serve a holy God. He is holy. He is infinitely unique and set apart from everything and everyone else. There is no thing like Him. There is no one like Him. Across the landscape of time, across the far reaches of the galaxies, our great God stands alone. He is set apart. He is holy.

His Word is holy.
His ways are holy.
His name is holy.
His nature is holy.
His promises are holy.
His Spirit is holy.
His Son is holy.

The world around us is broken and corrupt and dirty, but God is holy. He is perfect and matchless in every single way.
He's unparalleled.
He's unbeatable.
He's unstoppable.
He's indescribable.
He's immeasurable.

In Isaiah 6, we're given a glimpse of God's holiness. It is a vision of heaven—the actual throne room where God reigns in all of His glory. God is surrounded by mighty angels whose awesome size and power we can't even begin to imagine. Legions of these mighty angels are gathered in worship to God, surrounding His throne, shouting praises with such intensity that it literally shakes the very foundation of heaven like deep thunder rolling across the sky. HOLY! HOLY! HOLY! Over and over and over again, forever and ever and ever they shout praise and adoration to God. HOLY! HOLY! HOLY!

God is holy.
Ponder that.

God Is Love | Cavan Carlton

"Dear friends, let us love one another, for love comes from God. Everyone who loves has been born of God and knows God. Whoever does not love does not know God, because God is love." –I John 4:7-8

At the very center of our heart, in the deepest recesses of who we are, we want love. We want to know love. We want to feel love. When I was younger, there was a popular song, "I Want to Know What Love Is," by the band Foreigner. It hit #1 when it was released in 1984, and really has never stopped being popular over nearly four decades. Around the world, it's played tens of thousands of times a day. I use Spotify to listen to music, and "I Want to Know What Love Is" has been played, just on Spotify, nearly 700 million times. Part of the reason why the song is so popular is because it resonates deeply with something inside of us. We want to know love. We want to feel love.

The Bible says that God is love. The Bible says that love comes from God. He is the one and only pure source of love.

The Bible says that anyone who does not love does not know God. If we live a life fully surrendered to God, our love for Him and for others will grow more and more perfect.

Paul beautifully describes love in 1 Corinthians 13.
Love is patient.
Love is kind.
Love is not jealous or boastful or proud or rude.
Love is not irritable, and it keeps no record of being wronged.
Love does not rejoice about injustice, but rejoices whenever the truth wins out.
Love never gives up, never loses faith, is always hopeful, and endures through every circumstance.

This is God's love, and there is nothing like it. It's wonderful, beautiful, powerful, matchless, limitless, and everlasting.

God's love never changes because He never changes. God is love.
Ponder that.

God's Holy Love | Cavan Carlton

"There is no one holy like the Lord" –I Samuel 2:2a
"Because your love is better than life, my lips will glorify you." –Psalm 63:3

God's holiness and God's love: these two core attributes of God stand high and mighty as beacons of light defining who He is. God is holy! God is love! God's holiness—and His love—are forever intertwined, bound together as His DNA: the divine nature of Abba. They cannot be separated. You cannot accurately define God's holiness without also proclaiming His love. You cannot accurately define God's love without also proclaiming His holiness. Every time we think or speak of God's love, we are thinking and speaking of His holiness.

In both the Old and New Testaments, God commands us to be holy like He is holy. We are also commanded to love perfectly, just like Him. Both! At the same time! This is a high calling!

There's a beautiful tension between holiness and love. God holds them in perfect balance. His holiness blazes with such intensity that we cannot even comprehend, while at the same time He loves us with a love so great we cannot even comprehend.

This tension between holiness and love is difficult to grasp. God holds it perfectly because He is God. But we are not God, and we struggle. In our own strength, we fail. Without the Holy Spirit, it's impossible. But with God's Spirit it's not impossible, because we can do all things through Christ who lives in us and gives us strength.

This is God's righteous pathway of holy love. And through His Holy Spirit in us, He equips, enables, and empowers us to faithfully walk on His path. He gives us the authority and the power to be holy and to truly love one another like Jesus. But maintaining the balance, walking on God's righteous path, is difficult. It's a narrow path.

This difficulty often leads people to slide off the path in one direction or another. They slide towards holiness, waving the banner of holiness while minimizing God's love, or they slide towards love, waving the banner of love while minimizing God's holiness. When this happens, the Christian will slide off God's righteous path of holy love and fall into one of the two ditches that line the sides of the road. The ditches are no good. The devil is in the ditches. Yet God's holy love shows us how to stay on the road.

Watch Your Step! | Torrie Slaughter

"Jesus said to his disciples, 'Things that cause people to stumble are bound to come... So watch yourselves.'" –Luke 17:1, 3

Are you facing temptations in your life? Take heart, for Jesus teaches us in Luke 17:1-10 about the power of forgiveness, faith, and humility. I want to share some insights I gained from reading Luke 17:1-10. This passage contains some powerful teachings from Jesus about trespasses, temptations, and the power of faith.

First, Jesus warns His disciples in verses 1-2 about the dangers of causing others to stumble. He emphasizes that it would be better for them to have a millstone tied around their neck and be thrown into the sea than to cause someone to stumble. This is a powerful reminder that we should prioritize the well-being of others and avoid leading them astray.

Jesus also instructs His disciples in verses 3-4 to forgive those who sin against them, even if they sin against them seven times in a day. This teaching highlights the importance of prioritizing forgiveness and reconciliation in our relationships with others.

In verses 5-6, the disciples ask Jesus to increase their faith. Jesus tells them that even a tiny amount of faith can move mountains. This teaching reminds us of the power of faith and our need to trust in God in all situations.

Finally, in verses 7-10, Jesus tells His disciples that when they have done all that God commanded, they should say, "We are unworthy servants; we have only done our duty." This teaching reminds us of the humility and obedience required of us as followers of Christ.

The teachings in this passage are powerful and profound. They remind us of the importance of being mindful of our actions and their impact on others. We must quickly forgive and seek reconciliation with those who have wronged us. We must also have faith in God and trust in His power to move mountains in our lives. Finally, we must approach our relationship with God with humility and obedience, recognizing that we are unworthy servants who have only done our duty.

As we go about our lives, facing trespasses and temptations, let us remember the power of faith and the importance of forgiveness, humility, and obedience. May these teachings guide us daily and bring us closer to God.

SABBATH

A RHYTHM OF REST

¹⁷ *How precious to me are your thoughts,[a] God!*

How vast is the sum of them!

¹⁸ *Were I to count them, they would outnumber the*

grains of sand—

when I awake, I am still with you.

Psalm 139:17-18

Bad Days | Camelot Shuff

"Today, do not harden your heart as you did in the rebellion..." –Hebrews 3:8

Do you ever feel pressured? Pressured to conform, pressured to perform? Pressured by expectations that others have or even that you have for yourself? Our natural instinct when pressured is to resist, push back, push through. We never give up or give in.

Our culture highlights and demands this sort of persistence if we want to achieve best results and earn our rightful promotions and recognitions. It is mostly obvious that this is counter to the way of humility, so, when these pressures come, we usually cast our cares on Jesus, confessing our sins and allowing Him to be our Peace. In that balance, there is the quiet contentment that comes. That contentment says, "I am so glad I am not what I used to be. Thank you, Jesus, that you have lifted me out of a pit and onto solid ground." At the same time, within contentment, we might give way to complacency.

I wonder if now that my feet have been on solid ground for quite some time I still need to remove my sandals. Do I walk with reverence before almighty God?

Or has my walk on solid ground become a party that I attend with other solid-ground walkers, resisting the need to go to Jesus and conforming to the outward appearance of "rock walkers"? Do I pray only when I lead? Do I follow only when someone is following me? Do I worship only when we worship? Thank God for the body of Christ. But Lord forbid that I would allow my heart to harden, to become complacent all while serving in the house of the Lord!

Prayer: Lord, you know my heart. Soften it. Lord, you see my pride. Forgive me, Lord, you were my first love. Remind me, Lord, you are the resurrection. Refresh me. Lord, give me eyes to see you until I am humbly grateful always.

Honoring a "Man of God" | Deb Huff

"Now we ask you, brothers and sisters, to acknowledge those who work hard among you, who care for you in the Lord and who admonish you. Hold them in the highest regard in love because of their work. Live in peace with each other." –I Thessalonians 5:12-13

Elisha called her "the Shunammite woman." She called him "the man of God."

A godly prophet traveled the countryside, and a Shunammite woman often invited him to have a meal with her family. We do not know her name, but she had money and must have been a good cook, as Elisha made it a routine to stop there to eat.

One day she said to her husband, "I know that this man who often comes our way is a holy man of God. Let's make a small room on the roof and put in it a bed and a table, a chair and a lamp for him. Then he can stay there whenever he comes to us" (II Kings 4:9-10).

She put her decorating skills to use to make a welcoming place for "the holy man of God." This woman could have given him money to stay at a nearby inn. Instead, she gave him a tangible gift of her time, treasure, and talent.

How do we reach out to the pastors in our lives? Do we pray for them daily? Do we speak words of encouragement? When was the last time we said thank you for all you do?

Pastors do so much more than deliver Sunday sermons; there are meetings, preparation, counseling, weddings, funerals, and so on. Then there's the list we don't even think about—answering phone calls in the middle of the night about all kinds of emergencies, finding food and shelter for someone in need, handling complaints from an unhappy church neighbor who wants attendees' cars not to block their driveway, and so on.

Pastors carry a heavy load, and we need to thank them, encourage them, and if possible, bless them in a tangible way. At the very least, we can say thank you, we can send a card of encouragement, and we can tell them about the impact they have had on our lives.

Be Very Patient With Everyone | Kerry Willis

"And we urge you, brothers and sisters, warn those who are idle and disruptive, encourage the disheartened, help the weak, be patient with everyone."
–I Thessalonians 5:14

Patience is perhaps the most underestimated and most undesired slice within the fruit of the Spirit. Some even foolishly say things like, "Don't pray for patience." Well, love is patient, so we cannot have the fruit of the Spirit apart from patience, and that alone makes me desire it.

I am beautifully challenged towards patience by the commentary that Oswald Chambers gives for 1 Thessalonians 5:14. Let me again share the verse and then the commentary.

The verse is 1 Thessalonians 5:14 with emphasis added: "We [earnestly] urge you, believers, admonish those who are out of line [the undisciplined, the unruly, the disorderly], encourage the timid [who lack spiritual courage], help the[spiritually] weak, be very patient with everyone [always controlling your temper]."

The Oswald Chambers commentary: "Don't lose patience with others if they do not see at once what you already see. God's word exhorts us to be patient with all people. It brings to mind the question; How long did it take God to put me (to put you) where I am (where you are) now?"

So I pray: God, you are love and you are patient. Please make me like you! Amen!

Hurry Up and Wait | Andy Scoles

"Wait for the Lord; Be strong and let your heart take courage; Yes, wait for the Lord."
–Psalm 27:14

"The Lord is not slow about His promise, as some count slowness, but is patient toward you, not willing for any to perish, but for all to come to repentance." –II Peter 3:9

"Therefore be patient, brothers and sisters, until the coming of the Lord. The farmer waits for the precious produce of the soil, being patient about it, until it gets the early and late rains." –James 5:7

For as long as I can remember, people in my life have jokingly told me never to pray for patience, because if I do God will give me opportunities to learn it. So naturally, I decided long ago to pray for patience because I wanted to learn a virtue that everyone else avoids. And yes, that has led to many opportunities to learn patience.

Instant gratification is a hallmark of our culture, so it's no surprise that our ability to wait on the Lord is imperfect. Throughout Scripture, people's inability to wait on the word got them into trouble. For instance, Abraham and Sarah waited imperfectly and got ahead of God by trying to have a son their own way—which ended badly.

What happens when we don't wait on the Lord? We do things we regret. We disobey and end up in sin. We rush in without considering the consequences because we can't see what lies ahead and are wise in our own eyes. God can see all outcomes, and He wants to make the way straight before us, a way that we often aren't ready for.

But why does God want us to wait in the first place? Surely not just to make us squirm. No, God wants to transform us in the waiting and prepare us for what He has planned. If we look back, we can often see the patterns through which God worked as we waited. Without those periods of waiting, we would never become who we need to be in order to be ready for the fulfillment of God's promises.

What are you waiting for? What do you want? Let us pray for the ability to wait well, to be patient as the Lord works in unseen ways to bring about His fulfilled promises for the whole world.

Greater Still | Stephen Willis

"I pray that you, being rooted and established in love, may have power, together with all the Lord's holy people, to grasp how wide and long and high and deep is the love of Christ." –Ephesians 3:17b-18

Our prayers are a window into our priorities. I think some people tire of praying because they spend most of their prayer time asking for things that don't really help them in the spiritual realm. In Paul's letter to the Ephesians, we see that his priority was for the early church to grow spiritual roots established in the love of the Father. Paul believed that if the early church discovered the true love of the Father, they would receive "power together" when they began to "grasp how wide and long and high and deep is the love of Christ" (v. 18). Can I ask: Do you spend much time sitting and trying to grasp the width, length, height, and depth of the love of God? If not, you should make it a regular part of your activity. Paul was right. It will bring an incredible amount of encouragement and power.

Recently, I received a discouraging email just hours before bed. It was one of those emails that the enemy wanted to use to attack my worth as a person and pastor. I went to bed thinking about it, and it quickly came back to my mind early the next morning. I sat down just moments after getting up to start my time with the Lord. As I sat down, a song that had never caught my attention came streaming through my AirPods. The song written by Brandon Lake declares,

My sin was deep. Your grace was deeper.
My shame was wide. Your arms were wider.
My guilt was great. Your love was greater still.
How deep, how wide, how far, how high the love of my Savior. The love of Christ.

As I played the song again, the phrase "greater still" became the anthem of my soul. My circumstances had not changed, but I sat rediscovering that His love is greater still. Follow my lead. Go ahead and make a list of all the things that the love of God is greater than. Warning: The list will get really long.

Prayer: Abba Father, help me gain power in the discovery of your love that is "greater still."

Do Not Let the Small Things Trip You Up | Reenie Peppers

"If you are right with God, He strengthens you for the journey; the Lord will be pleased with your life. And even though you trip up, you will not fall on your face because He holds you by the hand." –Psalm 37:23-24

As a rule, we usually do not trip over the big stuff. We do not trip over the couch, or the dining table, or our nightstand. We do, however, trip over the little things: the toy car, the backpack left on the floor, or the hastily discarded shoe.

Spiritually, we are very often tripped up by the seemingly small stuff. We skip our devotional time one morning. We dwell on an unkind thought about a brother or sister. We tell a little white lie. When we trip up over even the smallest thing, we lose our spiritual equilibrium. Equilibrium is the right balance between competing influences. We daily live under the competing influences of our flesh and the Spirit of God. Any accidental slip can give the influence of the flesh the upper hand.

God promises in Psalm 37 that He will strengthen us for the journey (our journey toward holy living) and keep us from falling on our faces. Though God promises His help, we have our part to do as well. We need to recognize and deal with the small stuff that can trip us up so it does not become a stumbling block to our spiritual equilibrium. When we trip over the same small thing again and again, it can become a big thing. Missing our devotional time once turns into missing our devotional time for a week or more. Our unkind thought about a brother or sister can morph into a critical spirit. The small things need our attention so they do not become the big things.

Prayer: Dear Father, help me to recognize and deal with the small things that so easily trip me up. I thank you that you strengthen me for the journey and keep me from falling on my face. In Jesus' name, Amen.

SABBATH

A RHYTHM
OF REST

It is good to wait quietly for the salvation of the Lord.

Lamentations 3:26

A Whiny Generation | Deb Huff

"Do everything without complaining or arguing, so that you may become blameless and pure, children of God without fault in a crooked and depraved generation, in which you will shine like stars in the universe as you hold out the word of life—in order that I may boast on the day of Christ that I did not run or labor for nothing." –Philippians 2:14-16

"Why does she have more…?" "Why can't I go…?" "Why does he treat me…?" "Why don't you…?"

Sometimes asking a question is reasonable, but how often do our questions become irritating or a means to badger someone into doing what we want them to do? How many times do our questions reflect a bad attitude or a contentious spirit?

Instead of being grateful for what we do have, do we want more? Instead of being happy with our circumstances, do we grumble about what should be?

Our children learned the fine art of whining from watching and listening to us. We set the standard for them to follow.

They know that if they ask "why" long enough and loud enough with a few "pleases" and puppy dog eyes thrown in for good measure that they will get their way. And our children have mastered this pattern much too well. How can we turn the tide away from this selfish behavior?

We have to control our own whiny ways. In the course of a week, take note of how often you find yourself whining. What caused the annoying reaction? Was it based on a prideful attitude? Were you seeing the fault in others without taking inventory of your own actions?

In your prayer life, pray for a troublesome situation. Ask God to change hearts, to redirect resources or whatever is needed to bring Him glory. Ask God to reveal your role in the situation. Ask for Him to direct your actions, words, and thoughts. While it's OK to ask God to change an employer who lacks a caring heart, we should also ask for His guidance in what we should do to make the situation more peaceful (or at least more bearable).

Instead of complaining to God about everything, we should go to Him with hearts full of gratitude for what we do have, counting our blessings.

The Art of Saying Thank You | Deb Huff

"In everything give thanks: for this is the will of God concerning you."
–I Thessalonians 5:18

"Thanks for cooking us dinner, Nana, especially the dessert."
"Thanks for my new shoes. Wanna see me jump high?"
"Thanks for taking me to youth group."
"Thank you for holding me through the storm."

All four of our grandchildren are good about saying thank you, and that makes me happy to my core. Yes, it's nice that they acknowledge gifts and acts of kindness from family and friends. But what's most important is that they have learned to have an attitude of gratitude even for the simplest of things. Why is this important? While this practice of good etiquette may seem trivial, learning how to say thank you to our Lord and Savior is the most important skill they can possess.

I know how good my heart feels when these children say thank you for an ice cream cone and give me a hug to go with it. I hug them right back and look forward to the next thing I can do for them to make them happy.

On a spiritual level, think about saying thank you to God for the blessings He has given you. It's easy to acknowledge Him for the food He has provided or the health problems He has carried you through. What about recognizing Him for help with the irritating neighbor or showing appreciation for the unexpected job promotion?

Above all the everyday matters, He has provided a way for us to spend eternity with Him through the death, burial, and resurrection of His Son Jesus Christ. When was the last time you humbly thanked Him for His great gift? He has provided for your needs and even your wants and so much more—up to and including the gift of eternal life. And He wants to hear from your heart full of thanks. He delights in doing so.

Counting your blessings enriches our prayer life and brings you into a deeper fellowship with God. Are you exhibiting the kind of manners towards Him that you expect from children in your life?

"The LORD delights in those who fear him, who put their hope in his unfailing love" (Psalm 147:11).

Gratitude | Todd Thomas

"Let everything that has breath praise the LORD." –Psalm 150:6

And then.

That phrase—"and then"—often prefaces an explanation of how gratitude fades away. An uninvited reversal comes. Circumstances in the lives of others have an adverse impact on our circumstances. Situations beyond the scope of our corrective influence turn life on its head. And gratitude fades.

The loss of gratitude does not leave a void in our hearts. The loss of gratitude allows for dark and negative attitudes to fill us. I know; I've been there. I have had to learn that my circumstances cannot be allowed to become my source of gratitude. If I allow circumstances to be the foundation of my gratitude, then my life becomes an exhausting cycle of being grateful one moment and grumbling the next.

My gratitude must rest on one foundation: the goodness of God.

It is not that God has goodness, like a spiritual commodity that is portioned out to me as I perform admirably. God is good and expresses Himself into my life in more ways than I am capable of recognizing. His goodness is not enhanced by the positive circumstances in my life. Neither is His goodness filtered out by the harsh circumstances of my life.

We know that in everything God works for the good of those who love Him. They are the people He called because that was His plan. God knew them before He made the world, and He decided that they would be like His Son so that Jesus would be the firstborn of many brothers (Romans 8:28-29).

Once we understand that the eternal God is taking all the events of our earthly life and weaving them into a life being formed in the image of Christ, gratitude arises irresistibly.

Let everything that has breath praise the LORD.

Faithful Love | Matthew S.E. Waggoner

"For I desire Faithful Love and not sacrifice, the knowledge of God rather than burnt offerings." -Hosea 6:6

Alicia, my wife of 18 years, sat at the table with me while we ate lunch one afternoon, and we began to have a conversation about how it felt when we went above and beyond for others but got little to no appreciation back. It can be frustrating when we work hard on something important and no one notices or appreciates it. What do you do when those moments come into your life? What do you do when it seems like relationships are just one-sided?

You pray for faithful love. Faithful love is a love that is committed and unwavering in its devotion. It is a love that endures through the ups and downs, the good times and the bad, and still remains steadfast and loyal— like Jesus in the Garden of Gethsemane, ridiculed by Pharisees, alienated by a people who had been waiting for His arrival but rejected Him, criticized, and left to pray alone in an olive grove while His closest friends slept against a tree. Jesus, in His faithful love to the Father, was still willing to go a little farther and fell to His knees to pray, "O my Father, Abba Father... if it be possible, let this cup pass from me. Yet, not as I will, but as you will." That's faithful love. It's love without conditions. It's faithful to the end, even when death is inevitable. Faithful love is dripped in grace and washed in mercy. And it continues on, even when others abandon you.

Alicia and I prayed that day that we would be more faithful in our love for others, even when we didn't feel loved by them in return. Perhaps today you can think of someone you can faithfully love like Jesus.

Abba Father, you promise to fully love us as you desire faithful love from us. Help us today to receive your love fully because we know you are faithful. Amen.

WWYDTJ | Matthew Lesniak

"For I was hungry and you gave Me something to eat, I was thirsty and you gave Me something to drink, I was a stranger and you took Me in, I was naked and you clothed Me, I was sick and you looked after Me, I was in prison and you visited Me."
–Matthew 25:35-36

There was a time when many in Christian circles owned and displayed WWJD merchandise. "What Would Jesus Do?" these bits of paraphernalia urged us to ask. There is no doubt that our Lord desires obedience from us, but obedience that has its root in the flesh is the enemy of God. Our obedience must be fueled by God, by His Son Jesus, and by His Holy Spirit. Only then does it give Him all the glory. Only then does His joy become our "complete joy."

How might this look in practice? When it comes to our interactions with others and our acts of love, for instance, Jesus teaches us that our left hand should not know what our right hand is doing. How would our interactions be transformed if we treated everyone—family, friends, and strangers alike—as if they were Jesus? Ponder that for a moment. Every interaction you have with another person is an interaction with Jesus. What Would You Do To Jesus (WWYDTJ)?

This is the power found in this teaching. We do not know our own hearts like Jesus does. Similarly, we cannot know the reality of the hearts of those with whom we interact day in and day out. Therefore, our proper response to the reality of Jesus' life within us is...LOVE. Our kindness and charity towards others are infinite, good, and selfless when rooted in Christ—they are what Jesus would do and they ought to be what we would do to Jesus. As we abide in Jesus, we truly don't even realize we are loving and serving Jesus when we love and serve others (see verse 37).

God help us! Help us realize that every interaction today is one with YOU. What Would You Do To Jesus?

God's Priority | Stephen Willis

"Then Jesus said to Simon, 'Don't be afraid; from now on you will fish for people.' So they pulled their boats up on shore, left everything and followed him." -Matthew 5:10b-11

I was a high school basketball coach who was running from a call to ministry, and the season had been over for a couple of weeks. The athletic director showed up at my classroom with our conference championship trophy. He said, "Here's your trophy, Coach! I didn't want it to get lost because it matters more to you than others." As he left the classroom, I heard the inaudible voice of God's Spirit ask deep within my soul, "Stephen, are you working for trophies that no one else cares about?"

In Luke 5, we see Jesus call the sons of Zebedee away from the fishing business on what was likely the biggest fishing day of their lives. As the son of a fisherman, I have often thought about the large amount of fish that the boys left their father that day. Sure, those fish represented a lot of money, but they also represented a lot of work. As I ponder the text, it makes me ask, "What are you working for?"

Don't misunderstand me. God doesn't call everyone to work in full-time ministry. However, he has called all of us to work with His priority in mind. Simon would leave his father with the fish in order that he could go and "fish for people." Like Simon's father, my own father was the last fisherman in our family. My brothers and I all became pastors. But my father's calling was just as real as ours, as he continued to work as a fisherman with God's priority in mind. As I examine the life of my Dad (who has gone on before us), I know full well that his legacy has little to do with the fish that he caught and everything to do with the lives he impacted. As my dad toiled on the seas and walked along the docks, he remained mindful of God's priority. In the end, the impact he had on others had far more weight than the fish he caught.

Prayer: Lord Jesus, help us to see beyond the circumstances of my life. Help me to live with your priorities in mind as I look to work in a way that glorifies you.

SABBATH

A RHYTHM
OF REST

When the Lord restored the fortunes of[a] Zion,

we were like those who dreamed.[b]

Our mouths were filled with laughter,

our tongues with songs of joy.

Then it was said among the nations,

"The Lord has done great things for them."

The Lord has done great things for us,

and we are filled with joy.

Psalm 126:1-3

Burning Heart | Matthew S.E. Waggoner

"Were not our hearts burning within us...?" –Luke 24:32

As I sat in the holiest of holies (the back row of the worship conference), I felt out of place. My friend who had invited me was fully immersed in the worship, but I felt disconnected and unsure of what to do. I watched as people laughed and cried, seemingly swept away by the power of the presence of the Holy Spirit. Despite the tangible energy in the room, I struggled to find my own connection to the worship experience.

Later that night, as I lay in bed replaying the events of the evening, I kept hearing these words: "Matthew, do you love me?" It was Jesus stoking the coals of my heart. I soon realized that my disconnection was not because of the worship style or the people around me, but because I was focusing on my own discomfort and unfamiliarity. I remembered the story of the two men on the road to Emmaus who, despite having heard the testimony of the resurrection, still walked away from Jesus until He Himself revealed the truth to them through the Scriptures.

I realized that my own heart was foolish and easily swayed by my own preferences, just like the hearts of those two men. My focus was not on Jesus but on myself and my own comfort. In that moment, I recognized that my true battle for a heart burning with worship was not external but internal. It was a battle against my own self-belief and desires.

From that moment on, I made a conscious effort to shift my focus towards Jesus and to surrender my heart to Him in every opportunity of worship. I learned that true worship is not about finding the right environment or style but about having a heart that is fully surrendered to Jesus. Is He not the "air that we breathe?" It is a choice to put aside my own preferences and fears and to surrender to the Holy Spirit to guide me into a deeper, more meaningful, and worshipful relationship. His holy presence lives within me, igniting me.

Abba Father, stoke the coals of my smoldering heart and ignite within me a consuming, passionate affection for only you, anywhere and everywhere. Amen.

Knowing God | Stephen Willis

"Dear friends, let us love one another, for love comes from God. Everyone who loves has been born of God and knows God." –I John 4:7

I recently encountered a Marine veteran who was visiting our community. Although it seemed like a pure accident that we would have had the chance to meet, as I talked to him, I learned that he had a sister who lived in the area and that she was a frequent attender of our church. As we talked, he shared with me parts of his story as a soldier who spent two deployments in some very dangerous parts of the world. He escaped with his life, but you could tell that he was now facing a new battle as someone looking to assimilate back into some type of normalcy in everyday life.

Before long, I felt like the Spirit was prompting me to demonstrate my gratitude in a deeper way than just thanking him for his sacrifice for our nation. As we departed, I found myself giving him a gift of appreciation in the name of Jesus. He was a little shocked by the gesture, but I could tell that it really touched him. I left grateful that I didn't talk myself out of the opportunity because I knew that my act of gratitude was nothing more than an extension of God's love.

Since this encounter I have spent some time thinking about the tradition of holiness that is such a vital part of my heritage. What is the relationship between holiness and the call for us to demonstrate God's love? Could it be that the most holy people among us are the ones who have learned to love others best? It may be a simple concept for some, but it isn't for me. You see, holiness can be so easily hijacked by standards, legalism, and false pretense. Could it be that when God proclaimed, "Be Holy for I am Holy" (I Peter 1:15-16), that He was mostly talking about how we choose to love the rest of humanity? Our text reminds us that it is impossible to know God without loving others.

Prayer: Lord Jesus, help your holiness grow in me as I strive to love as you have loved.

Pitching a Tent | Emily Heady

"Peter said to Jesus, 'Lord, it is good for us to be here. If you wish, I will put up three shelters—one for you, one for Moses and one for Elijah.'" –Matthew 17:4

I don't like camping much. I like the idea of it—the stars, a warm sleeping bag, a fire and marshmallows—but unless it's the perfect sort of fall day, I'd rather be in my own bug-free bed. But camping plays a significant role in Scripture. The Old Testament patriarchs often moved from one place to another, taking huge numbers of animals and people with them—and tents enough to accommodate everyone. When they fled Egypt, the Israelites began a generations-long camping trip on their way to the Promised Land. Every Sukkot, or Feast of Tabernacles, the whole nation camped for seven days, during which time they remembered how they had come from wandering in the wilderness to enjoying a bountiful harvest. And Paul, a tentmaker by trade, reminds us that these bodies we live in are only tents, soon to be replaced by an eternal house in heaven (II Cor. 5:2).

The word for "tent" that we see used so often in Scripture—"tabernacle"—has a rich history in our Christian tradition. Besides the obvious meaning, it is a moveable place of worship where God dwelled. In Exodus, Moses constructed this tabernacle with its twisted curtains, lampstand, and bread. And today, in church usage, the tabernacle is a vessel in which holy things such as communion elements are stored and transported. Tabernacles house something of great value, if only temporarily.

So when Peter, having just witnessed the Transfiguration, sees Elijah and Moses talking with Jesus, his natural response is to want to pitch a tent. Peter doesn't get what he wants, maybe because tents by their very nature are temporary. Our true home—like Moses' and Elijah's—is heaven, where we will enjoy the presence of our Lord forever.

Jesus, as we journey on, let us take time to "camp out" with you as we anticipate our final home.

Worship as a Spiritual Discipline | Ashley Gomez

"When you come together, it is not the Lord's supper that you eat. For in eating, each one goes ahead with his own meal. One goes hungry, another gets drunk. What! Do you not have houses to eat and drink in? Or do you despise the church of God and humiliate those who have nothing?... So then, my brothers, when you come together to eat, wait for one another— if anyone is hungry, let him eat at home—so that when you come together it will not be for judgment." –I Corinthians 11:20-22, 33-34

I was having lunch the other day with my husband and some other church family. As I was sitting there, I got into a discussion with one brother about music. In the course of our discussion, he made the off-hand comment, "To be honest, we listen to [some well-known church in our area that sings all hymns] before coming to church." And though I know he meant it as nothing marvelous, over the next couple days, the importance of what he conveyed hit home in the most significant of ways: My brother purposefully prepares himself with his wife to enter into community with me and our other brothers and sisters! I had never been so moved.

I often quote Richard Foster's Celebration of Discipline because it has encouraged me greatly in the pursuit of those practices which help build up not only myself, but those in the faith with me also. And in Foster's discussion of the act of corporate worship, he makes this comment about stepping into the community of believers in worship: that, in "hav[ing] a willingness to be gathered in the power of the Lord . . . I . . . learn to let go of my agenda, of my concern, of my being blessed, of my hearing the word of God. The language of the gathered [becomes] not 'I,' but 'we.'"

What we do in corporate worship says so much about the grace of the God we serve—how He works in us and moves in us to make us one body. So, let us come into worship in that Spirit of preparation, "eating before we gather," so that we may together partake of the sweet Communion Christ has prepared before us.

Too Much! | Kerry Willis

"For God so loved the world that he gave his one and only Son, that whoever believes in him shall not perish but have eternal life. For God did not send his Son into the world to condemn the world, but to save the world through him." –John 3:16-17

When our son Grayson started to talk as a young child, his two signature words were "too much!" I am not sure how he came up with these two powerful words when we would ask him how much he loved us. Nevertheless, his answer from the first time we asked him "How much do you love us?" was "Too much!"

The same words came whenever we asked him "How much does Jesus love Grayson?" "Too much!" My guess is that whenever he heard the word "love," the phrase "too much" triggered in his young mind.

These thoughts remind me of another question: "Is it even possible to love a loved one too much?" It's an interesting question, don't you think? Is it possible to care too much for others? If it's possible, I am probably guilty.

So, if it's possible to love and care too much for others, I probably owe an apology to some people across my lifetime. What am I talking about? Well, if it's possible to love and care about people too much, or so much that they miss the love of God, I would want to apologize for that kind of love and care. And if I loved or cared about others more than I loved and cared for the Lord, well, I am sorry for that especially.

Don't get me wrong: I want to love and care for others, and I want and need the love and care of others, but I do not want it to interrupt in any way the love of God! Without doubt, if we reflect on the truth of John 3:16-17, surely we would agree that God loved and cared for us "too much"—and for that we must surely be most grateful!

Thanks for thinking about loving and caring with me today. It seemed to come out of nowhere, but I am pretty sure it came my way from the mind of Christ. I hope I learn the lessons He wants me to know and to live.

Oh yeah! Our son Grayson's very first full sentence was spoken to me. As I held him after a life-saving surgery, he said with a laugh: "I love you." It was unbelievable; he was only four months old! "Too much," indeed!

Worship and Wheelchairs | Stephen Willis

"And we know that in all things God works for the good of those who love him, who have been called according to his purpose." –Romans 8:28

I recently had the honor of serving as a delegate to our denomination's General Assembly. It is always a great experience. This last assembly I experienced God in a way that will forever change me. We arrived at the second worship service a few minutes late (I'm never late) and found a seat on the far outside section of the arena. Even before I found my seat, I sensed the presence of God in an extra special way. As we joined the multitude of worshippers, we transitioned into the song "The Goodness of God." It was as if the volume of praise intensified as we proclaimed,

And all my life You have been faithful
And all my life You have been so, so good
With every breath that I am able
Oh, I will sing of the goodness of God
…'Cause Your goodness is running after
It's running after me…

As this anthem of truth was being proclaimed by thousands of people, I looked over my shoulder to see one worshiper whose posture taught me God's truth. This young lady, probably in her early 30s, was confined to a wheelchair. It was obvious that her body had been distorted by the effects of cerebral palsy. But I was overwhelmed by the countenance of joy that was on her face as she sang and proclaimed the goodness of her God. As I continued to join her in this anthem of praise, I was undone.

Romans 8:28 is often quoted. Do we believe it? I know beyond a shadow of a doubt that not all things are good. I see bad things all the time, and I don't like it. When a young couple some thirty years ago received the diagnosis of cerebral palsy for their baby, I know they didn't like it. Yet just recently in a multitude of worshipers, their daughter was a visible testimony that God can take the worst of things and use them for our good.

As the service closed I had to meet this young lady. I approached her and said, "Hi, I'm Stephen." She responded, "Nice to meet you. My name is Grace."

SABBATH

A RHYTHM
OF REST

And the God of all grace, who called you to his eternal

glory in Christ, after you have suffered a little while,

will himself restore you and make you strong, firm

and steadfast.

1 Peter 5:10

Jesus vs. Hypocrisy | Cavan Carlton

"Woe to you, teachers of the law and Pharisees, you hypocrites! You are like whitewashed tombs, which look beautiful on the outside but on the inside are full of the bones of the dead and everything unclean." –Matthew 23:27

Nobody likes a hypocrite. There's something deep within us that stirs in an unhealthy way when we see someone say one thing and do the opposite. It creates an inner distaste and distrust.

Throughout His recorded public ministry, Jesus demonstrated incredible mercy on the sick and the poor....even on sinners! His grace and strength saved the life of the woman caught in adultery from an imminent barrage of deadly stones, but after her accusers left He also clearly told her to go and sin no more. Grace, mercy, and justice! But Jesus had great contempt and little patience for spiritual hypocrites. Why?

Because Jesus knew that spiritual hypocrisy bears false witness. It corrupts the true message of God, leading to confusion, distrust, and unbelief. A single spiritual hypocrite can inflict tremendous damage, with the effects often lasting for generations. Is there generational distrust of Christianity in your family? If so, it can likely be traced back to an act of spiritual hypocrisy by a family member at some point in your family's past.

Jesus Christ is the King of truth. He is truth. "I am the Way, the Truth, and the Life" (John 14:6). The Holy Spirit of Christ is often called the voice of truth. Come to know Him personally and you will see that there isn't an ounce of hypocrisy in Him. Only truth! Don't let someone else's hypocrisy prevent you from experiencing the fullness of God.

A fleshly response would be to pause and think about who the hypocrites are in your life. It's not your job to find them out. That's God's job, not ours! Spend time today looking inwardly at your own heart. Invite the Holy Spirit to search the deep recesses of your soul. He has no tolerance for hypocrisy. It grieves Him. If you have it in your life, you've got to get rid of it.

Culture or Christ? | Stephen Willis

"Do not be conformed to this world, but be transformed by the renewal of your mind, that by testing you may discern what is the will of God, what is good and acceptable and perfect." –Romans 12:2

As a public school teacher, I discovered on a whole new level how a person's actions and opinions can impact those around them. This is true for both big and little things. If I had one student who decided he needed to use the bathroom, it seemed as if almost everyone else needed to do the same. If I had one student whose destination was mischief, his friends would likely take the trip as well. This phenomenon goes beyond school children. As relational beings, it is easy for us to conform to the opinions of culture in search of acceptance and freedom. However, as followers of Christ we must discover and remember that conforming to anything or anyone apart from the truth of Jesus Christ will lead to darkness and disappointment.

I once had a high school tennis coach present a question to the high school athletes he coached. He asked, "Is our image everything?" For many of us, our immediate response is, "Absolutely not." However, do our priorities and actions match our verbal response? These kids that he was coaching grew up in an upscale country club environment. Their lives were shaped by the newest trends, the newest rackets, and the latest and greatest tennis shoes. When he asked the question, some of the more intelligent athletes refused to answer, while several of the others answered, "Absolutely!" After receiving the affirmative response, he spent ten minutes explaining that looking like a good tennis player has very little to do with winning tennis matches. The true success of a tennis player centers on discipline, fundamentals, and work ethic.

As disciples of Jesus, let us hear clearly the words of Paul as he calls us to not conform to the patterns of this world, but to be transformed by the renewal of our mind that comes through Jesus Christ. As we hear the words of Paul, let our eyes remain focused on the Christ who sets us free from the temptation of conformity that leads to disappointment.

Prayer: Lord Jesus, free me from the temptation to conform to a culture that doesn't value what you value.

Ears to Hear His Voice | Bruce Gardner

"The gatekeeper opens the gate for him, and the sheep recognize his voice and come to him. He calls his own sheep by name and leads them out." –John 10:3

"'Go out and stand before me on the mountain,' the Lord told him. And as Elijah stood there, the Lord passed by, and a mighty windstorm hit the mountain. It was such a terrible blast that the rocks were torn loose, but the Lord was not in the wind. After the wind there was an earthquake, but the Lord was not in the earthquake. And after the earthquake there was a fire, but the Lord was not in the fire. And after the fire there was the sound of a gentle whisper." –I Kings 19:11-12

Have you ever prayed to hear God's voice? Have you ever wondered how to know it is Him?

I can't say it any better than Chris Tiegreen:

"Most people would love to hear God's voice clearly and consistently, but few think it's even possible. Perhaps we assume that sort of communication is only available to the supersaints who spend long hours in prayer and meditation. Or at least to those who have shown enough devotion and maturity to qualify. But scripture shows us a different pattern. God has spoken to pagan kings (Pharaoh and Nebuchadnezzar), persecutors of Christians (Saul/Paul), unwilling prophets (many), and people from idol-worshiping families (Abraham and Gideon). Historically, he has spoken to addicts clinging to one last hope, rebels stubbornly headed in the wrong direction, Muslims fighting against believers in Jesus, materialists who finally ask if this life is all there is, and normal, everyday people who pray to him for direction. He draws much fewer boundaries than religious minds do."

Never assume you are unable to hear God's voice. All you have to do is ask. It may take some practice and fine-tuning to hear Him well, but you can. You probably already do but haven't yet learned to distinguish what He is saying. He will speak into your everyday experiences through Scripture, conversations, prayer, desires, patterns of circumstances, and even the parables. Ask for ears to ear, and then open them. The world will come alive with the sights and sounds of His voice.[1]

Do you have ears to hear?

———

1 Tiegreen, Chris. "Ears to Hear." iDisciple.org. https://www.idisciple.org/post/ears-to-hear-2

I've Preached My Last Sermon | J. Philip Fuller

"Let the message of Christ dwell among you richly as you teach and admonish one another with all wisdom through psalms, hymns, and songs from the Spirit, singing to God with gratitude in your hearts." –Colossians 3:16

I have preached my last sermon. No, I'm not retiring or stepping away from ministry. But yes, I've preached my last sermon.

Words have an attitude that accompanies them, something often like a plus or minus sign—a little context added to the meaning of a word. For instance, though there is not much difference between the words "guy" and "man" in any dictionary, context changes everything. Try calling someone a "wise man" or a "wise guy" and note the contrast!

"Sermon" is one of those words—its connotations are often more negative than positive. Why? If ministers are honest, we take time to craft, create, and deliver the sermon. We seek a new angle, a clever point of entry, or a fancy alliteration to make the sermon memorable, relevant, and interesting. The danger is obvious— to get so lost in the art of the sermon that the message fades.

What does Christ's Church need today? Does Christ ask for cleverness or the delivery of a clear message? Polished visuals or prophetic voices? Every generation has preachers who, out the reservoir of Bible reading, prayer, and availability to the Spirit, have boldly proclaimed messages straight from the heart of God, who with clear hearts are able to say, "The Lord asked me to give you this word today..."

John Stott, addressing the issue of preaching, writes about a preacher of generations ago who captured his commitment to the faithful delivery of messages via this simple motto, "I read myself full. I pray myself hot. I let myself go."[1] A Frances Havergal hymn includes these two lines:

Take my hands and let them move at the impulse of Thy love.
Take my lips and let them be, filled with messages for Thee.

My prayer is that we have preached our last crafty sermons and instead we dedicate ourselves to prayer-saturated messages from His living and loving Word as willing instruments for God.

---

1 Stott, John. *Between Two Worlds: The Challenge of Preaching Today.* Grand Rapids, MI: Eerdmans, 2017.

Image Is Everything | Emily Heady

"The Son is the image of the invisible God, the firstborn of all creation." -Colossians 1:15

It goes almost without saying that we live in an image-saturated time. On the one hand, it seems like image is everything. Teens spend countless hours curating their social media profiles, and corporations engage in endless branding exercises as they try to project just the right image of themselves. On the other hand, all this imagery that surrounds us has made us skeptical, hungry for something deeper and more real than the sort of "relationship" an interaction on an online post might constitute.

Scripture takes the idea of an image very seriously. God made man in His own image. The Israelites were given a commandment, written by the finger of God, not to make for themselves a graven image lest they be tempted to bow down to it.

The key to this command is a little phrase buried in the middle: "You shall not make for yourself" an idol, image, or carved object resembling something created (Exodus 20:4). Later, when Israel does just this, casting a golden calf, God expresses His frustration in those same words: "How quickly they have turned aside from the way that I commanded them! They have made for themselves a molten calf and have bowed down to it" (Exodus 32:8).

Jesus was the image of the invisible God, and in Him the fullness of God dwells. He is the creator of all; all things were made by Him, and for Him. He made us, and not we ourselves. We are God's workmanship. Jesus took on flesh for us—He became the image of God for humanity so that humanity might again embody the image of God that was created in us in the beginning.

When we think about the image we project to the world, let's ask ourselves this—for whom am I branding myself? Who do I want to see me?

Dear God, please help me to remember that I am made in your image and for your glory.

God's Word Is Unchanging | Reenie Peppers

"So God has given us two unchanging things: His promise and His oath. These prove that it is impossible for God to lie. As a result, we who come to God for refuge might be encouraged to seize that hope that is set before us. That hope is real and true, an anchor to steady our restless souls, a hope that leads us back behind the curtain to where God is." –Hebrews 6:18-19

There is not much in this world that we can claim as unchanging. People and nations change their opinions and policies at the drop of a hat. It is difficult to determine which side is to the left, which side is to the right, which side leans conservative, or which side leans more liberal. Even vocabulary is constantly changing. In Virginia, if something is "wicked," it is bad. However, if something is "wicked" in Massachusetts, it is cool or good.

There is something that does not change, however, and that is the promises of God. We can take refuge in the promises of God in the midst of this ever changing, chaotic world. We can take courage in the fact that God's promises are true and will be accomplished. In a world where things continually fluctuate, we know that the hope we have in God and His promises is real and true.

Constant uncertainty and change can leave people unsettled and anxious. During COVID-19, we saw firsthand how the constant uncertainty produced an epidemic of anxiety and disquiet on a broad scale. Thankfully, as followers of Christ, we have the promises of God as our anchor.

Prayer: Dear God, thank you that in the midst of a chaotic and unsettled world, we have a refuge and anchor in your precious promises. Help us to seize and share the hope that your unshakable promises provide. In Jesus' name, Amen.

SABBATH

A RHYTHM OF REST

Lord, you have been our dwelling place

throughout all generations.

Before the mountains were born

or you brought forth the whole world,

from everlasting to everlasting you are God.

Psalm 90:1-2

The Great I Will Be | JJ Wyzinski

"But Moses said to God, 'If I come to the Israelites and say to them, 'The God of your ancestors has sent me to you,' and they ask me, 'What is his name?' what shall I say to them?' God said to Moses, 'I Am Who I Am.'" –Exodus 3:13-14

In biblical times, there was a god for everything. There were gods of sports, crops, natural disasters, seasons, and more. This is why Moses needed to know who he was speaking to. It wasn't a lack of trust that this bush was divine. His question was, "What domain of authority do you claim?" It makes sense in his world. If the God of shrubbery was sending him, the Israelites had no chance. If the sender had authority over the rain, his command wouldn't really carry weight in the dry desert of Egypt.

There's power in knowing a god's name. If you know who they are and where they have dominion, you know where they don't have dominion. Understanding this question makes God's answer make even more sense. God isn't just responding with a name. God is responding with a statement of dominion and power. God is saying, "You won't be able to figure me out like that. The moment you think you have me boxed in and you know what I am and what I am not, you're mistaken." God says it shortly and concisely: "I am who I am."

We need to know something else about this answer. It can also be translated "I will be whoever I will be." This name, God's name, Yahweh, is a promise to Moses, to the Israelites, and to us. It's not just about God's dominion, it's about God's character. The one who calls Moses to speak to Pharaoh will be enough. Always. No circumstance will come, no storm will rise, no kings will rule, and no time will come where God will not be what God's people need: "I am...and I will be." The rest of Scripture can be understood as God continuing to reveal this. God becomes everything, including our sacrifice. Why? Because it's who God is—the great I AM and will ALWAYS BE.

Prayer: Help me trust you. You are everything I need and you always will be. Amen.

Freely Love | Matthew S.E. Waggoner

"I will heal their faithlessness; I will love them freely." -Hosea 14:4a

There's a phrase I wish we as Christians would forget. I've combed the Bible and searched for a theological foundation for it, but I have never found one. It's this: "If you scratch my back, I'll scratch yours." I believe it's one of the most damaging phrases to hear within a group of disciples seeking to love God and love others. It sounds good, but it's actually faithless. It sounds like brotherly love and unity, but something's missing.

What is missing in such a phrase as this? One word: relationship.

That's why it's not my favorite phrase. When this phrase and motto infiltrate the heart of a disciple of Jesus, it immediately casts human interactions in terms of transactions and obedience rather than relationship and love. This is the kind of love that says, "Look at what I've done; now what will you do for me in return?" That doesn't really sound like a relationship to me. It's more like bondage.

God tells the Israelites, "I will freely love them." Freely loving them means without cost or payment, or given as a gift. Jesus told His disciples to heal the sick, raise the dead, cleanse the lepers, and cast out demons, and to do so freely, without charging any money for their services (Matthew 10:8). Paul tells us in Romans 3:24 that believers are justified "freely by God's grace." David worships in Psalm 54:6-7: "I will freely sacrifice unto thee." What David means is that he will give without being compelled or obligated. It indicates an attitude without obligations. He wants to freely give because there's no bondage.

To love freely, there needs—as the very word "freely" suggests—to be freedom. Freedom is the key to love, and the key to freedom lies in having complete trust in God's love. Let's ask this question: Am I living with a transactional mindset or a relational mindset? Choose relationship! Because that is where true, faithful, and freely-given love is lived out.

Abba Father, help me today to love freely as your love was freely given. Amen.

The River | Gary O'Shell

"He opened the rock, and water flowed out; It ran in the dry places like a river."
–Psalm 105:41

"Does a dry spiritual time mean the Lord has run out of water?" –Anonymous

Dry spiritual times come to the believer. None of us will be exempt from them. Sometimes they may come as a result of letting other things crowd out our attention and focus on Him. We, in the laxness of our walk, can be responsible for them and if so, we need to make a spiritual adjustment. However, there are times when He purposefully leads us through the dryness of the desert and the water of His Spirit can seem very scarce and hard to lay hold of. The enemy of our soul is very glad to come alongside us and accuse the Father of forsaking us, or accuse us of having angered Him and causing Him to withdraw from us. As always, he's a liar and the truth is not in him. Our Father has something far greater in mind for us in this place. It's His desire that we press on in the dry places, believing all the while that He will supply His living water through His Son, Jesus.

At Meribah, the Israelites were mad with thirst and on the verge of full rebellion against God. In His mercy, God directed Moses to strike the rock with his staff, and when he did, water flowed out. It sated the thirst of the people. If He was willing to do so even with the rebellious, what will He do to supply us with all the water and bread of life that we need? Wherever we are, Christ the rock is with us. His water will never run out. If He has led us into a dry desert, it is for us to learn that even in deserts, He will work miracles. In the driest place, His river of life will flow into the deepest and driest parts of our souls. In that place, we will come to know that His water will never run out, no matter where He leads us.

If you're in that place today, press on! Out of the Rock will come His life saving water. He will never run dry. Let the river flow!

Absolute Encourager | Chad Moler

"So encourage each other and build each other up, just as you are already doing."
–I Thessalonians 5:11

Have you ever had someone who was an absolute encourager to you? I remember when I first began preaching at my church in Arizona. I was extremely nervous, in part because it was new to me and in part because I never had been that good at public speaking. Despite working for a month on my first message, I still had butterflies in my stomach.

As I walked into the sanctuary early that Sunday morning, I was greeted by two of the most wonderful people, Steve and Lyn (affectionately called Lynnie). Steve possessed a hearty laugh and strong handshake, and Lynnie just beamed with the love of Jesus. Lynnie said, "Oh honey, we have been praying for you today!" Steve then pulled me aside and prayed with me.

When I was finished with the message, the first people to greet me as I came off the stage other than my family were Steve and Lynnie. Steve shook my hand and smiled, while all 5'2" of Lynnie was bear hugging me. "My sweet boy, that was wonderful!" Lynnie said.

It didn't matter what I was doing at the church, whether preaching, leading new membership classes, or meeting visitors in the lobby, Steve and Lynnie were always there to cheer me on and to introduce me to others. Their hearts were devoted to their calling as absolute encouragers.

Encouragement is infectious. As you encourage others, they in turn will do the same. That's why Paul encouraged the church in Thessalonica to continue doing just that: building each other up. If everyone were to work on being encouragers, then discouragement would not be given a foothold. So, who are you encouraging today? Who is in your life that you can build up instead of tear down? In what ways can you come alongside another person and walk with them through difficulties? Encouragement won't solve their problems, but it helps you pray with and be present for them as they navigate life's challenges.

Father, help us to always be encouraging to others, never looking to tear another down, but always looking to build up. Amen.

The Great Cloud of Witnesses | Emily Heady

"Wherefore seeing we also are compassed about with so great a cloud of witnesses, let us lay aside every weight, and the sin which doth so easily beset us, and let us run with patience the race that is set before us." –Hebrews 12:1

The end of October brings Halloween, or "All Hallows Eve," the day when— folk tradition holds—evil spirits of all sorts were thought to be at their most active. The next day, November 1, is All Saints Day, the light and encouraging counterpoint to the havoc and hobgoblins of the previous evening. On All Saints Day, we celebrate all the saints of the church, known and unknown, and honor their faithful witness.

While our holiness tradition does not elevate human saints beyond the level that's scripturally appropriate, Wesley's quadrilateral (Scripture, Tradition, Reason, Experience) makes room for the richness they add to our faith. Personally, I have benefited from the work of the saints in promulgating our Christian traditions, both on macro and micro levels. The writings of Saint John of the Cross and Saint Teresa of Avila, for example, have taught me that the ways I experience God could be so much deeper; they model a way I can grow. St. Thomas More's courageous defiance of King Henry VIII reminds me to stand strong even when it is likely to cost me. And the model of hospitality provided by my first Sunday school teacher shows me what a life given in service to others might look like.

The great cloud of witnesses is cheering us on; we are not alone. They are in the seats beside us at church, and we can hear them cheering if we take time to listen. They are speaking to us from books on our shelves and writings passed down from the pulpit, and we can learn from their example. They are watching God's kingdom coming and His will being done, and we are a part of it! The Christian life is a marathon and not a sprint, but we are surrounded by many others who are running well. Let us lean on them for support.

Jesus, as we live our lives, grant us patience and a sense of the larger kingdom of which we are a part, that we might run well the race set before us.

Alone | Ashley Gomez

"Then [Hagar] went off and sat down about a bowshot away [from her son], for she thought, 'I cannot watch the boy die.' And as she sat there, she began to sob...[A]nd the angel of God called to Hagar from heaven and said to her, 'What is the matter, Hagar? Do not be afraid.'" –Genesis 21:16-17

There are different types of solitude described in the Bible. Often I have sought that solitude described with Isaac in his field in Genesis 24: the kind of gentle reprieve from the pressures of life and all the demands for attention, simply to attend to the Lord our God. Richard Foster, in his book Celebration of Discipline, writes, "Christian meditation leads us to the inner wholeness necessary to give ourselves to God freely," through first detaching from the world and then reattaching ourselves to the one true God.[1]

More often, though, I find myself caught in the other type of solitude the Bible describes: noise and distraction, which keeps my eyes from the Lord. Hagar is in this state of being alone. She is harried and lost, first running from abuse then later forced out for the threat her son presents to Isaac. Both times, though, God seeks her; He sees her and He speaks to her. I don't know the relationship that Hagar had with the Lord. But in both of these situations, God moves first. Genesis 16 reveals to us that not only does God see her, but that Hagar herself sees Him. Somehow, in the noise of her despair, Hagar has forgotten or given up on this promise from the Lord, but God still sees her. In her moment of deepest solitude, God encourages Hagar once again, guiding her to life-giving water that sustains them for God's promised future.

Sometimes life looks different. It isn't that we shouldn't strive for moments to get away with the Lord; Christ Himself shows us the importance of this. But when life does look different and we cannot find the familiar quiet, it is comforting to know that our God is still there and will still speak. He does not leave us without comfort or guidance, although the way may not be obvious at first. Perhaps we need only to wait on Him.

---

1 Foster, Richard. 1978. *Celebration of Discipline: The Path to Spiritual Growth*. London: Hodder & Stoughton, 2008.

SABBATH

A RHYTHM
OF REST

"I, Jesus, have sent my angel to give you[a] this

testimony for the churches. I am the Root and the

Offspring of David, and the bright Morning Star."

The Spirit and the bride say, "Come!" And let the one

who hears say, "Come!" Let the one who is thirsty

come; and let the one who wishes take the free gift of

the water of life.

Revelation 22:16-17

Fruit of the Spirit: Patience | Brad Billet

"A hot-tempered person stirs up conflict, but the one who is patient calms a quarrel."
–Proverbs 15:18

Patience can be understood as checking on your Amazon delivery only once an hour instead of every ten minutes. In our conflict-rich world, the willingness to wait is both incredibly valuable and incredibly difficult—especially when we try to apply patience to our words, as James 1:19 instructs. After all, the hardest thing to tame is not the house cat, which won't quit knocking things off the counter, but the tongue (James 3:8).

Practicing patience with our words is critical because "the tongue has the power of life and death" (Proverbs 18:21). The reality of this hits every time the recordings of what others have spoken over you plays in your head whether you like it or not. Speaking without thinking, or responding quickly out of anger or defensiveness, tends to speak death over others. It too often looks like name-calling, putting someone down, or responding with an emotionally satisfying zinger to win an argument. Wounds from hasty words lead to bad choices and broken identities, and they cause relationships to struggle. Our lack of patience may involve a much deeper level of cursing than saying the wrong four-letter word. How can we claim to love our neighbor when that is what comes out of our mouths?

Instead, may we reclaim our priestly heritage of speaking life over others by administering blessing. It requires patience to see where grace is needed in someone's life and then to give voice to that. It requires patience to help someone with whom you are in conflict see themselves with God's eyes. It requires patience to stay silent so that you can better be present with those hurting and grieving. Displaying patience may make us uncomfortable, but the power of patiently chosen words can help rewrite life stories, break curses, and heal long-lingering wounds.

Patient words require intentionality. But they are not simply a matter of will. They are evidence of the fruit of the Spirit that results from being in Christ. The Word that is God empowers us to know what to speak and when to speak it, so that the power of life may flow through our words to a desperate world. Today, before saying anything else, wait in awe of that fact.

Fruit of the Spirit: Joy | Brad Billet

"Rejoice in the Lord always. I will say it again: Rejoice!" –Philippians 4:4

Attention is powerful. What we notice and pay attention to typically directs how we feel. When we notice that we are in the presence of good health or delicious food or the people we love, we feel joy. What happens when we attend to the presence of life-shattering things? How can we express joy in those dark places?

Dark places may make Paul's command to rejoice in the Lord always feel unreasonable. Yet, joy is part of the fruit of the Spirit and has no off-season. But with our attention focused on the presence of suffering and loss, joy doesn't feel right.

Martin Pistorius was a healthy child growing up. Then at age twelve, his body just shut down. His parents were told to take him home, keep him comfortable, and wait for him to die. Instead, for four years he was completely lost in darkness. At sixteen, his mind suddenly came back, yet he was unable to move or communicate. Completely aware of everything that was going on, he was "entombed in his body," unable to stop the abuse he suffered at the hands of his caretakers.

It is hard to imagine the hopelessness he felt in that state. Incredibly, Pistorius learned to find joy by turning his attention from what was in his presence to whose presence he was in: "The only certainty I could cling to when so much didn't make sense was that God was with me . . . when I felt disappointed and powerless, my conversations with God taught me that gratitude could sustain me. When the smallest prayer was answered, I gave thanks to the Lord. Caught in perhaps the most extreme isolation a person can experience, I grew ever closer to God."[1]

After nine years, God miraculously answered Martin's prayers when a new caretaker noticed his responsive eye movements. Today, married and a business owner, Martin moves in a wheelchair and speaks through a computer; he has much to celebrate! While grateful for it all, Martin's attention is fixed on the only one worthy of rejoicing in, who took him from trapped to freedom.

Whatever you are walking through, when was the last time you rejoiced in and realized the intimate presence of God with you?

---

1 Pistorius, Martin. "Trapped Inside My Own Body for 12 Years." Christianity Today, 20 July 2015.

Let Pain Do Its Job | Nick Willis

"Count it all joy, my brothers, when you meet trials of various kinds, for you know that the testing of your faith produces steadfastness. And let steadfastness have its full effect, that you may be perfect and complete, lacking in nothing." –James 1:2-4

I have never broken a bone. Even as I say this I am realizing two things: that I might jinx myself, and that I am a very fortunate individual. Breaking bones hurts, and they don't stop hurting overnight. Healing takes considerable time, care, and rest, not to mention consultation with educated medical professionals, casts, and maybe rehabbing the surrounding muscles.

We all understand what it feels like to have brokenness—bones or otherwise. As a result of sin, we are all broken, out of joint with how the Lord made us to be in the Garden. We have harmful hurts, habits, hang-ups, character deficiencies. We make mistakes. We ruin relationships. As a result of our own brokenness, we break the things (and people) around us.

James is writing to a people who are experiencing trials and persecution. They (much like us) were broken and fighting to put their hope in Christ. How confusing it must have been for them to hear that God wanted to use that very brokenness to strengthen their faith and produce steadfastness! However, much as with a broken bone, they—and we—would have to allow the healing process to do its work. We have to endure the pain as doctors set the bone back in place. We have to deal with the incessant itching underneath the cast, and we have to wrestle through sleepless nights while the bone is restored. We have the choice to allow the healing process to have its full effect or reject it, with it never healing or healing improperly.

How are you looking at your trials? Are they just things to complain about? Or are you allowing "steadfastness to have its full effect" as God heals what is broken and makes you a strong reflection of our blessed Savior? The choice is yours—but know that the Great Physician is worthy of our trust!

Father, grant me to trust you in my trials, to know that you are growing my faith and producing a greater deal of steadfastness, all that I may enjoy you more.

Grace...Way Out Front | Bill Willis

"Deborah said to Barak, 'Go! This is the day the Lord has given Sisera into your hands. Has not the Lord gone ahead of you?'" –Judges 4:14

While our church has some wonderful articles of faith, there's one particular article of faith I've come to appreciate: 'prevenient grace.' Simply stated, it's grace that goes before us—'grace, way out front.'

I recently read of how Deborah, Israel's leader, was directed by God to attack Syria, whose army was led by Sisera. Preparing to face an enemy whose army had 900 iron chariots, Israel's general was quaking in his boots. On the other hand, Deborah's words to Barak revealed she was trusting in the grace of God: grace, way out front.

This story resonated in my heart as I pondered and prayed about the things I was facing. In the depths of my soul, God asked: "Haven't I always been way out front in your life?" He then took me back to a dock located on the shoreline of Harkers Island, NC.

As a young boy, I loved swimming with the older boys, though I couldn't swim. However, I discovered the water was chest deep at a certain spot on the pier. It was there I would jump, time and again, knowing my older brother or one of his friends would safely lead me through the deep water to the dock.

Over 45 years later, there's one day I'll never forget. I still recall how the wind was stronger and how the waves were washing deep into the marsh. Unbeknownst to me, the full moon was affecting the tides, including my spot. But as I had done many times before, I jumped into the water, only to realize the bottom had disappeared. In that moment I knew I was in trouble and that I could drown.

Well, it's obvious: I didn't drown. God's prevenient grace showed up that day in the person of Terry Yeomans, a friend and relative of my family. Having just climbed from the water and onto the dock, Terry dove into the water and saved me.

On this trip down memory lane, tears flowed down my face as God reminded me to trust and follow Him, to live and lead wherever He directs, and to never forget He is always with me and is always 'way out front.'

Acknowledge Him - Part One | Deb Huff

"Trust in the Lord with all thine heart; And lean not unto thine own understanding. In all your ways acknowledge Him, And He shall direct your paths." –Proverbs 3:6

In the front of most books is an acknowledgments page, a place where the author says "thank you" to those who inspired and shaped the content of the work. These acknowledgments can take on many forms, from simple statements to long explanations of how a source helped an author.

Like a book, we need acknowledgments that show everyone we meet who has inspired us and shaped the content of who we are. Of course, as believers we should display God's direction and blessings in our lives for all to see.

For some people, wearing a T-shirt with a catchy phrases like "I've read the final chapter and God wins" or "Normal isn't coming back but Jesus is" or "I can do all things through Christ who strengthens me" is an easy way to tell others that God is the source of their joy. Bumper stickers and jewelry quickly do the same thing. But these fashion statements are not enough.

Here are three other ways you can give a proper acknowledgment of God's influence in your life:

First and most importantly, acknowledge God personally. Start your day, or at least spend a specific time in your day, thanking the Lord for what He has done to save you, for what He has done in your personal life to make things better, for what He has done to help your family and friends, and so forth. You need to be sincere with God about what He means to you. Some days you may pour out your heart with an unending list that recognizes His great blessings, and other days you may feel like you are redundant in your thoughts. That's OK. Any honest conversation you have with God will help forge a deeper relationship with Him.

Before we move onto the second and third ways, take some time to ponder how you might make room in your day to acknowledge all God has done for you.

Acknowledge Him - Part Two | Deb Huff

"Trust in the Lord with all thine heart; And lean not unto thine own understanding. In all your ways acknowledge Him, And He shall direct your paths." –Proverbs 3:6

What are the other ways we can actively acknowledge God's work in our lives? Here are a few more suggestions. These build on the first from yesterday— taking time to thank God for all He has done.

Here is suggestion number two: When given the opportunity to testify about God's hand of blessing, be ready! Have a well thought-out testimony that gives highlights of how God has moved you through a dark time or guided you through a tough situation. Make your testimony clear and meaningful, and complete with a verse. It should be concise in the three-to-five-minute time frame. Pray about what God wants you to say about your relationship with Him. You may want to write it down and practice saying it. Ask God to use what He has given you to say to bless others. You may wind up sharing it with the person in front of you at the grocery checkout, or you may present it to your Sunday school class. You never know how sharing your experience with the Lord may influence or encourage others. In any case, you need to be ready with your testimony and let the Holy Spirit move in hearts.

Third, be looking for service opportunities God gives you to show others His wondrous love. It may be taking a missions trip with your church or volunteering at the local soup kitchen. Think about how you can get involved with your church in helping the elderly or serving in the nursery. Your service is an acknowledgment of the unexplainable love God has given you through His Son Jesus Christ.

"For God so loved the world that he gave his one and only Son, that whoever believes in him shall not perish but will have everlasting life" (John 3:16). How could we not acknowledge Him if we understand that?

SABBATH

A RHYTHM OF REST

³⁰ With my mouth I will greatly extol the Lord;

in the great throng of worshipers I will praise him.

³¹ For he stands at the right hand of the needy,

to save their lives from those who would condemn them.

Psalm 109:30-31

On the Scene | Stephen Willis

"Jesus came and stood among them and said to them, 'Peace be with you.'" -John 20:19b.

I got one of those calls this week. A young couple tragically lost their three-year-old son. I drove over, realizing my weakness, recognizing that I didn't understand and feeling overwhelmed about how it would go. When I got there, I was overwhelmed in a completely different way. The countenance and conversation of this young mom was saturated with the peace that can come only from Christ. Yes, she was broken, but at the same time she glowed and spoke of her confidence in heaven. No doubt she was grieving but she wasn't grieving as the rest of the world grieves (1 Thess. 4:13). Why? She has a hope that the world doesn't have. As I left the house of this special family I felt as if I heard the voice of God (not audible but louder than that) proclaim, "In the midst of their pain I remain on the scene."

The early disciples on the very first resurrection Sunday got a first-hand account of Jesus showing up in the midst of pain. They were hiding behind a locked door and fearful of what would happen next. The body of Jesus was missing. Would they be blamed? The Romans and religious leaders had crucified their Lord. What would prevent them from doing the same to the disciples?

All of us are faced with the fear of getting hurt. We are afraid of failure, afraid of not having enough, afraid of persecution, afraid of rejection, afraid of death and disease. However, in the midst of all of these fears, the resurrected King whose name is Jesus arrives to offer us peace. This peace He offers is Himself. He is the one who spoke creation into existence. He is the one who came from heaven. He is the one who is the Son of God. He is the one who atoned for our sin. He is the one who conquered the grave. He is the one who sends the Holy Spirit to dwell within our hearts.

Yes, we experience pain. However, He is the one who will always remain.

Lord Jesus, may you attune my mind to the reality that you remain even in the midst of my pain. I ask that you would fill me afresh with your Holy Spirit.

For the Comfort of Others | Tabitha Jernigan

"Blessed be the God and Father of our Lord Jesus Christ, the Father of mercies and God of all comfort, who comforts us in all our affliction so that we will be able to comfort those who are in any affliction with the comfort with which we ourselves are comforted by God." -II Corinthians 1:3-4

On New Year's Day of 2019, my sweet husbabnd was told he might have throat cancer. They took a biopsy. We would know the results on Friday (this was on Monday). He went back to work Tuesday night, and I sat in my recliner paralyzed by fear. Cancer is a scary word and hearing that the earthly love of my life may have it was paralyzing.

I had faith smaller than a mustard seed. Many questions filled my head and heart. I cried, cried, cried, and cried some more. That Wednesday, I found myself in my bedroom, standing there and deeply afraid. God whispered, "Kneel before Me." So I knelt there at my bed and cried out to Him, "Lord, please speak to me, I cannot handle this, I need You to speak to me." My Bible was there by my bed, and I felt a nudge to pick it up. The Lord led me to II Corinthians 1. The words from verses 3-4 jumped off the page at me, and immediately the fear left because God had not given me a spirit of fear. I thanked and praised Him as I was kneeling before Him and His Word, wiped my face, got up, and said, "Lord, use us."

That Friday, I got the call saying my husband did indeed have throat cancer. It was overwhelming. The hard part was going to church Sunday, needing to preach a faith-filled message even though I felt broken. However, I was determined that God would get the glory no matter what. I shared about II Corinthians 1 and that no matter the outcome, our faith and trust was in God.

My husband went through thirty-five rounds of radiation and two rounds of very potent chemo, lost over sixty pounds, and had to have a feeding tube, but by the grace and healing power of God, he is cancer-free today and was only out of work for seven months. All glory goes to the Lord.

Room Filled With Compassion | Tabitha Jernigan

"And He has said to me, 'My grace is sufficient for you, for power is perfected in weakness.' Most gladly, therefore, I will rather boast about my weaknesses, so that the power of Christ may dwell in me." -II Corinthians 12:9

During the SuperBowl, our little Pekingese fur baby Pancake got sick, and we had to take him to a twenty-four-hour vet. As we sat there, we watched the beauty of God's grace and humanity come together.

We arrived and they checked his vitals. We sat there for a couple of hours, but since he seemed stable, we decided to go home and take Pancake to his vet the next morning instead of waiting another four to eight hours at the emergency clinic. We got back home at one in the morning.

Many people may have gotten upset, especially getting home so late. However, my husband and I know we were there in that vet's office by divine appointment. One couple had to have their little dog who was having seizures euthanized, and we got to pray with them. Another couple brought their cat that passed away before they arrived, and we prayed. Many others were concerned about their fur babies, and we prayed.

Everyone in that waiting room cried together for those who were mourning, and it was so sad but so beautiful. This mutual compassion helped our pain and worry over our own fur baby. Perfect strangers mourning together and getting the blessing of praying for others was a divine opportunity.

In the midst of that experience, I wrote a Facebook post asking for prayers for Pancake. I shared, "I am not sure if I can take more loss, but even in this hurt, God's grace is sufficient. Always take time to pray for others. It changes your perspective." The next Saturday, we had to have our sweet Pancake put to sleep. It was almost unbearable but God's grace was and is sufficient.

Father God, thank you for shining your light in and through others in times of sadness and despair. Help us to be mindful of those around us as we seek you in all our ways. We give you glory and praise. Amen.

Growth Through Crisis | Linda Shepherd

"Though he slay me, yet will I trust in him: but I will defend my own ways before him." –Job 13:15

Have you been in a crisis? Are you able to say what Job said: "Though he slay me, yet will I trust him?" Here is a man who had lost everything, yet his trust was still in God. Maybe you feel like Job in some ways. A crisis can serve as a test to learn where our faith lies. Our faith must be in God. Are we taking it upon our own selves to figure things out and handle our own emotions? Only through Christ can our emotions be handled. God gives us wisdom, and He wants to give us wisdom instead of leaving us to think things through in our own minds. We must ask Him to give us this good gift.

The extent to which we understand and believe the Word of God will also be tested in our lives when we go through crisises. With the Word of God in our hearts, we can be established, strengthened, and settled while going through difficult times (1 Peter 5:10). We must not wait until we find ourselves in a crisis to go to God's Word. Staying and living in His word will prepare us for the crisis that each of us will surely face one day—and we cannot wait until then to learn what God's Word says.

A crisis can be a great teacher for us. We can be broken and healed through a crisis, or we can be hardened and embittered. A crisis will teach us humility, faith, perseverance, and a deep trust in God if we choose to learn from it. A crisis can be the best thing that happened to us, giving us wisdom and compassion for others, an understanding of our own relationship with God, and a soft heart that allows us to minister out of our own troubles. Remember—God is not trying to hurt us when we go through these things. He is trying to teach us and grow us up in His might. He wants us to be more like Him.

Restored | Priscilla Tomlin

"Remember not the former things, nor consider the things of old. Behold, I am doing a new thing; now it springs forth, do you not perceive it? I will make a way in the wilderness and rivers in the desert." –Isaiah 43:18-19

Making my way through a Celebrate Recovery Step Study for the fifth time now, I'm finding out things about myself that I don't particularly like. However, if we allow God to do it, He will reveal things in our past that we need to just lay at the foot of the cross. For instance, I carried around for years the pain of failed relationships and marriages. I laid awake at night scheming and trying to figure out how I could get back at those who had hurt me deeply. Of course, I thought I had no part at all in these failed relationships and marriages. It was always someone else's doing, not mine!

But some time ago, Jesus allowed my heart to soften. Ever so gently, He helped me understand that yes, I did play a part in all those broken relationships. He has forgiven me for my sins and I no longer feel like a victim. I'm a child of God, and I am loved by the King.

And now as I co-lead and sit through another Celebrate Recovery Step Study, I see women making great strides toward loving themselves again. We are working through our hurts and pain that some of us have endured for years. We are there for one another to help deal with the emotions that boil over. We love one another because we can relate to the pain. We are getting stronger in our faith, moving ahead slowly and taking baby steps as God leads and guides.

Joel 2:23 says, "I will repay you for the years the locusts have eaten..."

God Promises Strength | Reenie Peppers

"The Lord will give strength to His people. The Lord will bless His people with peace."
–Psalm 29:11

This will age me, but do you remember the song lyric "What the world needs now is love, sweet love"? Of course, our world still needs love, and a lot of it. However, what our world desperately needs right now is peace: peace in Ukraine, peace in the Middle East, peace in our political institutions, and peace in our homes. The antithesis of peace is conflict, uncertainty, and chaos. Our world can definitely be described as fraught with conflict, uncertainty, and chaos.

Our world has experienced many conflicts and times of chaos. Starting back in the Old Testament, the people of God were forced to wander. They fought numerous battles; they were dispersed and enslaved. God's people are not novices when it comes to conflict, uncertainty, and chaos. But through it all, God gave His people strength and peace in the midst of all the conflict and chaos.

God promises His people peace and strength throughout His Word. God's peace protects our hearts and minds, keeping us strong and safe through some of life's most difficult moments. As Philippians 4:7 assures us, "And the peace of God, which transcends all understanding, will guard your hearts and you minds in Christ Jesus."

Being at peace in the midst of chaos and uncertainty is our strength: a strength that knows that God is with us, and that God is for us. The joy is in not just knowing this, but in living it day in and day out, no matter what is happening in our crazy world.

Prayer: Dear God, thank you that despite the craziness of our world, we can walk in your peace and your strength. I pray peace over our world, especially in the places of conflict and chaos. I pray your strength over those who are walking through difficulties and uncertainties. Guard them with your peace that transcends all understanding. In Jesus' name, Amen.

SABBATH

A RHYTHM
OF REST

He got up, rebuked the wind and said to the waves,

"Quiet! Be still!" Then the wind died down and it was

completely calm.

Mark 4:39

The Same God | Chris Shalter

"We glory in our sufferings, because we know that suffering produces perseverance; perseverance, character; and character, hope. And hope does not put us to shame, because God's love has been poured out into our hearts through the Holy Spirit, who has been given to us." –Romans 5:3-5

"Therefore we will not fear, though the earth give way and the mountains fall into the heart of the sea, though its waters roar and foam and the mountains quake with their surging. The LORD Almighty is with us; the God of Jacob is our fortress." –Psalm 46:2-3, 7

One of my closest friends passed away from cancer at just 29 years old. She was a wife, a mother, and a lover of Jesus. It's incredible just how different the world looks through the eyes of someone who has experienced deep, soul-penetrating grief. I've heard it described as your world coming to a halt while everyone else's is business as usual. It's almost as though you're not living in the same reality as everyone else. It's confusing and complicated, and it's why no one truly understands another's grief.

I wonder if those in deep grief have an advantage in experiencing God on levels deeper than many of us have experienced. The book of Job is the dissertation for such an experience. Even the apostle Paul encourages us to glory in our sufferings, for there is a deeper connection to be found with the Father in our pain and grief.

It's an incredible thought, then, that the God who was before your grief is the same God in the midst of it, and the same God on the other side of it. While every aspect of your life is inexplicably impacted and transformed by grief, there is still the constant, unwavering, unfailing, steadfast, comforting, loving presence of the living God sheltering you within His refuge, sustaining you with His strength. As the psalmist reminds us, "The LORD Almighty is with us; the God of Jacob is our fortress" (Psalm 46:2-3, 7).

To those walking through grief of all forms, know that you are loved by a God who desires for you to know He is unchanging in your grief, and He wants to be the steadfast anchor through your storm, the hand that guides you to quiet waters. You will never be more loved than you are right now.

Jesus Cares and Carries | Melba Willis

"They brought to Jesus many who were demon-possessed. And He cast out the spirits with a word, and healed all who were sick, that it might be fulfilled which was spoken by Isaiah the prophet, saying: 'He Himself took our infirmities and bore our sicknesses.'" –Matthew 8:16-17

One of my favorite songs is "No One Ever Cared for Me Like Jesus." The lyrics say this: "I would love to tell you what I think of Jesus,/since I found in Him a friend so strong and true./I would tell you how He changed my life completely./ He did something that no other friend could do./No one ever cared for me like Jesus./There's no other friend so kind as He./No one else could take this sin and darkness from me./O how much He cared for me."

As a young wife, I noticed the love my mother-in-law, Margery, and sister-in-law, Edith, had for Jesus. The Spirit spoke to me of how they had a personal relationship with Jesus, something I knew I did not have. It was clear; they knew of His personal care and how He carries the infirmities of His sheep.

God worked through their lives to save my soul. Since then, I have understood the wonderful care of a Savior who cares for the lost and carries His children. For over 55 years, I have lived with the wonderful truth that no one ever cared for me like Jesus. His care for me did not stop when He saved me from sin. Daily and through the years, He has given me the strength to carry the burdens of life.

My life in Christ has often led me to think of how terrible it must be for those who don't have Him as their Savior and friend. God has used this to put a burden on my heart for the lost and lonely.

Looking back, my prayers for God to save my sons and make something out of their lives were intertwined with my burden for others. I never dreamed that in answering my prayers for them, God would also fulfill the burden I had for the lost and lonely.

I am humbled God would call my sons to share the good news: Jesus is a friend who sticks closer than a brother," a Savior who cares for us and carries us!

Substituted Joy | Chad Moler

"I will shout for joy and sing your praises, for you have ransomed me." –Psalm 71:23

I am going to go out on a limb and say that almost every single person who has ever had to decide on what to buy has experienced some kind of buyer's remorse. I have experienced buyer's remorse on almost every vehicle that I have ever purchased. Something that should bring joy usually ends up becoming a headache over time.

How many times do we go into a situation thinking that we will get some kind of joy out of it, only to be left empty? That pleasure we are seeking ends up being less than expected, if we receive any at all. We think that if we can only experience the joy that a particular experience will bring, then we'll finally be happy. C.S. Lewis once said, [1]"I sometimes wonder whether all pleasures are not substitutes for joy."

Think about that for a moment. All earthly pleasures promise to bring us joy, yet that joy is elusive. So often we are brought to a low point when we get caught chasing after everything the world dresses up and presents as joy. I would submit that if we are not careful we can exchange eternal joy for temporal pleasure. We can sacrifice the satisfying joy for a pleasure we have to keep on chasing. David writes in Psalm 71 that he will shout for joy because of the incredible ransomed life he has. That ransomed life is something that we can forever be joyful about.

Father, help us to remember the incredible value that we have to you. You made the greatest sacrifice in sending your son to pay our ransom. Let us take joy in that act instead of substituting it for earthly pleasures. Amen.

---

1 Lewis, C.S. *Surprised by Joy: The Shape of My Early Life.* 1955. New York: HarperOne, 2017.

Remember Joy! | Kerry Willis

"...The joy you have in the Lord is your strength." –Nehemiah 8:10

Do you ever feel overwhelmed by life? Well, you can drop the false guilt and exhale, because feeling overwhelmed is a very real part of being a human being. I've personally had moments throughout my life where it seemed the cares of the world and the details of my day would drown me in despair. But thanks be to God, I'm still above the flood.

When we feel overwhelmed, what do we do? I don't know what you do, but I whisper the name of Jesus over and over and over again. Knowing that Jesus will not abandon His own causes my overwhelmed human feelings to shift to the overflow of His holy joy.

In fact, this verse continuously reminds my heart of the promise of God: Nehemiah 8:10 says, "...the joy you have in the Lord is your strength."

Let's remember that "the joy of our LORD is our strength" and let us always remember Jesus cares.

With hearts of gratitude, let us claim and sing these song lyrics today and forever:

"No one ever cared for me like Jesus,
There's no other friend so kind as He;
No one else could take the sin and darkness from me,
O how much He cared for me."

Joy Travels | Lynne Goodwin

"Suppose one of you has a hundred sheep and loses one of them. Doesn't he leave the ninety-nine in the open country and go after the lost sheep until he finds it? And when he finds it, he joyfully puts it on his shoulders and goes home. Then he calls his friends and neighbors together and says, 'Rejoice with me; I have found my lost sheep.' I tell you that in the same way there will be more rejoicing in heaven over one sinner who repents than over ninety-nine righteous persons who do not need to repent. Or suppose a woman has ten silver coins and loses one. Doesn't she light a lamp, sweep the house and search carefully until she finds it? And when she finds it, she calls her friends and neighbors together and says, 'Rejoice with me; I have found my lost coin.' In the same way, I tell you, there is rejoicing in the presence of the angels of God over one sinner who repents." –Luke 15:4-10

In this passage, Jesus tells two stories about how valuable sinners are to God. The first is a public, commercial story about the loss of something expensive that represents money, a commodity. Men in the audience would certainly identify with the urgency of the man in the parable and his need to find the missing sheep. Jesus wanted them to understand the heart of God as He seeks His lost sheep, and His willingness to do whatever is necessary to bring them home.

Then Jesus tells another story—a private, domestic story, about the same thing— the effort to find a treasured possession. I think He was showing the women in the audience that God understood their world too. In the same way that they would search the house, He will focus His effort on the precious thing until it is found.

Both stories end in rejoicing. The thing of value is restored, the finders are filled with joy, and calling their friends together, they celebrate. Jesus tells us that the angels in heaven rejoice together when a sinner repents. They rejoice together. Maybe joy just isn't joy until it's shared. When we begin to think of others as valuable, if we can see them as God does, then we will be able to share His joy in their repentance and rejoice with the angels.

Unspeakable Joy | Deb Huff

"Though you have not seen him, you love him; and even though you do not see him now, you believe in him and are filled with an inexpressible and glorious joy, for you are receiving the end result of your faith, the salvation of your souls." –1 Peter 1:8-9

It's Monday morning. You drag yourself out of bed, looking for that first cup of coffee. You struggle to get ready for the day. Pack kids off to school. Prepare for what you have to do. Make plans to visit a shut-in and to meet up with friends later in the week. Check your calendar for the next committee meeting at church and don't forget choir practice. Lots of busyness.

In all of your activities, have you thought about joy? Has anyone in your household seen any joy in your heart? Or on your face? In the place where you work or spend most of your time, would folks there know that you are filled with joy? Or would they wonder what caused your grumpy attitude to rain on everyone else's day?

Think about the people you come in contact with through the course of a day. At a restaurant, do you grumble at the waitress when your favorite dish is not available?

When you are in line at the grocery store check out and you spot a man from church whose wife is going through cancer treatment, do you look away or do you at least let him know you are praying for the family?

If you have given your life to Christ, His spirit lives in you. Your sins are forgiven. You will reign with Christ forever in heaven. Nothing could be greater. The light of the joy from knowing that should radiate from you. Your every breath should exhale joy.

A reminder of the joy that Peter describes can be found in the song "Joy Unspeakable" by Barney Elliott Warren (1900): "I have found His grace is all complete; He supplieth every need. While I sit and learn at Jesus' feet, I am free, yes, freed indeed. It is joy unspeakable and full of glory, full of glory, full of glory. It is joy unspeakable and full of glory, O the half has never yet been told!"

May this be your testimony.

SABBATH

A RHYTHM
OF REST

Restore to me the joy of your salvation, and grant me

a willing spirit to sustain me.

Psalm 51:12

I Remember When... | Steven L. Guizar

"In the year that King Uzziah died, I saw the Lord seated on a throne, high and exalted, and the train of his robe filled the temple. Then I heard the voice of the Lord..." -Isaiah 6:1;8a

I have had a lot of "I remember when..." moments in life. I remember when I learned to ride a bike. I remember when Jennifer, my wife, said "yes" to marrying me. I remember when our two sons were born.

I also remember my Nannie who lived to be 101 before her earthly body died. I remember she was challenged with dementia. Early on she would look at us, smile, tap each side of her head, and say "The dementia is not as bad on this side as it is on this side." She couldn't remember everything, though. She could remember the love of her life, my Pop-Pop, to whom she was married for 67 years. She could not remember his death.

I remember the year was 1999, and I remember Pop-Pop's last words to me. He said, "Steven, I am looking forward to hearing you preach." How did he know? I didn't tell anyone about the encounter I had had with Jesus the year before and His call to shepherd His people.

In the year that my Pop-Pop died, I heard the Lord remind me of His calling, and I saw the Lord, and His presence mattered most!

Since then, there have been other years I remember seeing the Lord too. In the year my niece died at birth, I was six, and I remember He cared for me. I remember the year I was laid off from work. In ministry, I remember walking through life with people who remember the year when they received a challenging health diagnosis; when their loved one died; when they were laid off and finances dried up; or when the divorce/betrayal happened.

Maybe you too remember the year when someone or something died too? The Word of the Lord invites us to remember that these tough times can also be the year when...we see the Lord and hear His voice call us. He calls us to see that He still sits on the throne and can fill our hearts with life.

Prayer: Jesus, may this year be the year that I remember when I see you, hear you, and am filled by you!

If | Brian Charette

"If we confess our sins, he is faithful and just and will forgive us our sins and purify us from all unrighteousness." –I John 1:9

If you're a geezer like me, you might remember the song from 1971 with the shortest title of any top ten song in U.S. chart history. If you'll permit some sappiness, sing along: "If a picture paints a thousand words, then why can't I paint you? The words will never show, the you I've come to know..." (Millennials will have to YouTube it.) The song had a one-word title, "If," and it was originally recorded by the group Bread. (Ironically, the song was from their album called Manna.) One word, two letters. A short title but a big word biblically.

If...

It's not just for pop songs.

In fact, has a word so tiny ever loomed so large as a biblical promise when we read I John 1:9? When we consider the act of confession and its power, we are faced today with John's dramatic conditional declaration. One thing is conditional upon another. If we confess our sins, He will then act because He is so faithful and just. He will forgive us. Just let that sink in. And He will purify us from all unrighteousness. That little word—"if"—packs a punch that echoes across eternity. It's a tiny word that calls us to a big, important act: confession.

The implication, of course, is that, if we haven't been forgiven and if we haven't been purified from all unrighteousness, it may be because we haven't fulfilled our part of the promise. We haven't confessed.

Freedom is right there for you... if.

Hidden in the Garden | JJ Wyzinski

"They heard the sound of the Lord God walking in the garden at the time of the evening breeze, and the man and his wife hid themselves from the presence of the Lord God among the trees of the garden. But the Lord God called to the man, and said to him, 'Where are you?'" –Genesis 3:8-9

I still remember the first time I took a bite out of the tree. It was called "The Tree of Popularity," and it was beautiful. For years I'd come back to that tree, tasting its fruit. It started with giving up the way I dressed. "They were just clothes," I'd tell myself. "God didn't say that I can't dress this way."

Next came the way I consumed: "I'm not hurting anyone by looking or tasting," I thought. Slowly but surely, I was changing. Small bites became gluttonous feasts. One visit to the tree each day became living under its branches. I convinced myself that I just wanted to enjoy what God had created.

Then, God had nothing to do with it. I had experienced everything the tree had to offer and whether God was in the garden didn't make a difference. The tree gave me power, friends, and confidence. But it couldn't last.

One day a storm came that this tree hadn't prepared me for. The knowledge, the shade, and all of the sweet-tasting fruit wasn't enough. I found myself with a belly full of fruit but nothing to withstand the storm.

I'm sure you've been here before. I wish that I had thrown myself down in repentance at the feet of the Lord God. But instead, I hid. I heard the sound of the Lord God walking in the garden and I ran to the trees and I hid.

But the greatest moment of my life came when, in my hiding, God asked a simple question: "Where are you?" The God who created me and knows me better than I could ever imagine came after me. When I hid away, God didn't let me keep hiding. God did it for Adam and Eve, and God is still calling in the garden for you and me.

Prayer: Oh precious Lord, thank you for not letting me stay hidden.

"I APPROACH YOUR BANQUET TABLE"

Lord Jesus Christ,
I approach your banquet table in fear and trembling,
for I am a sinner and dare not rely on my own worth
but only on your goodness and mercy.
I am defiled by many sins in body and soul
and by my unguarded thoughts and words.
Gracious God of majesty and awe,
I seek your protection,
I look for your healing.
Poor troubled sinner that I am,
I appeal to you, the fountain of all mercy.
I cannot bear your judgment,
but I trust in your salvation.
Lord, I show my wounds to you
and uncover my shame before you.
I know my sins are many and great
and they fill me with fear,
but I hope in your mercies,
for they cannot be numbered.
Lord Jesus Christ, eternal king,
divine and human,
crucified for humanity,
look upon me with mercy and hear my prayer,
for I trust in you…
Have mercy on me,
full of sorrow and sin,
for the depth of your compassion never ends.
Praise to you, saving sacrifice,
offered on the wood of the cross for me and for all.
Praise to the noble and precious blood
flowing from the wounds of my crucified Lord,
Jesus Christ and washing away the sins of the
whole world.
Remember, Lord, your creatures,
whom you have redeemed with your blood.
I repent of my sins
and I long to put right what I have done.
Merciful Lord, take away all my offenses and sins;
purify me in body and soul,
and make me worthy to taste the holy of holies.
May it spur me on to works pleasing to you and be
profitable to my health in body and soul and a firm
defense against the wiles of my enemies.
Amen.

St. Ambrose

Still Hovering | JJ Wyzinski

"In the beginning God created the heavens and the earth. Now the earth was formless and empty, darkness was over the surface of the deep, but the Spirit of God was hovering over the waters." –Genesis 1:1–2

What a start to the story! Here we are, two verses in, and the ancient writer of Genesis 1 has already given us a glimpse into the entire biblical story. In two verses, less than 30 words (a remarkable feat for any pastor), we are given a promise that will be explored and proven over the rest of Scripture and over the course of our own lives. To boil it down even further, this promise can be summed up in two words: "but God."

The earth was formless and empty...but the Spirit of God was there. Darkness was over the surface of the deep...but God was there. Later we will see the story of Abraham and Sarah begin in barrenness...but God. We will see Joseph sold to his brothers...but God. We will see a world turn from its creator and in need of a Savior...but God will be there.

Have you ever experienced a "but God" moment? Maybe it was a moment so formless, so empty, and so dark that you can't describe it as anything other than "deep." Have no fear. Moments like that are God's specialty. It's so much a part of God's character to step in that, when the entire biblical narrative opens, we see God's Spirit hovering over it all. It's just what He does.

Maybe you can recall the chaos, or maybe you're in it now. Maybe it was physical pain, emotional turmoil, financial uncertainty, or a hurt so deep that it felt impossible. Maybe you're in the deep even now. Maybe your family, your church, your friends, or your work just feels...deep. If so, rest in the first promise God ever made. Rest in one conjunction that reverberates through Scripture, through life, and can still be heard today. Rest in the promise that the Spirit of God isn't done hovering over the deep.

Prayer: Holy God, thank you for always being present and bringing order to your creation. Amen.

The Distance | Brian Charette

"And everyone went to his own town to register. So Joseph also went up from the town of Nazareth in Galilee to Judea, to Bethlehem the town of David, because he belonged to the house and line of David. He went there to register with Mary, who was pledged to be married to him and was expecting a child." –Luke 2:3-5

Have you ever noticed how much of the biblical Christmas story is about people going somewhere?

In Luke 2, the Christmas story starts with Zechariah traveling from his home in Judea to the temple in Jerusalem to serve his tour of duty as High Priest. Then they return home where Elizabeth conceives John the Baptist. The angel Gabriel is dispatched from heaven to visit Mary. Mary then goes from Nazareth to visit Elizabeth in Judea. Then, of course when it comes time for Jesus to be born, Mary and Joseph pack up and travel from Nazareth in Galilee to Bethlehem because of the census ordered by Caesar Augustus.

No one surrounding the biblical Christmas story seems to keep still. They are always covering ground. Pregnant Mary and her husband Joseph cover about 100 miles for the baby to be born, much of it on foot. The Magi likely traveled about 1200 miles.

The distance.

What is it about Christmas and distance? You can't ignore the fact that, if you study the biblical accounts of the birth of the Lord, you study people moving. You study distance.

Maybe it is because distance matters to people who are far away. And because just before the coming of a Savior, we were very far away. I'm not talking about the distance between Persia and Jerusalem or even the distance between heaven and a Middle East manger.

Dead in our sin, we were as far from God as we could possibly be. An insurmountable distance. Cut off from God. Far from His favor.

Then, Jesus came, covering the greatest distance that could be imagined and all on our behalf. The distance between death and life.

SABBATH

A RHYTHM
OF REST

"It will be a sign between me and the Israelites

forever, for in six days the Lord made the

heavens and the earth, and on the seventh day

he rested and was refreshed."

Exodus 31:17

God Is With Us in the Valley | Reenie Peppers

"Watch for this—a virgin will get pregnant and bear a son; They will name him 'Emmanuel' (Hebrew for 'God is with us')." –Matthew 1:23

Valleys are the low points in our lives: the points when we are afraid, confused, and most vulnerable. The valleys of life are unpredictable and unavoidable. So how do we navigate the valleys of life? While in the valley, we must keep our minds fixed on God and the things above.

Paul gives us good advice: "Don't shuffle along, eyes to the ground, absorbed with the things right in front of you. Look up, and be alert to what is going on around Christ—that's where the action is. See things from his perspective." –Colossians 3:2

Here's a story to help us imagine what this might look like: "Corrie Ten Boom personifies how one walks through the valley with eyes continually fixed on God. In 1944, during WWII, Corrie Ten Boom and her sister, Betsie, endured ten months of unimaginable suffering while imprisoned by the Nazis for their resistance work in aiding and hiding Jews. Betsie would never leave prison alive. She died in the infamous German concentration camp, Ravensbruck, in December 1944. After Corrie's release on New Years' Eve, due to what she would later discover was a clerical error (a week later women her age were sent to the gas chambers), Corrie devoted her life to sharing the love of Jesus around the world." [1]

As Corrie Ten Boom herself said, "I've experienced His Presence in the deepest darkest hell that men can create ... I have tested the promises of the Bible, and believe me, you can count on them."

Prayer: Dear Lord, when I travel the valleys of life, help me keep my eyes fixed on you. I pray that during this season of Advent that I would experience you in a new, fresh way as Emmanuel, God with us. In Jesus name, Amen.

---

1 Yet I Will Praise You. Hope for Mommies. https://hopemommies.org/yet-i-will-praise-you-corrie-ten-boom)

God Is With Us in the Wilderness | Reenie Peppers

"Watch for this—a virgin will get pregnant and bear a son; They will name him Emmanuel" (Hebrew for 'God is with us')." –Matthew 1:23

The wilderness is a place of spiritual, mental, and emotional challenge. While we're there, we often experience isolation, fatigue, and self-doubt. We feel far from God, spiritually dry, and that our prayers are ineffectual. It can also be a place of increased spiritual awareness and depth.

God often uses the wilderness times to get our attention so He can speak to us. God spoke to Abraham while he was in the wilderness. God spoke to the Israelites at Mount Sinai while they were in the wilderness. God met a ready-to-give-up Elijah in the wilderness.

"A voice is wailing, 'In the wilderness, get it ready! Prepare the way;
 make it a straight shot. The Eternal would have it so.
Straighten the way in the wandering desert to make the crooked road
 wide and straight for our God." –Isaiah 40:3

Estera Wieja reminds us, "In our Western cultures, we are very used to our comforts. Even as followers of Jesus, we try to avoid the wilderness. We don't like when life is hard, and barren, and dry. The wilderness makes us feel isolated, so we do what we can to escape it. But what if we asked God when is the right time to move on? Or is He trying to tell us something?" [1]
Marlena Graves (MDiv, Northeastern Seminary)states in her book A Beautiful Disaster that "the wilderness has a way of curing our illusions about ourselves and teaching us to depend more and more on God. When we first enter, we're convinced we've entered the bowels of hell. But on our pilgrimage, we discover the (wilderness) drips with the divine. We discover that desert land is fertile ground for spiritual activity, transformation, and renewal" (7).[2]

Prayer: Dear Lord, in my wilderness place, let me hear what you are saying to me. Let my time in the wilderness be fertile ground for spiritual transformation and renewal. Remind me that you are still Emmanuel, 'God with us' even in the wilderness. In Jesus name, Amen.

---

1 Wieja, Estera. Wilderness Meaning in the Bible: The Importance of Desert Seasons. Fellowship of Israel Related Ministries Learning Center. October 26, 2020. (https://firmisrael.org/learn/wilderness-meaning-bible-importance-desert-seasons/)
2 Graves, Marlena. *A Beautiful Disaster*. Ada, Michigan: Baker Publishing Group, 2014.

God Is With Us in the Storms of Life | Reenie Peppers

"Watch for this—a virgin will get pregnant and bear a son; They will name Him Emmanuel." –Matthew 1:23

Storms are often unexpected and unpredictable. One minute the sky is clear and the sun is shining. Suddenly, the sky darkens, clouds roll in, and a fierce wind begins to blow.

These spontaneous storms can cause us to panic because they are out of our control. Sudden storms cause us to doubt that we can make it through and reach our destination. We focus on the storm rather than the one who is with us in and through the storm.

In the midst of every storm, I AM, Emmanuel, is with us. He will get us to our destination if we trust Him and give Him complete control. It happens in Scripture: "Later that evening the disciples walked down to the sea, boarded a boat, and set sail toward Capernaum. Twilight gave way to darkness. Jesus had not yet joined them. Suddenly, the waves rose and a fierce wind began to rock the boat. After rowing three or four miles through the stormy seas, they spotted Jesus approaching the boat walking mysteriously upon the deep waters that surrounded them. They panicked. Jesus called out to His disciples 'I am the One. Don't be afraid.' They welcomed Jesus aboard their small vessel; and when He stepped into the boat, the next thing they knew, they were ashore at their destination" (John 6:16-21).

As Max Lucado reminds us, "Storms overtake us. And it sometimes seems they will never end. . . . Before Jesus stills the storms, He comes to us in the midst of our storms. . . .Yes, you want this storm to pass. Yes, you want the winds to still. But yes, you want to know, you need to know, and you must know that the great I AM is near." [1]

Prayer: Dear Lord, you know how the storms of life cause me to panic and doubt. Remind me that you are Emmanuel, 'God with us,' in the midst of every storm this life can throw at me. I know you will get me through the storm and to my destination if I trust You and give you control. Amen.

———————

[1] Lucado, Max. *You Are Never Alone: Trust in the Miracle of God's Presence and Power.* Nashville: Thomas Nelson, 2020.

Sacred Silence | Angelica Atkins

"This is what the Sovereign Lord, the Holy One of Israel, says: 'In repentance and rest is your salvation, in quietness and trust is your strength.'" –Isaiah 30:15a

"But when you pray, go into your room, close the door and pray to your Father, who is unseen. Then your Father, who sees what is done in secret, will reward you." –Matthew 6:6

One Christmas clearly stands out in my memory from my years growing up in Canada. My brothers and I went to sleep Christmas Eve and woke up the next morning to a world pillowed in white!

So much snow had fallen that the branches of a giant pine in our backyard bent all the way down to the ground. I remember crawling into the dark, quiet shelter created underneath, feeling like I had discovered a holy hiding place.

Many years later, I experienced the same sensation stepping off a busy summer street into a cool, quiet stone cathedral in Europe.

Christmas can be the noisiest, busiest time of year. But the first Christmas came 400 years after God's prophets had all fallen silent. And before angel choruses and rejoicing shepherds broke that silence, miraculous life began to stir in the secret and silence of one young woman's womb.

Whether it is a snow fort or church chapel, Jesus' invitation is to seek out quiet, secret places in prayer. There, we can return to the wonder of being seen and held in God's presence.

Prayer: Here I am, Lord. It's just me and you. Thank you for making room for me in your heart. Help me to make room for you this Advent season. Your presence is the most important place for me to be. I offer you this space and time, asking you to come in new ways in my life.

Chronos and Kairos | Emily Heady

"But when the fullness of time had come, God sent forth his Son, born of woman, born under the law, to redeem those who were under the law, so that we might receive adoption as sons." -Galatians 4:4-5

What is the fullness of time? The Ancient Greeks differentiated numerical clock-time, or Chronos, from the time that has to do with meaning, purpose, and story, or Kairos. September 21 might be the first day of Fall on the calendar (Chronos), but we all know that the fullness of Fall comes, Kairos-style, when you don a cardigan to watch college football.

By the time Jesus made His appearance, Mary had been waiting quite some time. All the signs were there—swollen feet, morning sickness, and aching muscles all pointed to the fact that she was, quite literally, making room for God's Son on Earth. Then, a birth pang! The time had come for Jesus to change everything. Surely Mary counted the days as she rubbed her aching feet. But she also knew she was part of something infinitely larger and more meaningful than an obstetric chart could summarize. She was under the law (Chronos), but she was also under grace (Kairos).

I find it so easy to get caught in Chronos—my schedule, my to-do list, my fear of falling behind. Pondering "the fullness of time," though, I recall that God is writing a story, not handing me a to-do list. Good novelists work in Kairos. If a novelist gives us a detail, it matters; it's a sign of how the story is going to unfold. John the Baptist's leap in Elizabeth's womb might, on any given Tuesday, have been the result of some bad broccoli—but on the day Mary visited her, it was a key plot point in the story of salvation. May we be ever ready to surrender our Chronos for the Kairos God is revealing.

Dear God, please help us to pay attention in the midst of our schedules to the big story you're writing.

Enter In | Kerry Willis

"God told us, 'Wisdom means that you respect Me, the Lord, and turn from sin.'"
-Job 28:28 (CEV)

Any season is the right season to turn from sin, but the Christmas season is especially a prime time to turn our backs on rebellion, to abandon our sin, and to turn our faces to the Lord. Will we surrender to God, desiring to be right with Him?

In the Old Testament book of Job, we read the meaning of wisdom according to God. God says that wisdom means we respect Him as Lord and turn from sin.

These words by Reinhold Niebuhr are a powerful prayer:

"God grant me the serenity to accept the things I can't change;
Courage to change the things I can; and Wisdom to know the difference.
Living one day at a time; enjoying one moment at a time;
Accepting hardships as the pathway to peace;
Taking, as Jesus did, this sinful world as it is, not as I would have it;
Trusting that He will make all things right if I surrender to His Will;
That I may be reasonably happy in this life and supremely happy with Him,
Forever in the next. Amen."

A few Christmases ago, an old Christmas Carol found new meaning in my own soul—O Little Town of Bethlehem. The words of the final verse of the beloved song remain fastened like an eternal embrace around my inner man to this very day:

"O Holy Child of Bethlehem descend to us, we pray.
Cast out our sin and enter in, be born to us today.
We hear the Christmas angels, the great glad tidings tell.
O come to us, abide with (within) us, our Lord Emmanuel."

God, I want to be wise in your eyes, loving you and loathing sin. Yes! Amen!

SABBATH

A RHYTHM
OF REST

Take my yoke upon you and learn from me, for

I am gentle and humble in heart, and you will

find rest for your souls.

Matthew 11:29

Life Together | Mike Lyle

"Even Elizabeth is going to have a child in her old age, and she who was said to be unable to conceive is in her sixth month for no word from God will ever fail. 'I am the Lord's servant,' Mary answered. 'May your word to me be fulfilled.' Then the angel left her. At that time, Mary got ready and hurried to a town in the hill country of Judea, where she entered Zechariah's home and greeted Elizabeth. When Elizabeth heard Mary's greeting the baby leapt in her womb and Elizabeth was filled with the Holy Spirit. In a loud voice she exclaimed: 'Blessed are you among women, and blessed is the child you will bear! But why am I so favored, that the mother of my Lord should come to me? As soon as the sound of your greeting reached my ears, the baby in my womb leaped for joy.'" –Luke 1:36-44

Pregnancy demands a certain amount of sacrifice. I remember that my wife gave up coffee when she found out she was pregnant (talk about a sacrifice!). When new life is growing within you, it changes everything—sleeping patterns, diet, habits, and even taste buds. The life of Jesus growing within the believer demands similar sacrifice. We must be willing to let go of other ways to live in order to embrace His way. I wonder if this level of surrender can even be done outside of the context of other people who are embracing this new life as well. Perhaps we need to be in a family of other people pregnant with the life of God.

When Mary is told that the life of God will be conceived in her, she is directed to another person who also has the life of God within her. Mary was a virgin, and Elizabeth was barren. They both received a miracle. Could this be a picture of the Church—a Holy Spirit inspired gathering of people who have received the miracle of new life from the Lord?

Luke depicts the scene when Mary and Elizabeth meet as joyful. Elizabeth shouts in a loud voice, and the baby in her womb leaps for joy. Likewise, when people who are living the "God with us" kind of life get together, they encourage and celebrate that life. We cannot live "God with us" alone. After all, God is with us.

May It Be As You Say | Wynne Lankford

"In the sixth month of Elizabeth's pregnancy, God sent the angel Gabriel to Nazareth, a town in Galilee, to a virgin pledged to be married to a man named Joseph, a descendant of David. The virgin's name was Mary. The angel went to her and said, 'Greetings, you who are highly favored! The Lord is with you.' Mary was greatly troubled at his words and wondered what kind of greeting this might be. But the angel said to her, 'Do not be afraid, Mary; you have found favor with God. You will conceive and give birth to a son, and you are to call him Jesus. He will be great and will be called the Son of the Most High. The Lord God will give him the throne of his father David, and he will reign over Jacob's descendants forever; his kingdom will never end.' 'How will this be, Mary asked the angel, 'since I am a virgin?'" -Luke 1:26–34

Have you ever stopped to consider the amount of faith Mary had to have to accept the news about Jesus for the first time? This kind of angelic interaction had happened only once during Mary's generation—to her cousin's husband, Zachariah. Before that there hadn't been any supernatural sightings for over 400 years.

Think about the request. "Don't be afraid. You will be given a son; by the way, you haven't been married and you haven't had sex, and this will be the Son of God."

Think about sharing the news with your fiancé, your friends, or even your parents. In that day, such talk could literally get you killed—and the angel wasn't there for those conversations!

Let's not forget the reality that Mary, just like us, had to accept Jesus' call to enter into the chaotic world and tell people her story. Mary stepped out boldly in faith and received Christ, knowing it could cost her her life. What would happen in our world if we, like Mary, received Christ and boldly lived the life He asks us to?

Have you taken that leap? Are you ready to respond as Mary did: "May it be to me as you have said."

Audacious Faith | Wynne Lankford

"This is how the birth of Jesus the Messiah came about: His mother Mary was pledged to be married to Joseph, but before they came together, she was found to be pregnant through the Holy Spirit. Because Joseph her husband was faithful to the law, and yet did not want to expose her to public disgrace, he had in mind to divorce her quietly."
Matthew 1:18–19

Can you imagine how it was for Joseph to receive Christ the first time? Understanding what it meant to be pledged or betrothed is essential to this story. In Mary and Joseph's culture, being pledged was just like being married without the sexual intimacy. Joseph would have been actively making preparations to receive his bride into a house. In the eyes of the community they were already as good as committed, so for Joseph to accept this news, he would either subject himself to the shame of people thinking he got Mary pregnant, or divorce and expose Mary to the community as an adulteress where she would then be punished with death.

Talk about a heavy decision. We know from Matthew 1:20 that an angel appeared to him with a message: "Joseph son of David, do not be afraid to take Mary home as your wife, because what is conceived in her is from the Holy Spirit." But he hears this only "after he had considered this." How long did he have to consider—a day, a week, three months while Mary went to visit her cousin?

Faced with these possibilities, would you have shown that kind of restraint? Would you have had the character to give God time to reveal the truth to you? Stop and consider how huge of a step of faith it was for Joseph to accept Jesus the first time—and not to rush out and make a decision that might have had disastrous consequences.

Abba Father, give me the same audacious faith that Joseph had. Help me to be willing to take a bold risk in believing and following your plan for my life. In Jesus' name, Amen.

Receiving the Gift of Christ | Wynne Lankford

"So they hurried off and found Mary and Joseph, and the baby, who was lying in the manger." -Luke 2:16

Really? This baby found in a dirty cave, lying in a slobber-soaked manger, is the deliverer of Israel? Really? Even for the shepherds, this had to be a leap of faith. You may be thinking about the fact that an angelic army told them to go so they had to believe, right? I'll admit that an army of angels shouting "hosanna" would pique my curiosity. But still, the message must have seemed odd—after hundreds of years of silence and oppression, they surely were not looking for the Messiah to come from a family so poor they couldn't find a place to stay the night.

The shepherds, while certainly blown away by the angelic host, were not stupid. They still had to embrace the fact that the Savior who was promised was, in fact, this child from a poor family, in this cave, lying in this manger. It doesn't take a lot of faith to go from the hillside with the angels to the cave. But to go out of the cave to tell your friends and neighbors—that's a different story. Luke 2:17-18 says that "when they had seen him, they spread the word concerning what had been told them about this child, and all who heard it were amazed at what the shepherds said to them."

Make no mistake. Going from the cave to the neighborhood took a lot of guts. What would happen if you accepted Jesus the way these shepherds did? Are you that zealous about sharing what you have seen and heard about Jesus? Are you spreading the word as rapidly as they did? Or are you worried what people might think of your stories that seem to go against conventional wisdom? Abba Father, will you give us the same courage you gave the shepherds to share their faith? Will you embolden us to become less worried about how our culture responds and more focused on what brings you glory? Help us share the message of Jesus with the world.

The Gifts of the Magi | Wynne Lankford

"On coming to the house, they saw the child with his mother Mary, and they bowed down and worshiped him. Then they opened their treasures and presented him with gifts of gold and of incense and of myrrh." -Matthew 2:11

Have you ever stopped to wonder what Mary thought of the gifts the Magi brought to Jesus? To say the least, these gifts provide a great deal of food for thought.

Gold makes sense, as it seems to be fitting for a king. And for sure, Mary and Joseph needed the income to afford the big move coming their way as they fled to Egypt. Incense was also a proper gift for deity, indicating that the Magi were giving God's son a great deal of respect. But what about myrrh? Myrrh was used in that day as a form of embalming fluid. Whether the Magi knew it or not, this gift would suggest that Jesus was born to die!

It's one thing to tell the world that the child you're carrying is God's baby. It's another to ponder all the attention this God-child is getting from the locals and distant travelers. But to embrace the reality that He was born to die...that is radical.

I'm sure Mary and Joseph knew the full prophesy of Jesus' birth and death, but to actually accept that this little gift from above would live and then be killed and in so doing, would somehow save the world, stretches the limits of what human minds can understand.

Mary had to embrace this truth, but what about you? Have you recognized Jesus came to die? Have you embraced that the true gift of Christmas is the eventual work Jesus did on the cross? Have you expressed your gratitude to God for sending His own Son to be born to die? Take some time today and worship the Lord.

Abba Father, give us the courage to accept the truth about your plans. Your ways are not our ways, and we must submit to how you desire to lead in order to receive what you desire to give. Thank you, Jesus, for your submission to the mission for us. Amen.

Giving: Our Holiday Feast | Carla Pollard

"... for God loves a cheerful giver." –II Corinthians 9:7

I sorted through cans, divided produce, and packed meat in coolers. I was exhausted and unsure if I had the stamina to greet the families coming to our food pantry. I knew they were counting on this. I had to push through and help them pack up the food and load their cars.

I was determined to help these families as much as possible. It is no fun being hungry, especially during the holidays. Brushing away the sweat rolling down my temples, I thought, God is so good. I was amazed at how I was now able to give, even in this small way. As I looked over the boxes, I remembered when I was a young and struggling divorced mother tasked with the difficulty of making ends meet. We faced discouraging days. I had faith, but it was faltering. I prayed, but God's answers never came as quickly as the "whys" that flooded my heart.

One Christmas was bleak for me and my son. I was certain there would be little food on our table. We decorated the tree and laid one wrapped gift under it. Yet, we were filled with joy. My son was ecstatic. It was as if that one gift were a room filled with glistening, gold and silver wrapped surprises. That was the year I found a $100 bill tucked inside my Bible. Someone thoughtful and kind changed our Christmas that year.

Now, I was able to bless others so they could enjoy a holiday feast. It was a joy to carry those boxes of food and pack it in their cars. I could not give them all a $100 bill, but I gave them my labor of love and food for their families. God had brought me full circle. God answered the "whys" of my difficult years. My life was touched by a generous act of kindness many Christmases ago. Now, I was able to touch lives with this act of generosity and kindness.

Prayer: Abba Father, when I face hard times help me to remember you meet my needs through it. Show me how I can share generously out of a thankful heart. Help me to be a cheerful giver, trusting you to take care of me. Amen.

SABBATH

A RHYTHM
OF REST

"Let us go to his dwelling place,

let us worship at his footstool, saying,

'Arise, Lord, and come to your resting place,

you and the ark of your might.'"

Psalm 132:7-8

In the Bleak Midwinter | Emily Heady

Christina Rossetti was an English poet who lived during the nineteenth century. She was a devoted, life-long Anglican who took seriously the calling God had placed on her life as a single woman with an artistic gift.

Although she grew up in a family with a stellar reputation for artistic output, she often found herself having to contribute to the family's finances, including assisting in running a school that did not succeed. After Christina's father died, the family's finances were even tighter, and Christina found herself as her mother's primary caregiver. She never married, though she was engaged twice.

In 1871, just one year before she published "In the Bleak Midwinter" under the title "A Christmas Carol," Rossetti had been diagnosed with Graves' disease, which both endangered her life and marred her beautiful features. She wrote this poem as an honest question—what could she, a poor, disfigured, single woman, give to the Lord of the universe? Here is her answer.

In the Bleak Midwinter

In the bleak midwinter, frosty wind made moan,
Earth stood hard as iron, water like a stone;
Snow had fallen, snow on snow, snow on snow,
In the bleak midwinter, long ago.
Our God, Heaven cannot hold Him, nor earth sustain;
Heaven and earth shall flee away when He comes to reign.
In the bleak midwinter a stable place sufficed
The Lord God Almighty, Jesus Christ.
Enough for Him, whom cherubim, worship night and day,
Breastful of milk, and a mangerful of hay;
Enough for Him, whom angels fall before,
The ox and ass and camel which adore.
Angels and archangels may have gathered there,
Cherubim and seraphim thronged the air;
But His mother only, in her maiden bliss,
Worshipped the beloved with a kiss.
What can I give Him, poor as I am?
If I were a shepherd, I would bring a lamb;
If I were a Wise Man, I would do my part;
Yet what I can I give Him: give my heart.

Nothing | Brian Charette

"Who, being in very nature God, did not consider equality with God something to be used to his own advantage; rather, he made himself nothing." –Philippians 2:6-7a

It's possible that one of the most important Christmas Scriptures isn't found where you would expect it. You won't read it in Luke or Isaiah or even Matthew. It's not likely the Scripture you will read around the tree before you open presents. It probably won't be the focus of one of your pastor's Advent sermons. Strangers won't show up at your door singing its words just a little off key.

But, perhaps, this Christmas it will make your list.

In the middle of Paul's letter to the Philippians, he includes a powerful poem that provides an anchor point for the book, and maybe even the New Testament. And it's really much more about Christmas than George Bailey or Buddy the Elf could ever dream about.

It's in the second chapter of the book, verses 5 through 8: "In your relationships with one another, have the same mindset as Christ Jesus. Who, being in very nature God, did not consider equality with God something to be used to his own advantage; rather, he made himself nothing by taking the very nature of a servant, being made in human likeness. And being found in appearance as a man, he humbled himself by becoming obedient to death—even death on a cross!"

I wonder if we realize just how much God sacrificed when He shed His majesty—which was rightfully His—for a manger. When He willing set down glory to make His home in the gutter. When splendor became shame so my sins could be erased.

Before He gave up His life, He gave up His rights. It makes me cringe at the number of times I have demanded mine.

Maybe this Christmas, you'll add a new passage of Scripture to your list. The one that carries with it the true—True—meaning of Christmas.

God Is with Us in the Manger | Reenie Peppers

"Watch for this—a virgin will get pregnant and bear a son; They will name him Immanuel." –Matthew 1:23

Jesus, God's Son, the fulfillment of Old Testament prophesy, was sent by God to bring man back into relationship with Him. Jesus, the long-promised Immanuel, came not as mighty ruler or military commander, but as a helpless infant.

Isaiah had predicted it: "All right then, the Lord himself will give you the sign. Look! The virgin will conceive a child! She will give birth to a son and will call him Immanuel (which means 'God is with us')" (Isaiah 14:7).

Jesus, the Word of God made flesh, was born in a stable and laid in a manger: "So the Word became human and made His home among us. He was full of unfailing love and faithfulness. And we have seen His glory, the glory of the Father's one and only Son" (John 1:14).

Anne Griffin reminds us of this: "The manger was a sign—When the angel appeared to the shepherds in the field to invite them to visit the newborn King, he told them to look for a baby in a manger. The manger wasn't just a sign for the shepherds; it's a sign to all of us that Jesus is accessible to everyone who seeks Him. The shepherds would not have had access to a baby born in a royal palace, and as strangers, they probably wouldn't even have had access to a baby born in the confines of a family home. But a manger was accessible to all—and still is."[1] Jesus, Emmanuel ('God with us'), accessible to everyone, then and now.

Prayer: Dear Lord, thank you for coming to us in a way that is forever accessible to us. I acknowledge how you humbled yourself in coming to us in human form, being placed in a lowly manger. You are Immanuel, "God with us", now and always. In Jesus' name, Amen.

---

1 Griffin, Annette. What Is the Meaning and Significance of the Manger? Christianity.com. October 27, 2022. https://www.christianity.com/wiki/holidays/meaning-and-significance-of-the-manger.html

A Child Is Born! | Carla G. Pollard

"Ye shall find a babe wrapped in swaddling clothes, and lying in a manger." –Luke 2:12

My husband, Joe, and I met our son, Nick, and daughter-in-law, Kim, at a local restaurant. Joe's father was visiting from Florida and wanted to see them. We were glad Kim's parents were able to join us too. The eight of us enjoyed laughter and lively conversation as we ate and fellowshipped together. The night flew by. As we were waiting for the check, Nick said that he and Kim had something for us. Kim reached into her bag and handed me and her mother one white bootie.

We eyed the gift with puzzled looks for a second or two. Then it dawned on us, and our group erupted into joyous screams, shouts, and laughter. Is it true? Yes, Kim was having a baby! We were going to be grandparents! The tables around us were caught up in our excitement, wondering what in the world had just happened. "She's having a baby!" we exclaimed, bringing the other tables of wide-eyed onlookers in on our joy.

Messages of new life bring excitement and wonder. Birth announcements from proud parents are a delight to receive. Hopes and dreams come alive as we look at the faces of those beautiful creations. When Jesus came into the world, God the Father sent a heavenly host of angels to proclaim the joyous gift of His Son's birth.

The shepherds' initial fear soon gave way as they looked on the face of Jesus. Their souls were filled with new hope and expectations of the grand work and plan of God birthed in a baby lying in a manger amid the bulls, rams, ewes, and lambs.

As they left the stable, those shepherds must have been filled with excitement and delight like we were when we received the news of the pending birth of our grandchild. Exuberant joy erupted in their souls and rose to their lips. Making their way back to their sheep those shepherds told the joyous news to any who would listen: "Christ the Savior is born! We've seen him here in Bethlehem, lying in a manger."

Prayer: Abba Father, we have the good news to share! Christ has come! And we are born again in Him! Open opportunities for us to bring others in on our joy. Amen.

Linger | Deirdra Jones

"The angel said to them, 'Don't be afraid! I have good news for you, a message that will fill everyone with joy. Today your Savior, Christ the Lord, was born in David's city.'" -Luke 2:10-11

To linger means "to stay in a place longer than necessary," or "a reluctance to leave" (Lucado 46). The shepherds lingered long enough to hear what the angels had to say, but what if they had not? What if at the sight of the heavenly hosts they took off instead? The angel's command—"Don't be afraid"—makes sense. Surely fear would have been a legitimate response to seeing what Luke describes in Chapter 2. It's not every day that an angel of the Lord appears with a message from God. What if they had let their fear outweigh their faith? What would have happened if the shepherds hadn't lingered to hear what the angels had to say next?

We have the same choice that the shepherds did. When God moves in our lives to call us deeper with Him, we have the choice to flee or linger. Max Lucado says, "Change always brings fear before it brings faith. We always assume the worst before we look for the best. God interrupts our lives with something we've never seen, and rather than praise, we panic! We interpret the presence of the problem as a the absence of God and scoot."[1]

If we choose to scoot, we will miss the greatest things God has for us. Had they not lingered, the shepherds would have missed being the first to know about the arrival of The Shepherd and the invitation to meet Him.

He came, and He's still coming, into our ordinary for the ordinary—us!—and if we are willing to linger with Him, He will lead us into the extraordinary that is only possible with Him because of Him.

Prayer: Father, fear is a natural reaction to something we've never seen, done, or been. May our faith be bigger and louder than any fear we can imagine. May we linger as long as it takes to hear and accept the invitation to go deeper with you. May your mission for us not go undone or pass by because we chose to scoot rather than linger. Amen.

---

1 Lucado, Max. "Chapter 12: Linger Near the Manger." *In the Manger: 25 Inspirational Selections for Advent.* Nashville: Thomas Nelson, 2012. 46.

Amazing Love | Kerry Willis

"For you know the grace of our Lord Jesus Christ, that though He was rich, yet for your sakes He became poor, so that you through His poverty might become rich."
-2 Corinthians 8:9 (NIV)

Incarnation is much more than a theological word. It is the foundation of our faith. Christianity does not teach reincarnation, but it does teach the Incarnation. In other words, we do not believe that after this life on Earth we will return once again as rats. We do believe, however, that God willingly entered our rat race. The Incarnation is explained in verses like John 1:14 and Matthew 1:23: The Word became flesh and dwelt among us; that is, the Second Person of the God-head, the Son of God, was born as a baby in Bethlehem. Therefore, He is Immanuel, God with us, as one of us. Mind-boggling stuff! The Creator became His creation? Wow!

2 Corinthians 8:9 is, in fact, a three-part proclamation of the Incarnation that leads us to celebration:

1. God the Son was rich.
2. God the Son became poor.
3. God the Son was rich and became poor so that we might become rich.

Yes, Christmastime reminds us of this heartwarming reality: Jesus left His heavenly glory to join our earthly story. What God did for us is indeed amazing, but why God did what He did for us is even more amazing. What God did for us is called amazing grace. Why God did what He did for us is called amazing love! There's no other way to say it. Hallelujah!

Dearest Abba Father: Your Love for us was and still is amazing. Amen.

SABBATH

A RHYTHM
OF REST

Therefore my heart is glad and my tongue rejoices;

my body also will rest secure.

Psalm 16:9

God Comes in Unexpected Places (Sometimes) | Mike Lyle

One of the main parts of the Christmas story is the birth of John the Baptist. Every single gospel writer tells us about the ministry of John before they tell us about the ministry of Jesus. His role was one of preparation. He was sent to make people ready to hear the gospel. When I hear the phrase, "make ready a people prepared for the Lord," I think about doing religious things. It conjures up feelings of guilt and how I need to stop that bad habit and start going to church more.

Here's the thing: Zechariah was a priest and represented religion in all its glory. In fact, the prophecy we read above took place in the holy of holies, which was in the middle of the Temple, which was in the center of a complex religious system. The context of this prophecy would lead us to believe that John was going to be a great religious leader speaking from pulpits and calling people back to "church." Zechariah's whole religious system was built around "disconnecting yourself from certain behaviors and people to make you good enough for God."[1]

But instead, John the Baptist lived in the desert, ate locusts, and wore sackcloth. Yes, he called people to repentance and rededication to the Lord. But his ministry took place in the wilderness—in the Jordan river—away from the Temple. There was something brewing that was taking place outside the realm of the Temple and the religious system. People weren't accustomed to looking for God's activity in new areas. I don't think we are either. This Christmas, are you looking for God to show up in surprising places? He just might be in the wilderness.

---

1 Chalke, Steve. *The Lost Message of Jesus*. Grand Rapids: Zondervan, 2003.

The Gospel According to Christmas | Mike Lyle

"The Virgin will conceive and give birth to a son, and they will call him Immanuel (which means God with us)." –Matthew 1:23

The gospel that I heard growing up was what Dallas Willard in The Divine Conspiracy calls the gospel of sin management. In this concept, Jesus is reduced to a vial of blood that we take like a pill to cure us of our sin-guilt. Then, people in Christendom become what Willard calls "vampire Christians"—only interested in Jesus for His blood. But, what if the gospel were more than that? For sure, atonement for sin is good news. But if Jesus came only to be killed by rulers, why did God tell Joseph to move to Egypt while Herod was looking to kill him? I believe Christmas presents us with a vital part of the good news without taking anything from the gospel of Easter.

Christmas reveals a God who comes close. Sometimes, the gospel story we tell begins with a God who is somewhere else, far away in heaven. This version of the gospel centers on going to heaven when we die so we can be with God in God's place. It is curious that none of the gospels begin their story like that. In fact, they all begin not with a God far away, but with a God who has come close. They speak of His kingdom that is at hand. The gospel writers reveal that we don't have to go anywhere to find God, we simply have to open our eyes to see Him. This is a vital part of the gospel according to Christmas—God is already here and wants to be with us.

Did you catch that? God wants to be with us. There is nothing we have to do to get God's attention or to earn God's love. I don't know about you, but that sounds like good news to me. Maybe you feel like your life isn't special or noteworthy—God has come close. Perhaps you believe you're too sinful or dirty to be worthy of God's love—God has come close. There's a chance you think God doesn't see you—God has come close. Listen to the gospel according to Christmas. "The Virgin will conceive and give birth to a son, and they will call him Immanuel (which means God with us)."

Joy in Waiting - Part One | Russanna Cook

"'The days are coming,' declares the Lord, 'when I will fulfill the good promise I made to the people of Israel and Judah. In those days and at that time, I will make a righteous Branch sprout from David's line; he will do what is just and right in the land. In those days Judah will be saved and Jerusalem will live in safety. This is the name by which it will be called: The Lord Our Righteous Savior.'" –Jeremiah 33:14-16

Uggghhhh. Advent.

That used to be my sentiment about Advent. Christmas is my thing. Ask anyone who knows me and they will tell you that I LOVE all things Christmas. I squeeze in every December tradition under the sun from gingerbread houses to Christmas light tours to hosting our annual Christmas Eve party. I count down the days until twinkle lights start to appear and this year, I'm already planning a third Christmas tree for my home. I love the joy and festivity the season brings. We're celebrating the arrival of a king after all—and not just any king—King Jesus.

As an extrovert, I find in the holiday season all the things I love—front and center. Sure, I get tired but the season goes by so quickly, I want to celebrate our Savior's birth as much as I can. But...enter Advent and the season of waiting. When our church started to honor the tradition of Advent, I was annoyed. It's Christmas! I felt like Advent was an invitation to be quiet and stare at the candlelight. That's not how I like to party. Hadn't Jesus already arrived? What were we waiting for exactly? As more people I knew started to embrace the season of Advent, I felt internally attacked. Did this mean I couldn't do all the Christmasy things I loved? Were all my traditions and events anti-Advent? How did I balance the waiting with the celebrating?

Little did I know, I was about to find out about the joy that comes in waiting well.

Joy in Waiting - Part Two | Russanna Cook

"'The days are coming,' declares the Lord, 'when I will fulfill the good promise I made to the people of Israel and Judah. In those days and at that time, I will make a righteous Branch sprout from David's line; he will do what is just and right in the land. In those days Judah will be saved and Jerusalem will live in safety. This is the name by which it will be called: The Lord Our Righteous Savior.'" –Jeremiah 33:14-16

I wrestled with this question about waiting for a while, and then something happened: COVID. Most of the things I loved about the season were canceled. I had a lot more time to sit and, you guessed it, stare at the candlelight.

But with this extra time on my hands, I came across an Advent Bible study that the Lord prompted me to order. I recruited a few friends to do it with me and each morning leading up to Christmas, I sat quietly by my twinkling Christmas tree studying Advent in detail. It was through this study that I realized that it wasn't so much that we were waiting to celebrate Jesus' arrival as a baby. Instead, it was that Advent allowed us space to wait for Him to return as the King of Kings and Lord of Lords. We were living between two advents: the promise fulfilled in Jesus' birth during the first Advent surely means that we can trust in His promise to come for the second one. I needed to rest in that promise more than I realized.

Embracing Advent, especially in a year when there was little else to hold on to, taught me that making room in my heart was more important than making room in my December calendar. But if the calendar eclipsed what God wanted to do in my heart during the waiting, then I was willing to surrender that. Now, I see Advent as a welcome addition to the joy Christmas brings, even the candlelight that now adds a welcome glow to the twinkling trees.

My Expectation Is from You | Carla G. Pollard

"My soul, wait thou only upon God; for my expectation is from him." –Psalm 62:5

By the night Jesus was born, Israel had waited in expectation for their coming Messiah for centuries. Held under bondage to Rome and by the decree from a foreign ruler, Mary and Joseph made their way to Bethlehem to register for tax purposes. They had no place to stay but were given permission to sleep in a barn, a stable. There in that dirty, smelly place where animals were housed and fed, Mary delivered Jesus. I wonder if Joseph expected it to be different. I wonder what was going on in Mary's heart. I wonder if anyone expected Messiah would come this way.

Jesus rarely met the expectations of others. He taught in the synagogue, and the religious crowd despised Him. He gathered disciples who desired an insurrection against Rome; instead, He taught them to forgive others and to love their enemies.

Christmastime is a time filled with expectations. Children expect Santa to deliver all the toys on their list. Families expect this year to be different. No disappointing PaPa or arguing with Uncle Mike! "Surely my husband picked up on my hints and knows what I want THIS year!"

We expect our children to visit us, our spouses to love and be faithful to us, our pastors to shepherd us, our friends to be loyal to us. But many times, our expectations fail us. They leave us broken and hurting. Year after year, most of us live with unmet expectations.

Unmet expectations cause us to miss the power and presence of God in the reality of our situation because expectations tend to define the story. But when we let go of our expectations and embrace God's power and presence, we can look to the future with anticipation instead. Maybe you are not where you expected to be this Christmas. Take heart and know Jesus is there with you. He appears in unexpected places. Jesus works in unexpected ways.

Abba Father, help me to let go of my expectations this Christmas. Forgive me for desiring my plans, my way. Let me trust in the fact that you show up in the unexpected. Grant me your grace to anticipate your presence in every situation I face. Amen.

Treasuring Christmas | Kerry Willis

When I glance in the rearview mirror of my life, many of the things I miss most have happened during the season of Christmas.

One of those memories is strong in my mind now. When our children were five and three years old, after tucking them into bed on Christmas Eve and while Kim was wrapping gifts, I drove to my dear friend David's house.

David was an exceptional artist and called himself "Santa's elf" at Christmastime, because he always painted artwork through the night each Christmas Eve, completing late projects for his customers to pick up by daylight on Christmas morning.

I miss the strong memory of sitting until about midnight on that particular Christmas Eve with my dear, kind, and talented friend. I still remember the peace of the companionship we enjoyed and the depth of the conversation we shared.

Little did I know it would be my last Christmas Eve as a resident of my native North Carolina island home. In 1992, we moved to Colorado Springs for Bible College and then on to Virginia. And little did I realize David would pass away a few years later.

I treasure especially that specific season of Christmases past. Our children are now 34 and 32, and while David is in heaven and I presently live in Cape May, New Jersey, I still own enough of David's artwork to warm my heart and inspire my soul.

I am doubly blessed by yesterday's Christmas memories and today's Christmas moments. In fact, my treasured memories remind me of this verse from the first Christmas story:

"But Mary treasured all these things in her heart and often pondered what they meant." -Luke 2:19

All joy to your world! Treasure the season! Let us pray in adoration: Dearest King Jesus, you are the season and we are the reason! Amen!

SABBATH

A RHYTHM
OF REST

Come, let us bow down in worship,

let us kneel before the Lord our Maker.

Psalm 95:6

Seagulls | Reenie Peppers

"So be careful how you live; be mindful of your steps. Don't run around like idiots as the rest of the world does. Instead, walk as the wise! Make the most of every living and breathing moment because these are evil times. So understand and be confident in God's will, and don't live thoughtlessly." –Ephesians 5:15-17 (The Voice)

Seagulls: You either love them or hate them. You are looking out toward a beautiful sunset and a couple of seagulls are lazily drifting along the horizon—you love them. You are on the beach with your kids having a snack and a chip falls to the sand and immediately you are surrounded by screeching, grasping seagulls—you hate them.

Recently I was vacationing in Clearwater, Florida. A father on the fifth floor of the resort decided it was a harmless diversion to allow his two young children to feed a seagull some Cheerios. Within seconds, chaos erupted.

This father's seemingly harmless diversion got me thinking of the times I may have entertained a "harmless" diversion that lead to an undesirable conclusion. I have sat down to watch a "little" television and found myself squandering away three hours of my time. I've taken out my phone for a "quick" game that turned into a dozen not so quick games. I have allowed myself to get diverted, detoured, and distracted by things that have whittled away my time and my focus.

Now, diversions are not a bad thing in themselves. Diversions are needed to relax us, refuel, and refresh us. I am talking about a diversion that takes control of our time and our focus. I need to be mindful of what I do and how I use my time, especially my unstructured time, as that is when I am most likely to be thoughtless in my steps and my intentions. The times we live in lend themselves to evil. I must be wise about my focus and the usage of my time and guard it from the evil influences of the present age.

The father who used feeding seagulls as a diversion was not entirely mindful of the undesirable result of his actions. I do not want my diversions to put me in unwise and wasteful situations. The times are evil, and sometimes, so are seagulls.

Eternal Life | Kerry Willis

"Now this is eternal life: that they know you, the only true God, and Jesus Christ, whom you have sent." –John 17:3

To know God is to have eternal life. Eternal life is not just about then and there, it's also about here and now. If we know God in right relationship through His Son, eternal life is already underway for us.

True, eternity is yet to come; however, eternal life is already available. Jesus is our eternal life.

Hear the words of Jesus spoken in John 6:47: "I assure you, anyone who believes in Me already has eternal life."

Christ in us gives us the hope of glory. Yes, the hope of heaven, eternal life, right here and right now (Colossians 1:27b).

Enough said. Be encouraged.

Printed in the USA
CPSIA information can be obtained
at www.ICGtesting.com
LVHW022123300923
759798LV00011B/580